Ethnicity and Assimilation

Robert M. Jiobu

State University of New York Press

Published by
State University of New York Press, Albany

©1988 State University of New York

Printed in the United States of America

For information, address State University of New York
Press, State University Plaza, Albany, N.Y., 12246

Library of Congress Cataloging in Publication Data

Jiobu, Robert M.   Ethnicity and assimilation / Robert M. Jiobu
   p.   cm.
   Includes index.
   ISBN 0-88706-647-X.   ISBN 0-88706-648-8 (pbk.)
   1. Ethnology—California.   2. Ethnicity—California.   3. Social
mobility—California.   4. California—Social conditions.   I. Title.
F870.A1J56 1988
305.8'009794—dc19   87-16983
                                                        CIP

To Karen and Eric

Contents

CHAPTER 8

Preface

I had two goals in mind when writing this book, neither of which took precedence over the other. One was to learn more about ethnic groups based on an extensive analysis of quantitative data. This goal derrived from my predilection for crunching numbers and, more important, from what I have long observed about the field of ethnic relations. While volumes and volumes have been written about the topic, surprisingly enough, empirical voids still exist, especially when studying groups other than blacks. Data are sporadic, inconsistent in format and source, and limited in scope. This makes directly comparing ethnic groups difficult, sometimes impossible, and that in turn, seriously interferes with attempts to explain ethnic relations. I hope, therefore, that this volume will help to fill the void in knowledge.

My second goal was to examine contrasting ethnic groups from a particular viewpoint: the infrastructure. By adhering to this viewpoint, I do not mean to imply that prejudice and discrimination are unimportant. As an ethnic minority myself, personal experience leads me to believe that nothing could be further from the truth; yet at the same time, I do not believe that spiteful people determine the course of ethnic history, at least not in the long run. To explain that, we must look at the structural features of the group and of the society in which the group exists.

In analyzing ethnic infrastructures, I used the simplist statistics that answered the theoretical question being posed. Means and percentage tables sometimes sufficed; in other instances, however, "simple" statistics were not sufficient, and so I used more complex ones. Unfortunately, describing the complexity sometimes interfered with the argument's flow, and, to avoid that, I placed some material in appendices. I hope the nonspecialist will find the data interesting and useful, while the specialist, who might wish to know more about the details of the procedures, will have access to them.

In carrying out this research, Dick Haller provided technical assistance with computer-related matters, William Form read Chapter 7, and Simon Dinitz critiqued the entire manuscript. Their generosity is deeply appreciated, and I thank them for it.

Robert Masao Jiobu
The Ohio State University

Prologue

For approximately 100 years after the founding of the United States of America, the door to this country was wide open and people could enter and leave as they pleased.[1] Starting around the mid-nineteenth century, however, the open door began to slowly swing shut. Rather than being welcomed additions to the labor pool, immigrants, first from Europe and later from Asia, were increasingly viewed as competitors for jobs and land, and before long, the federal government was actively regulating immigration. The government set health standards and prohibited certain forms of contract labor. Ellis Island in New York harbor was designated as the processing center for European immigrants and became a symbol of America's new tougher policy. Not everyone could get in anymore, and in fact, one-third of all arrivals were sent back. Angels Island in San Francisco Bay performed the same function on the West Coast and had the same symbolic significance to Asian immigrants. When, in 1882, Congress passed the Chinese Exclusion Act, the precedent was set not only for Asian exclusion, but for exclusion in general. Sentiment in favor of restrictive immigration continued to grow throughout the decades, finally culminating in the 1924 National Origins Act. It established a quota system heavily favoring western European nations, and for all practical purposes, it ended Asian immigration.

By the time the quota system went into effect, ethnicity was already a fact of American life. Ethnic groups of all kinds dotted the American landscape. Cajuns, transplanted French settlers from Nova Scotia, lived in Louisiana swamps while gypsies travelled the highways. Armenians farmed the Central Valley of California, Chinese worked the cotton fields of Mississippi, and Puerto Ricans and Portuguese worked the sugar cane fields of Hawaii. That these groups existed and continue to exist is *de facto* obvious. That they might assimilate was hoped by some and dreaded by others. The tension generated by the conflict between that hope and that dread has shaped the history of American ethnic relations for more than one century.

Antiethnic furor used to be relatively straightforward. There was a "Negro problem" and a "Chinese problem," for instance, and the response of the dominant group could be directed at each group separately and regionally. The "Negro problem" was viewed as a Southern problem, and the "Chinese problem" was viewed as a California problem. While racism is always deplorable, it was relatively simple compared to today's situation. Now, different immigrant streams are converging on a few places during a time when sensitivity to racial issues is far greater than before, and although that is gratifying on ideological grounds, it does introduce complications into sociological explanations. The economic situation is also different. Large proportions of recent immigrants come from the upper social levels of their home societies, while the lower-level jobs that previously absorbed immigrants are disappearing. New immigrants are being grafted on to extant ethnic communities, and often the graft is taking poorly, or not taking at all. The gravity, complexity, and range of ethnic issues currently confronting American society can be gathered from incidents that have occurred, as the following news items illustrate. That I made no special effort to find these stories—they come in a steady, daily stream—suggests the volume and drama of the problems now confronting us.[2]

• "In a reversal of a postwar trend, resentment of the Japanese appears to be growing among Americans. Indications are found that the increasing success of Japan in a wide range of industries and the looming presence of Asian industrial competitors such as Taiwan and South Korea are causing growing uneasiness and self-doubt about this country's long-time dominance of many industries."[3]

• A Vietnamese man was arrested for theft in Gainsville, Georgia, at the same time that another Vietnamese man living in the same area was arrested for murder. When the murder trial began, the man arrested for theft was brought to the court room and the prosecution began. The defendant, who understood enough English to realize he was not being tried for theft, could not speak well enough to convince anyone he was the wrong man.

"For a day and a half, Justice turned literally blind. While Hen Van Neguyen, 21 years old, smiled and quaked and told the court interpreter, 'Not me, not me,' witnesses identified him as Nguyen Ngoc Tieu, 27, the man accused of murder. Mr. Tieu, meanwhile, remained three blocks away in the county jail.

"To a degree, the miscarriage recalls the racial perspective that ruled an earlier time in the South. 'It's like the colored race—most of them look exactly alike,' said Jeff C. Wayne, who was District Attorney for 33 years. 'I've seen this happen one time before.'

"'The wrong colored boy had come up and sat down,' Mr. Wayne said. 'Fortunately,' he added, 'the judge recognized him.'"[4]

• "Despite opposition from civil rights groups and ethnic organizations, efforts to declare English the official national language appear to be gaining strength in parts of the country.

"In California, advocates of limiting the use of Spanish and other foreign languages recently gathered more than a million signatures on a petition."[5] When placed before the voters, the proposition passed by a 3-to-1 margin.[6]

• "Minorities constitute more than 20% of the nation's college-age population, but according to Sheila Biddle, program officer of the Ford Foundation, they accounted for only 8% of the 31,190 Ph.Ds awarded in 1983. Blacks, Puerto Ricans, Mexican Americans and American Indians together accounted for a bare 4.4%. At the M. A. level, blacks, who make up 13% of the college-age population, were awarded 6.5% of the degrees in 1979 and 5.8% in 1981. Educators say the statistics show few signs of improvement and in many cases have been getting worse."[7]

• At the Sanyo plant in Forest City, Arkansas, Japanese management techniques failed with American workers. Unable to cope with unions, the plant was riddled with unrest and strikes.

"After ten years, there's still little compromise and little understanding between the 26 Japanese managers and the engineers and their U. S. workers."

During a recent strike, "pickets carried signs that read: 'Japs Go Home', and 'Remember Pearl Harbor'. Japanese managers were shocked."[8]

• When Los Angeles Mayor Tom Bradley proposed renaming Weller Street in honor of Ellison S. Onizuka, the astronaut who died in the explosion of the spacecraft *Challenger,* he touched off a furor. Weller street runs through Little Tokyo.

"Colonel Onizuka was the first Asian-American astronaut and is regarded as a hero by Japanese-Americans. His photograph hangs in the shops and offices of this neighborhood.

"The dispute pits most of Little Tokyo businessmen and community leaders who favor the name change, against a handful of merchants on Weller Street, which is a block long and is lined by fashionable stores and restaurants that cater to Japanese tourists.

"Many feel that part of the present controversy comes from a mild but long-standing tension between Japanese nationals and the four generations of Japanese-Americans who have built up the area over the past 80 years.

"'People in Japan don't identify with Japanese-Americans,' said

Datsumi Dunistugu, executive secretary of the Japanese American Community and Cultural Center. 'I think that they respect Ellison Onizuka, but they don't have the same emotional feeling for him that others do.'"[9]

These news items do not prove a scientific proposition, of course, but they do remind us how much ethnic relations have changed, and at the same time, how constant some issues have remained. "They all look alike" is a bit of old racism while the controversy over naming a street for a Japanese American astronaut is new. The demand for an official national language is old while labor unrest at a Japanese plant in Arkansas is new. Because more than ten years have passed since the civil rights movement, the visible gains made by minorities can too easily detract our gaze from the undramatic but very real racism that persists in American society. We can only hope that the future will be more enlightened than the past, even the recent past, but no one can guarantee it.

1

Introduction

This book concerns ethnic groups in California, specifically, Chinese, Filipinos, Japanese, Koreans, Mexicans, Vietnamese, and whites. In the course of studying these groups, various and disparate topics are broached, possibly giving the appearance of random choice. But that is not the case, for the study follows an underlying thread, namely, the assumption or thesis that the upward mobility of an ethnic group is determined by its infrastructure, and by the infrastructure of the situation the group encounters. The history chapter, for example, devotes more space to economics and demographics than to subcultural values and attitudes. Other chapters similarly emphasize infrastructure, covering the groups' demographic composition, intermarriage rates, residential segregation, and labor force characteristics. These data speak to many hypotheses, and, when viewed collectively, they permit us to determine each group's level of assimilation and success.

While further amplification of this assumption will eventually be required, to do so now would be premature. Rather, I will wait until each group's history has been presented, and the plethora of specific hypotheses and statistical facts have been detailed, tasks to which the other chapters are devoted. Here, however, discussing the background leading up to the assumption or ascertaining why the assumption is important in the first place is appropriate.

Prejudice, Discrimination, and Values

For many decades, sociologists have believed that any group subjected to persistent, systematic, and intense discrimination will eventually become a problem minority. This belief explains the situation of American blacks, Mexican Americans, native Americans, Puerto Ricans, and many other groups, both in the United States and elsewhere. The obviousness of the explanation and the widespread support for it found in everyday observation and formal research have made it part of the conventional wisdom of sociology. Almost 50 years ago, Gunnar Myrdal articulated this explanation, calling it the principle of cumulation.[1] It, or variations of it, are among the most commonly cited sociological explanations for the failure of minority groups to achieve middle-class standing.[2]

Principle of Cumulation

In formal terms, the principle works as follows: discrimination by the majority keeps the target group in a state of low income, poor housing, inferior education, and the correlates thereof: disorganized family life and widespread involvement in crime and deviance. Discriminators, usually cast as the white majority, use these outcomes to justify discrimination, which results in more deprivation, disorganization, and deviance. This then promotes additional discrimination, and so on in a vicious circle. The prejudices of the majority and the situation of the victims thus mutually reinforce each other. From this principle, it follows that the majority determines the fate of the minority, for if majority discrimination disappeared, the minority would then be free to rise socioeconomically. The majority, therefore, bears the blame.

Over time, the principle of cumulation will work its way through until a state of balance or equilibrium is reached. Myrdal wrote the following:

> White prejudice and discrimination keep the Negro low in standards of living, health, education, manners and morals. This, in turn, gives support to white prejudice. White prejudice and Negro standards thus mutually "cause" each other. If things remain about as they are and have been, this means that the two forces happen to balance each other.[3]

Equilibrium is not perfectly stable, however. Changes in either the minority group or in the intensity of the majority discrimination will trigger a new cycle of mutual cause and effect, moving the system towards a new equilibrium. Myrdal called this cumulative causation: "The whole system will be moving in the direction of the primary change, but not much further. This is what we mean by cumulative causation."[4] The concept implies that a small change in earlier periods can coalesce with a small change in subsequent periods, and that combined, the total effect will be much larger than would be predicted on the basis of either change considered separately.

The change need not be downward. If prejudice and discrimination can be reduced, that would lead to a rise in the level of living for the target group, which would decrease prejudice and discrimination, and so on—each factor mutually causing the other in an upward spiral, the result of which would be higher socioeconomic status and improved interethnic relations.[5] For obvious reasons, the upward spiral has not been considered a social problem, while, for equally obvious reasons, the downward spiral has been considered an entirely different matter. Many minorities have found the downward spiral difficult to slow and impossible to reverse. Myrdal used the principle of cumulation to explain the plight of American blacks during the 1930's and 1940's, but the principle easily generalizes to more recent times and other groups. We could substitute Mexican American into Myrdal's formulation, and the argument would remain largely intact. To be sure, some details will differ because Mexican Americans have a different history and subculture, but those differences modify rather than change the basic logic of Myrdal's argument.

In sharp contrast to the groups just mentioned, other groups have been the targets of majority antipathy but have somehow managed to avoid the negative socioeconomic consequences. Explaining these cases has always been difficult scientifically and uncomfortable ideologically. Analysts have commonly argued that such groups possess subcultural values which predispose them to succeed in American society, for example, values favoring hard work, education, and self-help. Considered strictly as a scientific matter, this hypothesis might or might not be sustainable, but the political implications still cause concern. A group succeeds because it has the requisite values; it fails because it lacks them. In either case, the solution and consequences lie with the minority, allowing the majority to "get off free."

The issue of "who is to blame" raises the broader question of explaining *ethnic group mobility* in general. I refer to upwardly mobile minority groups as "exceptional groups," and the broader issue as "ethnic exceptionalism." The last chapter explores the idea further; the next section simply introduces it.

Ethnic Exceptionalism

Any explanation must, to be scientifically true, explain all the units within its domain, but that is far from easy. The American ethnic scene consists of a potpourri of racial, cultural, religious, and geographic groups, and although a given explanation might account for one group, it usually cannot account for very many other groups. The notion of ethnic exceptionalism is therefore relevant. It refers to groups which have, for various reasons, managed to escape the downward spiral and, further, have achieved significant upward mobility. Notable among such groups are some (and I emphasize *some*) Asian Americans—Chinese, perhaps, and especially Japanese.[6] We can call such groups "successes."[7]

Both the Chinese and Japanese experienced intense racial hostility beginning in the mid-nineteenth century and continuing, some say, to the present. While I would not want to become involved in a contest to determine which, of all the groups in America, have the most scars, the Chinese and Japanese Americans have certainly had their share. Despite that, they have attained the position and lifestyle of the white middle class and so contravene the principle of cumulation. These groups are a profound puzzle, and the dimensions of their exceptionalism constitutes a vitally important area of inquiry. If these dimensions can be isolated and compared among successful and unsuccessful groups, a new way of conceptualizing assimilation may begin to emerge. This hope underlies much of the data to be presented later.

Ethnicity and Assimilation

In the course of this study, many concepts will be used, but two are particularly basic: ethnicity and assimilation. Although commonly encountered, no consensus exists as to what they mean, and therefore, they require more discussion.

Ethnicity

While observers often feel confident that a given group is an ethnic group, they cannot always articulate the criteria they are using. This is not the case with *The Harvard Encyclopedia of American Ethnic Groups*, an authoritative compendium listing more than 100 distinct groups ranging from Acadians to Zoroastrians.[8] Rather than offering a one- or two-sentence definition, the *Harvard Encyclopedia* developed a list of defining characteristics. The characteristics were shared:[9]

- geographic origin;
- migratory status;
- race;
- language or dialect;
- religious faith;
- ties that transcend kinship, neighborhood, and community;

- traditions, values, and symbols;
- literature, folklore, and music;
- food preferences;
- settlement and employment patterns;
- special interests with regard to politics in the homeland and the United States;
- institutions that specifically serve and maintain the group;
- internal sense of distinctiveness; and,
- external perception of distinctiveness.

This list is comprehensive and, to judge by the results of the *Encyclopedia*, highly useful. William Petersen adopted a similar approach in his textbook on demography. He called the groups *subnations*:

> Except for their smaller size, these subnations [ethnic groups] have the main features that we associate with nationality: a common territory, an easier communication inside than outside the group, an actual or putative biological descent from common forebears, a sentimental identification with insiders and thus often a relative hostility toward outsiders. As with nations, not all subnations need show every distinguishing characteristic.[10]

That two widely disparate sources—an encyclopedia and a demography textbook—use the same approach suggests its generality. The *Harvard Encyclopedia* lists all the groups studied here while Petersen discusses Japanese and Chinese Americans as subnations.[11]

Even the comprehensive definition under discussion cannot completely expunge the ideological overtones that ethnicity has acquired throughout the years, and completely expunging them would not be desirable anyway. To do so would leave the concept so narrow that its importance would be diminished. Perhaps acknowledging the ideological overtones and in the process taking them into account is preferable.

Assimilation

Assimilation is sometimes called *acculturation, amalgamation, Americanization, or nondifferentiation.* Rather than extensively discussing each term, a task really not germane to the overall study, I circumvent the problem by not using all of them. Unless the context requires it, I use only *assimilation* and *differentiation.* The latter term is especially appropriate when discussing statistical indexes.

As used here, *assimilation* means to blend the culture and structure of one ethnic group with the culture and structure of another group. Assimilation has two possible outcomes. (1) The minority loses its distinctiveness and becomes like the majority. In the process, the majority group does not change. This is called *Anglo conformity*. Or, (2) the ethnic and majority groups blend homogeneously. Each loses its distinctiveness and a unique product results, a process called the *melting pot*. These concepts have their origin partially in scientific theory, partially in utopian wish, and partially in political ideology.

Melting Pot. In 1908, Israel Zangwill, himself an immigrant, wrote a play popular at the time but which is now forgotten except for its title, *The Melting Pot*. According to Zangwill's vision, the United States was a great crucible. In it, cultural and genetic blending inevitably took place to produce a product unique among the peoples of the earth. Many shared Zangwill's belief about the outcome of the process, but unlike him, they disliked it. Assimilation would debase and weaken American character, they argued. Prominent among such people was Alsworth Ross, a noted member of the then-new discipline of sociology. (Ross once served as president of the American Sociological Society.) He articulated his antiassimilation views in *The Old World in the New* (1914), a book which the *Harvard Encyclopedia* described as the " . . . intellectual counterpart of the Ku Klux Klan."[12] The following quotation illustrates Ross's feelings on the matter:

> When a more-developed element is obliged to compete on the same economic plane with a less-developed element [Mediterranean immigrants], the standards of cleanliness or decency or education cherished by the advanced element act on it like a slow poison. William does not leave as many children as Tonio, because he will not huddle his family into one room, eat macaroni off a bare board, work his wife barefoot in the field, and keep his children weeding onions instead of at school.[13]

If nothing else, Ross was consistent. His beliefs about Mediterranean immigrants echoed his beliefs about Asians. Earlier, in 1911, he had written the following about Chinese immigrants:

> . . . the yellow man can best the white man because he can better endure spoiled food, poor clothing, foul air, noise, dirt, discomfort and microbes. Reilly can outdo Ah San, but Ah San can underlive Reilly. Ah San cannot take away Reilly's job as being a better workman; but, because he can live and do some work at a wage on which Reilly cannot keep himself fit to work at all, three or four Ah Sans

can take Reilly's job from him. And they will do it, too, unless they are barred out of the market where Reilly is selling his labor.[14]

Ross was not the only social scientist to oppose open-door immigration. Jesse Steiner of the University of Chicago believed that the Japanese (and certain other races) were so marked physiologically that they could never assimilate. "This makes inevitable the establishment of a color line between the East and the West, no less real than that between the White and the Black."[15] While Steiner's aim was similar to Ross's, Steiner's writing was much less strident.

Approximately ten years later, Robert Park, the leading sociologist at the time, proposed a race relations cycle, maintaining that all ethnic groups go through the stages of contacts, competition, accommodation, and finally assimilation. This cycle " . . . is apparently progressive and irreversible."[16] Park believed in the inevitability of the cycle but had reservations. "It does not follow that because the tendencies to assimilation and eventual amalgamation of races exist, they should not be resisted and, if possible, altogether inhibited."[17]

R. D. McKenzie, a sociologist at the University of Washington, shared Park's ambivalence toward assimilation. In 1928, McKenzie published a study entitled *Oriental Exclusion.*[18] While he disagreed with the notion that some races were biologically inferior to others, he nevertheless opposed the policy of open-door immigration. About that he was explicit: "Human migration must be controlled," he stated.[19] He also wrote:

> It has been pointed out on numerous occasions that the quota principle, as at present applied to Europeans, if applied to Asiatics, would admit such a negligible number that the practical end of exclusion would be achieved and without sacrifice of international good-will.[20]

In his belief about immigration, McKenzie mixed sociology with political ideology. That he did it with more scholarly trappings (his treatise contains standard jargon, references, and statistical tables) does not hide the fact.

The melting pot theory assumes that, in the process of blending, both majority and minority will change. Other possibilities exist, however, and one such possibility has constituted the major alternative to the melting pot.

Anglo Conformity. The majority group remains the same while the ethnic group changes to become like the majority. With regard to the United States, this is called *Americanization* or *Anglo conformity.*

Throughout history, Americanization has been the goal most often written into law, the clearest example being the National Origins Act of 1924. Senator Johnson cosponsored the act and reflected the sentiment behind it when he said:

> The United States is our land. If it was not the land of our fathers, at least it may be, and it should be, the land of our children. We intend to maintain it so. The day of unalloyed welcome to all peoples, the day of indiscriminate acceptance of all races, has definitely ended.[21]

In theory, Anglo conformity may be achieved by the complete assimilation of the minority into the dominant culture. Assimilation could conceivably be so complete that their ethnicity totally disappears and the minority becomes identical to the majority. In practice, another strategy has been followed. As the 1924 immigration law implies, Anglo conformity was to be achieved by excluding certain groups which, for various reasons, were seen as unassimilable or undesirable. Without their presence, Anglo-Americanism becomes the *de facto* standard.

The new law was effective. Soon after it went into effect, immigration fell to its lowest level since the 1830's. During the Great Depression, more people left the country than arrived, a situation unprecedented in American history. The immigration door, once so wide opened that everyone could walk through, was now shut to all but a select few with the "right" racial background.

Even though the 1924 law quelled many political issues, a large extant ethnicity remained, and it required scientific explanation. Unquestionably, the notion of cultural pluralism proved to be the most popular alternative to the notions of Anglo conformity and the melting pot.

Cultural Pluralism. As with assimilation, cultural pluralism originated more in idealistic vision than in scientific analysis. Psychologist Horace Kallen, writing on the topic from the 1920s up to the 1950s, did much to advance the idea. He envisioned a utopian society in which ethnic groups would maintain their distinctiveness but coexist in harmony and respect. This would come about because each group would participate in common culture while the federal government provided common rule. The result would be akin to a federation of ethnic groups or, as he termed it, cultural pluralism. Ironically, Kallen coined the term in an essay published in 1924, the same year Congress passed the National Origins Act. To the extent that cultural pluralism would be the operative organizational scheme for ethnic relations, it would apply only to those groups already here.

A glimpse of Kallen's vision can be discerned from the following quotation taken from an essay inveighing against the Ku Klux Klan:

> Cultural growth is founded upon Cultural Pluralism. Cultural Pluralism is possible only in a democratic society whose institutions encourage individuality in groups, in persons, in temperaments, whose program liberates these individualities and guides them into a fellowship of freedom and cooperation. The alternative before Americans is Kulture Klu Klan or Cultural Pluralism.[22]

Although this quotation comes from a book with a subtitle suggesting science (*Studies in Group Psychologies of the American People*), Kallen never rigorously defined the concept nor empirically tested it, and so it has been used in many ways since that time.

Forty years after Kallen's initial writings, Milton Gordon attempted to clarify the concept. By and large, he succeeded. He began by observing that it is possible "for separate subsocieties [ethnic groups] to continue their existence even while the cultural differences between them become progressively reduced and even in a greater part eliminated."[23] On the surface this statement appears self-contradictory. How can an ethnic group be both separate and assimilated at the same time? Gordon said it was possible because assimilation takes place along different dimensions, the most fundamental being structure and culture. For example, ethnic groups quickly adopt the dominant group's culture: food, dress, customs, and even language. After a relatively short period, they may become almost culturally indistinguishable from the majority. Nevertheless, the group can still maintain its structural uniqueness: have its own social life, practice endogamy, move into uniquely ethnic occupations, and live in ghettoized neighborhoods. Furthermore, "structural pluralism . . . is the major key to the understanding of the ethnic makeup of American society, while cultural pluralism is the minor one."[24]

This point struck a responsive chord. It described American race relations with uncanny accuracy. It explained the anomaly of ethnic groups assimilating while remaining separate and unequal, a process visible to everyone but which had never been so neatly analyzed.

Gordon also analyzed socioeconomic status. He argued that the dominant group imposes its social class system on the ethnic group. The result was *ethclass*. For example, upper-class Chicanos may have the same socioeconomic attributes as the Anglo upper-class (same level of formal schooling, income, occupational prestige, and the like) but confine their structural relationships (family groupings, recreational clubs, religion) to other Chicanos with the same class attributes. In a similar way, other cells of the ethclass structure can be filled in. Chicanos of lower socioeconomic standing confine their structural relations to other Chicanos of the same standing, as do middle-class Chicanos, and so on.

From Gordon's analysis, it follows that the ethnic group can have a class structure mirroring the dominant group's and still not be structurally assimilated. In subsequent chapters, this possibility lies behind much of the interpretation of the data.

Assimilation as a Group Property. Individuals exist; they are important. While this is undeniable, it does not mean we cannot or should not recognize the group, organization, or society. They too exist, *sui generis*. This assumption is fundamental to the sociological perspective because it leads us away from studying individuals to studying social structure. In his monograph on residential segregation, Stanley Lieberson makes the point in the following way:

> Knowledge that an Italian immigrant is a barber, by itself, is insufficient to classify him as assimilated or not. By contrast, it is possible to determine the degree of similarity between the occupational distribution of all Italian immigrants and the native population's distribution in a city and then use the results as an indicator of an immigrant group's assimilation.[25]

An individual's occupation, even one which is traditionally associated with a particular ethnic group, tells us little about a person's assimilation. Empirically, the person may be an exception, assimilated in all respects save that one, and logically, the individual's situation does not always generalize to the group. The group is not, as the saying goes, the simple sum of its parts. It is more; it is an entity unto itself, and the same is true of other group level entities. An ethnic ghetto, for example, has no individual counterpart. It is a group concept *sui generis*.

If we accept that the ethnic group is real, that it exists *sui generis*, then assimilation can be treated as a group property. It describes the state of the ethnic group apart from the individuals who comprise it. Researchers working in this tradition sometimes operationally define *assimilation* as *the extent to which one group differs from another along a distribution*, such as residential location, income, or education.[26]

Demographic studies of assimilation use a similar approach. Do black infants die at a higher rate than white infants? Do Filipino Americans have a higher fertility rate than whites?[27] Problems such as these fall within the subarea of demography known as differential analysis; or the study of ethnic groups, subcultures, communities, and other units of analysis smaller than the total society.[28] The present book uses differential analysis liberally. It provides a way to make interethnic group comparisons while simultaneously adhering to the concept that the ethnic group exists *sui generis*.

Ethnicity can be thought of as an empirical phenomenon: the data either support the proposition that it exists, or the data do not support the proposition. If ethnicity does exist, we usually consider it to be permanent and real, especially when dealing with characteristics such as occupation, formal organizations, and community structure. It is possible, though, for ethnicity to be both real *and* ephemeral; insignificant *and* important. When that occurs, it is called *symbolic ethnicity*.

Symbolic Ethnicity. In the past, ethnicity was ascribed. It dominated a person's life in terms of friendship, family, occupation, residence, and in many other ways, some subtle and unconscious, others not. As time went on, later generations matured, broke away from their group and assimilated. By the third and fourth generations, assimilation may have progressed so far that ethnicity no longer bound members to the group. Italian Americans provide an illustration. Richard Alba has noted that the rate of intermarriage among Italians has declined approximately 10% since the 1960s. Based on this and other facts, he says, "the obvious conclusion, then, from this surge of marriage across national and religious lines is that the force of ethnicity is dissipating."[29] Consistent with this conclusion, Alba subtitled his monograph *Into the Twilight of Ethnicity*.

Rather than disappear entirely, which Alba and several others have argued will be the case, ethnicity might become voluntary, as Herbert Gans suggests in the following passage:

> Symbolic ethnicity can be expressed in a myriad of ways, but above all, I suspect, it is characterized by a nostalgic allegiance to the culture of the immigration generation, or that of the old country; a love for and a pride in a tradition that can be felt without having to be incorporated into everyday behavior.[30]

The Irish, for example, may be structurally and culturally assimilated, but on St. Patrick's Day, they would not dream of foregoing the traditional green regalia, green beer, parties, and parades celebrating

Irish ethnicity. On St. Patrick's Day, it is said, there are only two kinds of people, the Irish and those who want to be.

In some respects the term *voluntary* ethnicity is a misleading one. While it is voluntary in that one consciously chooses to exhibit ethnicity, that does not mean that one makes the decision without regard to structural forces. The Cajuns of Louisiana illustrate this. Originally French settlers in Nova Scotia, the British drove them out at bayonet point in 1775. Many eventually settled in Louisiana and there maintained their ethnic distinctiveness for more than 200 years. By the mid-1950s;, their ethnicity was diminishing and a movement to revive it developed. Cajuns especially feared the demise of the French language. Consequently, an organization was formed, several prominent Louisiana politicians joined the effort, and in 1965 the legislature passed a bill which supported the principle of bilingualism. Concurrently, a series of Cajun festivals began to publicize and popularize Cajun culture.[31] Thus, to say that Cajuns volunteered their ethnicity does not mean they did so in the absence of structural prompting and support.

Discussions of symbolic ethnicity seldom mention blacks, Mexicans, Asians, native Americans, or other nonwhite groups. Because of physiological distinctiveness, they cannot become an invisible part of the white mass, and so they cannot volunteer away their ethnicity as easily as many European groups. On the other hand, one can overemphasize physiological distinctiveness. Hair color and eye color are physical differences among people, yet they are not the basis for ethnic groupings. Moreover, there is nothing to prevent nonwhites from expressing symbolic ethnicity. Third generation Japanese Americans can hardly understand Japanese yet assiduously attend Japanese film festivals as a way of communing with their past.

Relevant to the search for roots is the "Hansen effect." Historian Marcus Hansen proposed a process of ethnic identification anchored in the fundamental problem encountered by each immigrant generation. The first generation faced the problem of establishing an economic and social foothold; the second generation faced the problem of shedding its ethnic past, or assimilating; and the third generation faced the problem of establishing its identity. "What the child wants to forget, the grandchild wants to remember."[32]

Up to this point, the purpose has been to clarify the major issues which will be addressed in later pages. During the discussion, different groups were referred to by various terms, but the terms were taken for granted. They ought to be clarified now because they are especially important for ethnic relations, a topic replete with emotional loadings.

Definitions of Ethnic Groups

Throughout the study, I try to be consistent in the usage of terms, and the following definitions, while not universally agreed upon, are fairly common.

Asian American. By *Asian* I mean no more or less than the following: Persons who identify themselves as Chinese, Filipino, Japanese, Korean, or Vietnamese. *Asian American* refers to persons who identify themselves as members of one of these groups and who are either citizens or long-term residents of the United States. To use a dated but serviceable phrase, they are Americans of Asian ancestry.

I am deliberate in choosing the word *Asian.* In some circles, the word *Oriental* has pejorative connotations. Out of respect for those who feel that way, I avoid the term whenever possible. Occasionally that is not possible or would introduce awkward syntaxes (such as Asian rugs instead of Oriental rugs). Under those circumstances, I do use the word with full awareness of the usage.

Even in the very narrow sense in which I use the term *Asian American*, it still may be problematic. It includes all Asians as homogeneously one, and to a certain extent different Asian groups do share a common background. Nevertheless, that commonality should not be allowed to obscure the substantial historical, cultural, and geographic differences that exist between the groups.

Recognizing this point, however, does not solve the terminology problem. A shorthand term is still required. Listing all the groups whenever making general statements would be awkward, inconvenient, and tedious in the extreme. I have therefore retained the collective term, *Asian American*. I hope I do no offense. The historical review and data to follow will amply demonstrate just how different those groups are.

Mexican American. The term *Mexican* refers to those persons who trace their ancestry to, or closely identify with, the country of Mexico. Like Asian Americans, *Mexican Americans* are those Mexicans who either have lived in the United States for a long period or are citizens. Occasionally, I use the term *Chicano* for variety. I suspect the term is becoming more widespread and has lost much of the militant ring that it had during the 1960s. Regardless of whether my suspicions are accurate, when I use *Chicano* I am not implying militancy.

Black. Following current practice, I use the term *black* or *Afro-American* interchangeably. In the past, the nonpejorative term was *Negro* and before that *colored*. Those terms sometimes appear in historical material. When that happens, I use them. To do otherwise would distort the record, particularly when the terms appear in the names of organizations.

White. I refer to *Caucasians* as whites, or *Anglos*, the latter usually as a contrast to Mexican. The reason is that the Census Bureau classifies Mexicans (and other Hispanics) as racially white. Anglo emphasizes that the term *white* does not include Hispanics.

Ethnic terminology continually changes. Yesterday's pejorative may be today's compliment, such as *black*. At one time, the term was used derogatorily, but currently it is the accepted term. Sometimes members of an ethnic group use a derogatory term among themselves but take offense when nonmembers use the same term. Teasing out the implications and nuances of such usage requires considerable study and goes well beyond the scope of this work.

The California Setting

A major goal of scientific inquiry is to provide general explanation or one which can be applied to many cases under many circumstances. Given this goal, the most fundamental methodological reason for using California data is that the groups being studied live there. The possibility of using other states may initially come to mind, but upon closer examination, that strategy has a major limitation. For instance, while many Asians live in Hawaii, the black and Mexican populations there are minuscule. Conversely, while many blacks and Mexicans live in the Southwestern border states, there the Asian populations are minuscule. Only in California are there large enough numbers of Asians, blacks, and Chicanos for statistical analyses.

Under these circumstances, a national sample might seem appropriate, but such a sample would result in little gain of generality, and possibly, much loss. Any national sample would contain so few Asians, especially Filipinos, Koreans, and Vietnamese, that very little could be done with their data. In addition, those Asians who did appear in the sample would be predominantly from California and Hawaii, but now the effect of location would be confounded in the data. For instance, Asians living in Hawaii have much different fertility patterns than those living in California.[33] Disentangling the state effects would be necessary, but in doing that, the California data would have to be isolated, which is tantamount to studying California in the first place. Another alternative is to oversample the ethnic groups. However, the

Census Bureau did not do that, and in any event, oversampling would not solve the problem of confounded state effects. Thus, somewhat paradoxically, a circumscribed sample can sometimes produce a firmer basis for generalization than a national sample.

In addition to the goal of making general statements about ethnicity, California data are important because they have implications for social issues. The state's ethnic mix began during the mid-nineteenth century when whites rushed in to stake out the gold fields, and in the process overran the indigenous Mexican and native American populations. Later immigrations added to the mix while the 1965 Immigration Act opened the way for a new influx of Asian immigrants. Southeast Asian refugees, predominantly Vietnamese, also arrived as a result of the Vietnam War. Although initially dispersed throughout the nation, most Vietnamese have quietly migrated to California. According to estimates, 37% of all Vietnamese live in Los Angeles County.[34] A news article said, "Los Angeles has recently become a world city: a symphony of languages, a mixture of cooking smells, a palette of skin colors, a tossed salad of cultures. There are no fewer than 28 nations represented at Ramona Elementary school in L. A.'s inner city. That's not unusual. Los Angeles County schools cope with an estimated 80 to 90 languages, most spoken by recent immigrants."[35]

The old ethnic mix was not without its problems (as the next chapter shows) and the new mix is bound to have problems too. New immigrants have not found an open-armed welcome from their earlier arriving brethren. Robberies, shakedowns, and gangland style killings have become common in Chinatown. Much of the problem seems to come from conflicts between newly arriving Chinese and the long-established Chinese American community.[36]

Conflicts are not confined to the Chinese. Americanized Filipinos are sometimes standoffish to new arrivals. Second, third, and fourth generation Japanese Americans find fresh immigrants from Japan "strange" and vice versa undoubtedly. Says one report: "The 'ABCs' (American-born Chinese) tend to be contemptuous of the 'FOBs' ('fresh off the boat'). L. A. Filipinos have their own snickering Tagalog language acronym—'TNT'—for their new and often illegal arrivals. Nisei, or U. S.-born Japanese are embarrassed by Japanese nationals who speak no English."[37]

Conflicts between ethnic groups also flare up. Koreans and Japanese have long-simmering antipathies going back to Japan's brutal occupation of Korea before World War I, and World War II hardly helped matters, to say the least. While World War II does not cloud the relations between other Asian groups, there is no reason to believe their relations are exceptionally harmonious. "Everybody picks on the

Koreans," says UCLA sociologist Harry Kitano; "they regard the Koreans as the Mortimer Snerds of America. They cannot learn the language, their food smells and they cannot express themselves."[38]

The relationships between blacks, Mexicans, and Asians must be regarded as largely unknown for lack of research. Anecdotal evidence, however, suggests that Mexicans and blacks may resent the special benefits given to Vietnamese immigrants, at least that is the speculation offered to explain recent violence between Vietnamese and blacks. According to *Time*, "The resentment is economic, with Blacks mad at Mexicans and Mexicans sore at Asians. 'They are all boat people who came into this country behind a war our kids fought,' complains James Ramirez of East L. A. 'The government gives them a 3% loan. If we had it so good, we'd be owner's too'."[39]

Nor is the hostility only between ethnic minorities. According to one news report, "Anti-Oriental graffiti speckles the Harvard Library; and at Berkeley a humor magazine last year drew the undergraduate library in the form of a pagoda. 'There's a thinly veiled racism here in jokes about ultrasmart, serious Asian students', says UCLA senior Brian Lowery."[40] Ted Tokaji, a Japanese American psychiatrist and expert on Asian American personality, perceives a subtle undercurrent of resentment. He says, "whites feel that Asians are taking over the place."[41]

The phrase "melting pot," despite its rhetorical effectiveness, does not describe California—if indeed it ever accurately described any state. California's ethnic melange never melded. If the imagery of the melting pot applies to California's new ethnic mix, it applies as a simmering caldron of disparate groups, all facing varying amounts and kinds of racism from the dominant group, from other minorities, and from elements within their own groups. A potential social issue of huge proportions is brewing. What the ethnic future of California will be is not yet clear, but if the past portends the future, it will be a time of trouble and pain.

About the Data

The major portion of this study is based on census data for 1980. Commonly called the Microdata or Public-Use Samples, the specific reference is *Census of Population and Housing, 1980: Public-Use Microdata Sample A, California*. This file contains information on 1,186,232 respondents living in California at the time of the Census. Because routinely analyzing the entire 1.2 million respondents was not practical, a subset of respondents was randomly drawn from the file and weighted. Weighted analysis was performed on this subset. The sampling ratios and weights are shown on the following table.

The weights were the reciprocal of the sampling ratio. In some instances discussed in the text, a second subset was randomly drawn using the same sampling ratios and weights. A weighted analysis was performed on one subsample and then replicated on the other. Various other methodological points are discussed as they arise throughout the book. In general, it should be noted, these points are cumulative: once discussed, they are not discussed again, yet they remain applicable.

Plan of the Book

The balance of the book is devoted to analysis, both statistical and theoretical. A longish chapter provides the historical background of each group. As will be seen, this chapter is selective. It is not intended to tell a group's entire story, but to highlight features that help explain the group's current position as revealed by the statistical analysis. The next several chapters present the statistical analysis. Some chapters are largely descriptive and exploratory while other chapters test specific hypothesis drawn from previous writings.

In presenting the data, I have followed a criterion suggested by the statistician, John Tukey. He wrote, "We can try to show either general behavior or detail. We should almost always choose one or the other."[42] Throughout the study, I have chosen general behavior. The overall relationships are emphasized through the graphs and tables. For that reason, I have also followed Tukey's dictum to round liberally. Usually, tables show only whole numbers because digits to the right of the decimal point rarely contribute to perceiving an overall

Table 1.1
Sampling Ratios and Weights

Ethnic Group	Sampling Ratio	Weight
Black	.10	10
Chinese	.50	2
Filipino	.50	2
Japanese	.50	2
Korean	.50	2
Mexican	.10	10
Vietnamese	.50	2
White	.01	100
Others	.10	10

relationship. On occasion, though, these digits are important, and they are reported.

Consistent with the goal of emphasizing overall relationships, the graphs are constructed in accord with the advice of Edward R. Tufte in his book, *The Visual Display of Quantitative Information.*[43] His basic criterion is simple: the graph should show the relationships in the data and all other considerations—aesthetics, labelling, footnotes— are secondary. An interesting consequence of applying this criterion is the suppression of details. The axes of the graphs do not have many tick marks or labels. Axes do not always meet at the origin, and occasionally axes are completely left off. The reason is that such details detract attention from overall relationships. Still, some readers may wish to examine the finer details of the data, and if that seemed likely, conventional tables have also been included, sometimes in chapters' appendices.

2

Historical Background

ecause I am a sociologist, my interest in history is undoubtedly
different from that of the historian; therefore, a few words
about the way I view it are appropriate. I view history as a
collection of analyzable facts. Episodes that historians, in their best
judgment, consider to be factually true are treated as data, and when
these data are assessed in light of sociological theory, explanation
results. This view of history is admittedly narrow. It ignores the broader,
humanistic lessons that history teaches. It places but little importance
on narrative and even less importance on developing a wholistic explanation. Nevertheless, the view adopted here should serve the present
purpose, which is to provide a sociological and historical backdrop
against which the data in subsequent chapters can be interpreted.
The following historical accounts are not, therefore, complete nar-
ratives, but selected abstracts intended to highlight sociological points.

Plan of the Chapter

The chapter is organized by ethnic groups and presented in the order
of their arrivals in California: Mexican Americans, first, then blacks,
Chinese Americans, Japanese Americans, Filipino Americans, and last,
Vietnamese Americans. This order, however, is approximate. Filipinos
are discussed next to last but were probably the first Asians to actually
visit California. They came as crewmen aboard Spanish galleons at a
time when native Americans were the only indigenous population.[1]
These Filipino visitors, however, did not stay.

The history of each group is divided into the following sections:

- introduction;
- economic impact of the group;
- laws and treaties directed against the group;

• violence directed against the group; and
• stereotype of the group.

These section divisions could not be maintained in every case. Some groups experienced less violence than other groups, for instance, and where information was accordingly sparse, I did not make a separate division, but included the information in other sections. Although this procedure makes for less uniformity in chapter headings, it more accurately reflects the group's experience. Also, groups with long histories in California obviously require more discussion than groups with short histories. This disparity is illustrated by contrasting Chicanos, whose history predates the founding of the state of California, with the Vietnamese, whose California history is little more than a decade old. More pages are therefore devoted to Chicano history, but that does not mean Chicanos are more important than Vietnamese. Koreans provide another illustration; their number was so small in California that, until the late 1960s, their history is the story of individuals (many of whom were political activists opposed to Japanese dominance of Korea).

Mexican Americans

One cannot study the growth of California's Mexican population in precise statistical terms because accurate immigration records and censuses simply do not exist. Even after the Southwest was settled, little effort was made to police effectively the U. S.-Mexico border, which was not even fenced until the 1950s. This situation has led one researcher to conclude that before 1910, Mexican immigraton data are essentially useless.[2] Although the accompanying statistics are based on census counts, they too should be taken as crude estimates. Table 2.1 shows the absolute and relative size of the Mexican population over the years.

The Mexican population has grown rapidly and consistently. From fewer than 8,000 in 1900, it quadrupled by 1910, tripled by 1920, and again quadrupled by 1930. The growth rate declined during the 1930s but increased with the onset of World War II. By 1970, the Mexican population in California was 1.9 million. This growth has exceeded that of the state as a whole. In 1900, Chicanos comprised less than 1% of the California population, but by 1970 the figure was slightly more than 9%. Of the groups being studied here, Mexican Americans are the largest, both in absolute number and as a percentage of the total population.

Table 2.1
Mexican Population
California*

Year	Number (1,000)	Percent
1900	8	.5
1910	34	1.4
1920	89	2.6
1930	368	6.5
1940	414	6.0
1950	760	7.2
1960	1,427	9.1
1970	1,857	9.3

*Census Bureau, Subject Reports, McWilliams, 1949.

The definition of the Mexican population has varied. 1940 data is estimated by interpolation.

Economic Impact

The expansion of agriculture and the building of railroads stimulated the demand for Mexican laborers while revolutions in Mexico were driving thousands of Mexicans north.[3] How many emigrated will never be known because virtually no one was guarding the borders, a situation that was not entirely unappreciated. Joan Moore and Harry Pachon write, "It now appears that much of this laxness was deliberate so that the border states could retain a flow of cheap labor so badly needed in the economy."[4]

Between 1900 and 1920, many Chicano immigrants worked on the railroad. Assembled in border towns, work gangs were sent out on six-month contracts. They lived in boxcars while on the move and founded shanty towns when work on the line temporarily slowed.[5] As early as 1900, the Southern Pacific employed 4,500 Mexicans on its California lines, and by 1906 the railroads were importing two and three boxcar loads of *cholos* per week. Writes Carey McWilliams in his history:

> Crews literally lived on the rails in boxcars . . . . 'Their abode,' as one railroad executive tersely phrased it, "is where these cars are placed". . . . Wherever a railroad labor camp was established, is where a Mexican *colonia* exists today.[6]

According to a 1912 government survey, most of the Mexicans in the Southwest had worked for the railroad at one time.[7] Wages were scaled by race: Mexican workers earned 20% to 50% less than Anglo workers for performing the same job.[8] In today's sociological jargon, this is called a "split-labor market."[9]

Mexicans also worked as laborers on the Southern California inter-urban trolley system. As with the railroads, the trolley companies built shanty towns at convenient points along the line. Some of these started in rural areas but later became barrios as the city expanded and surrounded them.

The railroads were important to Mexican economic life, but agriculture soon became more important, as historian Maldwyn Jones notes:

> Although some found work on the railroads, on the stock ranches, or in the mines, Mexican laborers were employed chiefly in the cultivation, harvesting, and packing of fruit, vegetables, cotton, and sugar cane. In the production of all of these commodities, they formed, indeed, the backbone of the Southwest's labor force.[10]

Sometimes employers used them to offset demands of other groups. A 1912 article states:

> Specific instances of the use of Mexicans to curb the demands of other races are found in the sugar-beet industry of central California, where they were introduced for the purpose of showing the Japanese laborers that they were not indispensable, and in the same industry in Colorado, where they were used in a similar way against the German-Russians.[11]

Despite being a source of cheap labor, opposition towards Chicanos began mounting. During the 1920s, welfare agencies, labor groups, and nativist organizations opposed unrestricted immigration from Mexico. The 1924 National Origins Act did not placate these groups because Mexico did not come under the quota system (neither did Canada). In 1924, however, the federal government did establish the Border Patrol. Five years later, American consular offices began rejecting many Mexican applicants for visas on the grounds that the applicants might become public charges. One Mexican American says, "My grandfather had to post a bond in order to immigrate."[12]

What would have happened were it not for the Great Depression makes for interesting, if empirically unresolvable, speculation. The declining economy reversed the immigration flow and increasingly forced those Mexicans who remained into direct competition with Anglos. Congress tried to resolve the conflict with the Repatriation Program. Under this program, some Chicanos returned to Mexico voluntarily. For those who did not, immigration officials undertook to either deport them or otherwise pressure them to leave, and according to estimates, 500,000 Mexicans repatriated. Immigration officials were draconian. One-half of all repatriates were American-born but were swept away anyway.[13]

Throughout the Great Depression, one-third of all Mexicans were living in California and 41% of the Mexican labor force was working in agriculture. As wages fell and jobs grew more scarce, agricultural workers increasingly turned to unionization. During the early 1930s, Mexicans established 40 agriculture unions, but most were short-lived. Perhaps the most influential was the Cannery and Agricultural Workers Industrial Union, "a creation of the Communist party."[14]

Strikes were common. In 1933, Mexican workers struck the El Monte strawberry fields; in 1934, the Redlands citrus groves; in 1936, the Salinas lettuce packers; in 1937, the Stockton canneries; and in 1941, the Ventura lemon groves. Ultimately, these strikes proved futile. Wages continued to fall and Anglos still displaced Mexicans. Before the Great Depression, Anglos comprised less than 20% of California migratory farm workers. By the end of the Great Depression, they comprised 85%.

Manpower was scarce during World War II, and the United States looked to Mexico for help. In 1942, Congress authorized the first *bracero* program, which allowed Mexican farm workers to enter the country on a short-term basis to perform agricultural labor. By the time the program ended in 1947, 200,000 braceros had entered the country and one-half had worked in California. In 1951, Congress reopened the bracero program and some 450,000 Mexican workers eventually used it. During the 1960s, braceros were 26% of the national agricultural labor force. Growers like them—they were cheap, docile and temporary.

Nevertheless, Congress ended the program in 1964. While growers liked braceros, native labor did not. Braceros dampened wages and acted as a brake on unionization. For instance, Caesar Chavez organized the National Farm Workers Association in 1962, but he waited until one year after the bracero program ended before launching the union against the Delano vineyards. The breakthrough for the union came the next year when the Schenley company, a major owner of vineyards, settled with the union.

Anti-Mexican Laws and Treaties

Mexicans lived in California long before Anglos did. The area now occupied by Arizona, California, New Mexico, and Texas became part of the United States as a result of the Mexican war fought from 1846 to 1848. Under the Treaty of Guadalupe Hidalgo, Mexicans residing in those areas could either return to Mexico or remain and be treated as U. S. citizens. The overwhelming majority, perhaps 80,000 (precise figures are not available), chose to stay. Of this number, between 7,500 and 13,000 lived in California.[15] They were the *Californios,* or the original Mexican residents of the state. Initially, Anglos were the foreigners, but that definition did not last long. In 1848, Californios were the power elite. Fifty years later they were a powerless minority. The laws and treaties of the times tell the story of how that came about.

California held a constitutional convention in 1849. Of the 48 delegates attending, eight were Mexican. Through collective efforts and political maneuvering, they thwarted some anti-Chicano legislation. They defeated a move to limit voting to Anglos, and they successfully supported a proposal requiring laws to be printed in Spanish and English (the law was later revoked). For a brief moment in California history, the position of Mexicans seemed, if not totally safe, at least defensible.

When gold was discovered in northern California, Anglo migrants— the 49er's—began flooding the area, along with several thousand Mexicans, Chinese, and some Chileans. State population swelled from 15,000 in 1848 to 100,000 by 1850. By 1852, it was 225,000, almost one-half of whom were prospectors. Ninety percent of the newcomers located in the north.[16]

Anglos took over the gold fields. To them, all nonwhites were foreigners and "therefore" without legitimate claims to civil liberties or property rights. The state government agreed and imposed a special tax on foreign miners in an open effort to discourage them. And even though the Treaty of Guadalupe Hidalgo guaranteed that Californios would be treated as citizens, they too were taxed. The state also passed a vagrancy law, popularly called "The Greasers Law," a colloquialism indicating its real intent: harassing Mexicans.

Although these laws were meant to drive Mexicans to the periphery of the economy, they did not attack the major base of Californio wealth: the land. Particularly in Southern California, elite Californio families held vast acreages. Some ranches dated back to grants made by Spanish kings. Soon the state began heavily taxing land. While common in American tradition, the policy was different from the then-prevailing Spanish-Mexican tradition of taxing production rather than land itself. Even more threatening, and ultimately devastating, were the attacks on land titles.

Congress created the Board of Land Commissioners in 1851. Holders of Mexican lands had to appear before the board and prove the validity of their titles. Between 1852 and 1856, the board heard 813 claims; 516 were ultimately held to be valid even though Government prosecutors appealed 80% of these.[17] But for most Californios, victory was pyrrhic. The typical case took 17 years to complete, and the legal costs mounted far beyond most ranchers' ability to pay. In the end, they lost their land anyway.

In Southern California prior to 1860, 50 old-line Californio families held all the land parcels worth $10,000 or more. A series of disastrous floods and droughts in the early 1860s aggravated their problems. By 1870, these families had lost three-fourths of those land parcels.[18] One wealthy rancher, Julio Verdugo, hoping to recover from the drought, took out a loan for $3,445.37 at an interest rate of 3% per month. This meant that at simple compound interest, (a concept he apparently did not understand), he would have owed almost $59,000 on the loan in eight years. At that time, Verdugo sold much of his ranch to pay the debt.[19]

The final blow to Mexican dominance in Southern California came in 1876 when the Transcontinental railroad arrived. The next year, the link to Santa Fe and the East opened. Anglo migrants, spurred by dreams of new wealth and the cheap fares due to competition between the two railroads, came pouring in. In one year (1887), 120,000 Anglos arrived.[20] At the beginning of the railroad era, about 25% of the population was Mexican. Ten years later, it was 10%, and, according to one study, their economic situation was bleak:

> The great bulk of Chicano workers in 1880 were either unskilled laborers or semiskilled manual workers, who had been displaced from traditional occupations in the pastoral economy. By 1880 nearly 88% of the Chicano workers in San Diego, 65% in San Diego, 82% in Santa Barbara, and 65% in Los Angeles, occupied the bottom of the socioeconomic structure.[21]

Anti-Mexican Violence

Violence against Mexican Americans has taken place routinely throughout California's past. Historians Matt Meier and Feliciano Rivera have this to say about the gold rush days: ". . . thievery, robbery, and murders were common throughout the gold mining period. Because of the stereotype most Anglos had of Mexicans, the latter provided convenient scapegoats for these crimes."[22] Another study describes the situation like this: "At Sonora an inflamed mob of 2,000 American miners attacked a camp of Mexicans. They killed many, burned the camp to the ground and rounded up hundreds of men, women and children to be driven like so many animals into a stockade."[23] Around the turn of the century, employers would openly march Mexican labor gangs down the main street of San Antonio under armed guard to prevent them from running away. Laborers threatening to break their contracts were chained to posts.[24]

The most famous incidents of anti-Mexican violence took place in Los Angeles during World War II: the Sleepy Lagoon Case and the Zoot Suit riot which followed. Rival Mexican American gangs fought a battle near a reservoir called the Sleepy Lagoon, and one man was killed. On June 3, 1943, a fight between Mexican youths and military servicemen broke out near a dance hall. During the following week, hundreds of servicemen swept through the Chicano sections of the city, harassing and threatening people, especially Zoot Suiters (youths, largely Mexican because the incident occurred in the Mexican district, who wore large baggy pants and coats called "Zoot Suits").

Although one is tempted to equate the Zoot Suit riot with the "race riots" of the 1960s, that would be a mistake. In the Zoot Suit riots, no one was killed or seriously injured. No pitched battles between Mexicans and the police were fought, and property damage was slight. The Zoot Suit riot was clearly an Anglo attack on Chicanos, and by present standards, a rather mild attack at that.[25]

Mexican Stereotype

The Chicano stereotype contains two contradictory themes. One image is of the Californio don; the other is of the Mexican peasant-bandit. Early travellers to California emphasized the former, often commenting on the gracious life style of wealthy ranchers. In *Two Years Before the Mast,* Richard Henry Dana described a fiesta:

> The great amusement of the evening—which I supposed was owing to its being carnival—was the breaking of eggs filled with cologne, or other essences, upon the heads of the company. . . . The women bring a great number of these secretly about them, and the amusement is to break one upon the head of a gentleman when his back is turned. . . . Another singular custom I was for some time at loss about. A pretty young girl was dancing . . . when a young man went behind her and placed his hat directly upon her head, letting it fall down over her eyes, and sprung back among the crowd. . . . Some of the ladies, upon whose heads hats had been placed, threw them off at once, and few kept them throughout the dance. . . . I soon began to suspect the meaning of the thing, and was afterward told that it was a compliment, and an offer to become the lady's gallant for the rest of the evening.

This aspect of the Mexican stereotype can still be seen in films and television programs such as "Zorro," "The Cisco Kid," and the local history play popular in Southern California, "Ramona." However romanticized, and therefore only partially accurate, this theme is, for the most part, flattering.

In direct opposition is the peasant-bandit theme. A historian says this about the Mexican war: "To the early writers the Mexican was just plain lazy and deserved to lose out, as he surely would to the energetic, productive Northerner."[26] In addition, Mexicans were also lawless, preferring to steal rather than work. The attribution of thievery to them was perpetuated by the image of the "bandito." Quick to plunder and be cruel when he had the upper hand, the bandito was cowardly otherwise. This stereotype may have originated in the Anglo mythologizing of the Alamo. Writes Joan Moore, "The Alamo is a Texas shrine and a standing monument to the Texas belief that Mexicans at heart are a very cowardly people."[27]

While one expects Mexicans to have a long history in California, one may not expect to find that blacks have been in California as long as Mexicans. For that reason, blacks are discussed next, although admittedly their number was not especially large.

Black Americans

Of the 44 persons who founded the city of Los Angeles in 1781, 26 were black. A Spanish census taken in 1790 classified 18% of the California population as being of African descent, and some of the leading families of the day were based on mixed marriages. California was sparsely populated then, however, so not too much should be made of the 18% figure, nor should too much reliance be placed on the early Spanish census.[28] The point is simply that blacks have been in California from the earliest of times.

By the time of the U.S.-Mexican war, the black percentage had dropped considerably. The Census Bureau estimates California's 1850 population at 92,000, 1,000 of whom were black.[29] The 1850 figure does not reflect the full impact of the gold rush, which was just getting underway. In two years, the state population more than doubled to 225,000, but blacks numbered only 2,000. By 1860, blacks still made up only a tiny percentage of the total population.

Slavery helps explain the small black population prior to the Civil War. They were not free to migrate. The reason blacks avoided California after emancipation is less clear. Distance may have been one factor, funds another, and the absence of a large black community might have made California less appealing. Whatever the reason, though, the black population grew slowly. By 1890, blacks made up less than 1% of the population.

Table 2.2
Black Population
California*

Year	Number (1,000)	Percent
1850	1	1.1
1860	4	1.1
1870	4	.7
1880	6	.7
1890	1	1.9
1900	22	.7
1910	23	.9
1920	39	1.1
1930	81	1.4
1940	124	1.8
1950	462	4.4
1960	884	5.6
1970	1,400	7.0

*Census Bureau, Historical Statistics of the United States.

The year 1890 marks the beginning of growth in Southern California, and the black population grew too. In that year, only 1,800 blacks lived in Los Angeles; ten years later the number had increased by more than 150%. Although the black population in the south was growing significantly, the same was not true in the north. Approximately 1,600 blacks lived in San Francisco in 1880, but only 200 more lived there in 1890. Slow growth also characterized other northern counties. The black population of Alameda, for instance, increased slightly from 690 in 1880 to 800 in 1890. The black population of Sacramento actually decreased over the same period, from 560 to 513.[30]

For the state as a whole, the table shows a moderate and steady growth increase between 1910 and 1940, a period including the Great Depression. During the 1930s, 41,000 blacks migrated to California, bringing the number to 124,000 by the end of the decade. Still, blacks comprised less than 2% of the population. California's growing defense industry was one magnet which attracted large numbers from other parts of the United States. During the 1940s, the black population increased to 462,000, but, of course, the white population grew too, and so the black percentage remained relatively small: 4%. By the end of the 1950s, the black population began approaching the million mark, and only then did the black percentage exceed 5%.

As these data indicate, blacks made up a relatively small proportion of California's population throughout the nineteenth century and for most of the twentieth century. However, that did not mean that blacks went unnoticed. As was the case with Mexicans, blacks found themselves occupying a powerless position in the infrastructure.

Economic Impact

Because there were so few blacks living in California during the nineteenth century, their economic impact was relatively slight. Unlike the Chinese, blacks did not compete with whites in the gold fields, a fact which may have reduced white animosity. As practiced by the '49er's, placer mining did not require large labor gangs composed of blacks (or any other group). Another reason for not using blacks seems almost fanciful, but white miners widely believed that blacks had a mystical ability to divine gold, and that it was therefore unfair to use blacks for prospecting. In one case, a white miner owned 15 slaves, and other white miners ordered him to leave the fields under the threat of violence.

Blacks were mostly urban. As early as 1852, San Francisco had enough blacks to support a segregated Methodist and Baptist church. Most blacks worked in the food and service industries, and they dominated barbering. ". . . All the barbers in the State were Negroes," reports one early history.[31] A few barbers became rich. In addition to service work, blacks worked around horses: smithing, grooming, and in a few instances, jockeying (an occupation later denied to blacks). Competition for jobs between different minorities sometimes helped employers bid down wages. A spokesman for the Los Angeles Railway Company once said, "We use a few Negro helpers. We use mostly Mexican workers because they work better and for less."[32]

The economic position of blacks was not particularly good, but after World War I it deteriorated further. The *Harvard Encyclopedia*, in a statement about the nation as a whole, said the following, which also applies to California:

> The decline of the black artisan may be traceable in part to his inability to upgrade his skills in a new industrial era. . . . But the primary cause of the postwar decline was racial prejudice. Whites began to prefer white barbers and waiters to black; craft unions excluded black workers and new manufacturing plants did not hire them.[33]

Southern California continued to attrack black migrants. Unlike many other places, blacks could find jobs in lower status civil service occupations. Their salaries were low compared to those of whites, but the economic situation was better than what it had been. Also, the absence of widespread unionism favored blacks.[34] A 1926 survey of 456 plants in the Los Angeles area found more than 50 employed blacks, a few of whom were low-level supervisors of Mexican and Anglo workers.[35] According to a study of department store personnel, "Management replaced white male 'attendants' and elevator men with blacks in order to stop time-wasting flirtation and conversation between male employees and white sales girls."[36] This is probably the only instance where taboos against interracial sex caused an upgrading of black male job status.

Although California was relatively open, it was no racial paradise. Restrictive covenants in housing deeds were commonplace and legal. Blacks were forced to live in segregated areas, that later became ghettos, the most famous of which is Watts, Los Angeles. Many movies, restaurants, swimming pools, and parks were understood to be off-limits to blacks. And economically, blacks faced competition from other ethnic groups. One writer claims that Japanese, Filipinos, and Mexicans gained an advantage by underliving blacks.[37] This claim is dubious, however, and is reminiscent of Ross's claim that Chinese and Irish immigrants underlived native whites.

During the Great Depression, nearly everyone fared poorly, but blacks more than most. Between 20% and 40% of California's urban blacks were on relief.[38] The pressures to push blacks down the occupational ladder intensified as unions gained power and systematically barred blacks. Whites displaced them in the service industry, and barbering, once exclusively black, became a segregated occupation, with black barbers for blacks and white barbers for whites.

In 1940, 12,000 blacks migrated to California, one-half to Southern California. World War II created a huge demand for labor, but blacks still met with resistance. For example, black organizations had to prod President Roosevelt to outlaw specifically racial discrimination in defense work. Although the population and economy of California had grown substantially by 1950, blacks remained on the bottom rungs of the socioeconomic ladder. By 1970, the income of a typical employed black in California was 37% lower than that of a comparable white.[39]

Anti-Black Laws

At the Constitutional Convention of 1849, delegates declared California a free state. The same convention also prohibited blacks from serving in the militia, voting, or giving testimony against whites in court. Like many other free states, California had a fugitive slave law, which meant that persons bringing slaves into the state could legally keep them, and runaway slaves were returned to their owners. Because the number of slaves in California must have been small (no one knows how many), the fugitive slave law was evidently ". . . intended to frighten blacks into leaving the state and it succeeded to a limited extent for some blacks did migrate to Canada, Mexico, Baja California, and Central America."[40] Authorities did not enforce the fugitive slave law consistently and a welter of contradictory legal precedents resulted. Legal issues were not resolved until 1857 when a fugitive slave named Archie Lee was finally freed after first being incarcerated as a runaway, then being forcibly rescued from custody by a pro-abolitionist mob, and then finally being acquitted by a U. S. commissioner on the grounds that his owner had voluntarily brought Lee into a free state with the intent of permanently residing there. After that, the fugitive slave law was effectively dead.

While one might think that suffrage would be the biggest political issue among blacks, it was not. Over an 11-year period beginning in 1852, blacks organized a series of "California Colored Conventions." At these gatherings, efforts to repeal the testimony law held center stage. The first convention authorized a petition campaign to influence state legislators.[41] The second California Colored Convention, held four years later, also focused on the testimony law, the campaign of the first convention having produced no result. Although neither Chinese nor native Americans could testify under the same law, the campaign did not include them. "The expression 'third-world solidarity' would not be heard until over a hundred years later."[42] This campaign also failed.

The third convention continued to fight the testimony law, but broadened its agenda to include the issues of black education, support for black newspapers, and defeat of the then-impending legislation that would prohibit black migration into the state (the bill did not pass). Like its predecessors, the campaign against the testimony law failed. Not until 1863—and the Civil War—was the law finally abolished for blacks (but not for Chinese and native Americans). With the repeal of the testimony law, the fourth California Colored Convention of 1865 shifted attention to suffrage, but that issue was not resolved until the passage of the fifteenth Amendment to the Constitution.

California also passed an antimiscegenation law in 1872. Evidently, the law caused little concern among blacks. It may have done little more than legally reaffirm a taboo so strong that no one was violating it anyway. (Later, the antimiscegenation law became an issue when applied to Asians).

Black Stereotype

Because California held out promises of being more racially tolerant than many other places, it is ironic that the state's most visible industry, motion pictures, should have contributed so much to the black stereotype. Arguably, no single work of popular culture did more to denigrate blacks than "Birth of a Nation," D. W. Griffith's revolutionary film about the Civil War.

In silent films, written text was interspersed with action sequences so the audience could follow the story line. A major part of "Birth of a Nation" takes place during the Reconstruction Period, and in one sequence, black representatives (played by whites in black face) become the majority of the legislature of South Carolina. The film text says, "Historic incidents from the first legislative session under Reconstruction"—which implies that what follows is factually accurate. The subsequent action scenes show black legislators sitting in session, joking and drinking, one with his bare feet on his desk. A black legislator, while munching on a chicken leg, addresses the chair. The chair makes a ruling: "All members must wear shoes," says the text. At the same session, legislators rescind the antimiscegenation law. Griffith shows black legislators covetously eyeing white female spectators in the galleries. "Later. The grim reapings begin," the text says.

The newly founded National Association for the Advancement of Colored People (NAACP) protested the film. While the San Francisco branch succeeded in getting some changes made, most people saw Griffith's uncut version. And Hollywood continued to perpetuate the black stereotype. Although not so mean as Griffith's portrayal, blacks were shown as happy-go-lucky, musically inclined buffoons, servants, or laborers. While always obsequious and often loyal, they needed whites to take care of them. Precisely what effect these portrayals had on fixing the black stereotype cannot be measured now. However, the effect must have been considerable.

During the nineteenth century, antiblack legislation was important in California, but the biggest campaign against nonwhites targeted the Chinese, and a little later, the Japanese. Asians provoked ". . . proportionately more white fear and violence than did the less numerous black residents."[43] One can debate whether the provocation was due to numbers or some other variable, but it is clear that the Asian presence became the main racial issue in California.

Chinese Americans

During the nineteenth century, some 2.5 million Chinese emigrated; the exact number is unknown, as is the exact number who went to the mainland United States. California conducted its first official census in 1850, but did not bother to count Chinese, Japanese, or native Americans. Data from the federal censuses are shown below.

As may be observed, the Chinese population has fluctuated considerably, increasing from some 34,000 in 1860 to 75,000 in 1880. Thereafter, it began declining, and not until 1960 did the Chinese population exceed that number again. The Chinese percentage of the population likewise first declined slowly, from a high of 9% in 1860, and then more quickly over the next several decades. By 1960, even though the number of Chinese had increased, the population of the state had also increased and so the Chinese percentage remained approximately what it had been over the preceding four decades. Immigration laws, enacted as a result of political pressures originating in California, were responsible for the decline of the Chinese population.

Economic Impact

Gold Rush. Like so many other groups, the Chinese immigrated for largely economic reasons. Says Betty Sung in her book on Chinese American history:

> The literal translation of the Chinese characters for the United States is 'Land of the Beautiful', but among the Chinese in the United States, the vernacular term for this country is Gum Shhan or 'Mountain of

Table 2.3
Chinese Population
California*

Year	Number (1,000)	Percent
1860	34	9.0
1870	49	8.8
1880	75	8.7
1890	72	6.0
1900	46	3.1
1910	36	1.5
1920	29	.8
1930	37	.7
1940	40	.6
1950	58	.6
1960	95	.6
1970	170	.9

*Census Bureau, various Volume IIs and Special Reports, Saxton, 1971, Tsai, 1983.

Gold'. The name originated with the earliest immigrants who came
to mine gold in the hills of California.[44]

At that time, Butte County in north-central California was the richest
gold field in the country. The 1860 census counted 2,177 Chinese in
the area. One resident of the area wrote, "I recall once while helping
drive some hogs to Oroville in 1860, when we got to town I thought
the whole town must be Chinese."[45]

Chinese were welcomed as long as they did the cooking, washing
and other menial tasks, but they were not welcomed as miners competing directly with whites. They were, however, "needed." White
miners worked the easy claims first. When those claims played out,
they sold the old claims to Chinese miners and moved on to the richer
sites. Through arduous work, old mines could be made to yield a
living, a living which whites scorned but of which the Chinese were
anxious to partake. If nothing else, mining old claims was better than
cooking and washing. The potential racial conflict was eased somewhat when gold was discovered in the Comstock Lode in 1859 and
white miners left to try their luck there.

As the California Gold Rush ran its course, the percentage of
Chinese miners steadily increased. Around 1850, Chinese miners were
less than 1% of all miners; by 1860, Chinese comprised 29%, and by
1870, more than 50%. At some point, of course, even the marginal
mines gave out, and the Gold Rush passed into history, a history which
has largely ignored, especially in its mythic elements, the role played
by the Chinese '49er's.

Railroads. While Chinese '49er's are not much remembered, the same
is not true of Chinese gandy dancers. The image of long gangs of
"coolies" in sack shirts and round, pointed straw hats laying rails
has survived to this day, in part because it has a basis in historical
fact.[46]

In 1862, Congress authorized the construction of the transcontinental railroad. The federal government financially backed the enterprise by issuing bonds and granting land rights. Construction was to
proceed from both the Pacific and Atlantic Oceans, meeting at some
unspecified place in the middle of the country. On the West Coast,
the rights to build the railroad went to the Central Pacific. Because
the government parcelled out payments as each mile of rail line was
completed, and because Congress had not fixed a meeting point
between the Pacific and Atlantic branches, the more miles of line
completed, the greater the wealth acquired. Speed was therefore
important, and in those days, the size of the labor gang was the critical
factor.

From the beginning, the Central Pacific had labor problems. The population of California was not large, economic times were basically good, and the gold fields still beckoned. A large pool of white laborers did not exist, and those whites willing to lay rails were unreliable. After two years, only 50 miles of track had been laid, and the Sierras still lay ahead. Out of desperation, the Central Pacific turned to the Chinese. In February 1865, the company hired 300 Chinese laborers as an experiment. The experiment went well, and by the end of the year, 3,000 more Chinese were hired. Even though the railroad drew Chinese from the gold fields and from farms and cities, there were not enough. The bulk had to be acquired through labor contracting firms which imported Chinese workers. One firm supposedly imported 30,000 under five-year contracts, but that figure is surely exaggerated. Nevertheless, it does suggest the great demand for Chinese labor.

The work was hard by any standard. Chinese gandy dancers literally toiled from sunup to sundown for a mere $35 a month, minus the cost of food and lodging. The Chinese cost the railroad two-thirds of what white laborers cost, and they were docile, hard-working, and noncomplaining. With them, the Central Pacific found the solution to its labor problems.

Fortuitously for the Chinese, the railroad was being built at a time when white workers were not suffering from high unemployment. If they had been, they undoubtedly would have objected to Chinese gandy dancers. Perhaps as important, Chinese labor had an upgrading effect on whites. As the Chinese flowed into the unskilled sector, whites moved up the socioeconomic ladder to become foremen, strawbosses, and skilled craftsmen. These jobs were understood to be for whites only.

There was also an atavistic factor stifling white objections. In his work on the anti-Chinese movement, historian Alexander Saxton notes that, "No man who had any choice would have chosen to be a common laborer on the Central Pacific during the crossing of the High Sierra."[47] Cutting across the face of cliffs and tunnelling through mountains during the dead of winter, amid freezing temperatures and huge snowbanks, was dangerous, and many Chinese lost their lives, although the exact number is unknown because no one bothered to keep records on the Chinese.

In her family biography, Maxine Hong Kingston writes of her ancestors, gandy dancers who worked on the cliffs of the Sierras. Her account provides an inkling of what it was like to ride a basket along the face of a cliff in order to plant explosive charges:

> The basket swung and twirled and [Ah Goong] saw the world sweep underneath him. . . . Suspended in the quiet sky, he thought all kinds

of crazy thoughts, that if a man didn't want to live anymore, he just cut the ropes, or, easier, tilt the basket, dip, and never have to worry again . . . . Swinging near the cliff, Ah Goong stood up and grabbed it by a twig. He dug holes, then inserted gunpowder and fuses . . . . At last his fuse caught; he waved, and men above pulled hand over hand, hauling him up, pulleys creaking . . . Ah Goong ran up the ledge road they'd cleared and watched the explosions, which banged almost synchronously, echoes booming like war. He moved his scaffold to the next section of the cliff and went down in the basket again, with bags of dirt, and set the next charge . . . . This time two men were blown up.[48]

The Chinese also worked on other lines. Between 1870 and 1887, Chinese gandy dancers laid the rails to San Joaquin, between San Francisco and Los Angeles over the notoriously dangerous Tehachapi Pass, and between Sacramento and Portland. And the transcontinental railroad finally connected with the eastern branch in Ogden, Utah, in 1869. One hundred years later, when the centennial marking that event was celebrated, no mention of the Chinese was planned until Chinese groups protested. The Chinese gandy dancer, like the Chinese '49'er, was being written out of the history.

Other Occupations. Not all Chinese worked on the railroad or in the gold fields. The following shows the percentage of Chinese in some other occupations:

Occupation	Percent Chinese
Truck gardening	33
Wool milling	70–80
Cigar making	90
Garment making	50

The Chinese constituted a larger proportion of the labor force than of the total population of California. During the 1870s they were 25% of the labor force.[49]

Labor found the Chinese domination of certain jobs, no matter how inconsequential in the overall economic scheme, intolerable. Moreover, the mere presence of the Chinese posed a threat. They provided employers with an alternative to more expensive white labor. Politicians quickly recognized labor's anti-Chinese sentiments, and "The Chinese must go" became the political rallying cry of the day. Anti-Chinese laws and treaties soon followed.

Anti-Chinese Laws and Treaties

California already had an infrastructure hostile to foreigners in general and nonwhites in particular. For instance, neither blacks nor Indians could bear witness against whites in a court of law. In 1854, this legal principle was extended to cover Chinese as well. In effect, a Chinese could not bring legal charges against a white without a white witness willing to testify in court.

Laws harassing Chinese were common. A newspaper article of the time describes a San Francisco ordinance thus: "Keepers of laundries and laundry offices who employ no vehicle drawn by animal power, shall pay $15 per quarter license—a tax applicable mainly to Chinese who carried their laundry loads in baskets rather than horse drawn vehicles." City law also required at least 500 square feet per person per room. Ostensibly for sanitation, this measure was actually directed against Chinese boarding houses. Another law required that persons arrested must have their hair clipped to a height of one inch. Also ostensibly a sanitation measure, the law was actually directed against the Chinese.

Much to the dismay of the anti-Chinese agitators, the courts often overturned these laws. Concerning the hair-clipping ordinance, the court ruling stated this:

> The ordinance being directed against the Chinese only, imposing upon them a degrading and cruel punishment, is also subject to the further objection, that it is hostile and discriminating legislation against a class forbidden by that clause of the Fourteenth Amendment to the Constitution, which declares that no State shall 'deny to any person within its jurisdiction the equal protection of the laws'.[50]

In 1880, Congress took the first step toward Chinese exclusion by declaring unto itself the power to regulate, but not to ban, Chinese immigration. Two years later, Congress decided that it did indeed have the power to ban immigration, and passed the Exclusion Act, which prohibited Chinese immigration for ten years. Chinese already in the United States could remain, leave, and re-enter the country, but Chinese could not become naturalized citizens. The Exclusion Act passed with " . . . almost complete absence of opposition to the measure."[51] Not until the middle of World War II, with China allied to the United States, did Congress pass a bill allowing Chinese to become naturalized citizens. The same bill also gave China an immigration quota for the first time. This number, 105 immigrants per year, was hardly immense.

With the passage of the Exclusion Act, anti-Chinese forces had won a major victory. Later, several laws were passed to tie up the loose ends of exclusion:

- In 1888, the Scott Act prohibited Chinese who left the United States from reentering. There was no grandfather clause. Those Chinese who were temporarily abroad suddenly could not return.
- The Geary Act passed six years later. It required the registration and identification of all Chinese residents and denied Chinese bail in *habeas corpus* proceedings. The Supreme Court upheld the registration requirement in 1893.
- In 1894, China signed a treaty with the United States agreeing to exclusion for ten years. Later, Congress unilaterally extended the Chinese exclusion laws until the 1924 National Origins Act rendered them moot.
- In 1904, Congress passed the Deficiency Act. It applied the principle and fact of exclusion to all United States possessions (with some exceptions for Hawaii).
- In 1906, California amended its antimiscegenation law, originally passed in 1872. When it became questionable whether the law applied to Chinese, the state legislature specifically included Mongolians in the statute.

So in fewer than 60 years, California and the federal government erected a legal infrastructure to keep the Chinese out, a structure which was extremely effective. Not until immigration laws were revamped in 1965 did the Chinese population begin to grow again.

Anti-Chinese Violence

Anti-Chinese violence was commonplace. Historians Victor and Brett de Bary Nee write this about the gold fields: " . . . in 1852 when Chinese miners joined the search for gold and found themselves for the first time in activities which were competitive with, rather than complementary to, those of white miners, [the] expression of anti-Chinese hostility began to erupt."[52] For instance, in the El Dorado fields in 1852, white miners went on a pogrom, pillaging Chinese mining camps. They also posted signs like this warning the Chinese to leave:

> Notice is hereby given to all Chinese on the Agua Fria and its tributaries to leave within 10 days of this date, and any failure to comply shall be subjected to 39 lashes and moved by force of arms.[53]

Violence was not limited to the fields. In Los Angeles, in 1871, two policemen were wounded when they intervened in a Chinese dispute over a woman. The incident triggered a riot which lasted four hours, during which 18 Chinese, including several children, were killed, some hanged on lampposts.[54] In San Francisco, a white mob, incensed because the Pacific Mail Steamship Company transported Chinese immigrants, attacked the company. The National Guard was called and could quell the riot only after engaging in a prolonged shooting battle with the crowd. (Curiously, no one seems to have been shot.)

Revenge, jealousy, greed—emotions such as these can explain occasional violence, or violence by a specific person directed at a specific person. But emotions cannot very well explain collective violence by a group directed at a group over a period of years. That requires broader structural and cultural explanations. One aspect of the broader explanation is the stereotype.

Chinese Stereotype

The Chinese stereotype centered around the themes of cruelty, filth, stagnation, opium addiction, and slavery. These were prominently played up in newspapers and in the penny press (wide circulation, low-cost magazines which were then becoming popular).[55] In what is the most detailed study of the anti-Chinese stereotype, historian Creighton Miller offers this illustration:

> One lurid eyewitness account of the execution of a woman who had murdered her husband described how the breasts, buttocks, and fleshy parts of her legs were removed before final decapitation. Indeed the association of cruelty with the Chinese was so general by 1856 that one American editor, on receiving the news that Chinese officials had erected the first imperial hospital, could not resist the chance afforded for a bit of sarcasm: 'Founding hospitals in China! What? In China, whose ditches, canals and rivers are reported to be strewn ever and anon with the bodies of infants that of course have been killed by their horrid mothers . . . . Is it possible that, in the breast of the Chinese, there can be one drop of the milk of human kindness, at least for children?'[56]

The reference to babies and mothers probably reflects the belief that the Chinese routinely practiced infanticide. Some reports claimed that Chinese mothers murdered one-half of all their babies.[57]

The Chinese were also stereotyped as being dirty, harboring unique microbes and a host of uniquely Chinese diseases. This "fact" was accepted virtually without question and found its way into reputable reference works. Then there was opium. Opium smoking had not been widespread in China until the British established control over certain aspects of Chinese commerce, including the opium trade, but the Chinese were blamed nonetheless. The image of cruel, inscrutable men cloistered away in filth laden dens sucking on opium pipes caught the people's imagination. Opium came to be unshakably associated with the Chinese and was taken as further evidence of their degeneration.

The negative stereotype of the Chinese occasionally encountered problems. Chinese culture had produced magnificent works of art, music, writing, and architecture. Even the most ardent anti-Sinophiles had to acknowledge those accomplishments. However, they did not have to give the current (that is, nineteenth century) generation of Chinese any credit. Anti-Sinophiles argued that at one time China was highly developed but had fallen into stagnation and could no longer support art and intellect. And if that explanation were insufficient, anti-Sinophiles further argued that Chinese accomplishments were due to a unique Asian facility for imitating rather than creating.[58]

These arguments found much support in the scientific community. The theory of evolution was gaining currency and was quickly taken up by social scientists. As field reports from faraway exotic places came filtering in, the idea took hold that some societies were at a higher level of evolutionary development than others. Western civilization stood at the top, while beneath it lay Mongolian (Asian) civilization, largely moribund. These ideas permeated the thinking of the time.

As if being cruel, filthy, and mentally and socially inferior were not enough, the Chinese were also accused of being slave dealers, especially of prostitutes. It just happened that Chinese immigration began growing at a time when the abolition movement was growing. Abolitionists feared the Chinese might become a new form of American slavery. As a result, in 1862 the United States outlawed the contract labor system under which many Chinese laborers first immigrated. In 1876, the Chinese government followed suit. Neither move quelled the concern or ended the stereotype.

The Chinese came under attack along with Californios, immigrant Mexicans, blacks, and other minorities. However, for some reason the Chinese threatened white hegemony more than Chicanos and blacks did. Perhaps the Chinese were perceived as more foreign, perhaps their number was perceived as greater than it actually was, or perhaps the Chinese were in more direct economic competition with whites. The intensity of the anti-Chinese movement has never been completely explained.

Japanese Americans

More than any other immigrant group, Japanese Americans emphasize generational standing. To each generation is attributed a particular social and political status, as well as unique psychological and
character attributes.[59] The generations have names. Original immigrants are called *Issei*. The children of the Issei are called *Nisei*, and
their children are called *Sansei*.[60] There is now a fourth generation,
Yonsei. Sometimes one hears the term *Nisei* being used to refer to all
Japanese Americans rather than to the second generation specifically.
This can be confusing, so more recently the term *Nikkei* is being used
when speaking of all Japanese Americans.

Demographers do not agree on the number of *Issei*. William Petersen has investigated this question in depth and points out much confusion about whether Hawaiian Japanese are included in the United
States totals and about whether immigration or census data are being
used.[61] The following table is for California only and is about as accurate a count as can be obtained.[62]

Before 1890, fewer than 1,000 Japanese lived in California. Not
until the turn of the century did the Japanese population exceed
10,000. Even today, at the peak, they number fewer than a quarter-
of-a-million. Moreover, unlike the Chinese, who at one time were a
significant percentage of the total population of California, the Japanese have always been a tiny population. Their highest percentage,
in 1920, was slightly more than 2%. From that point, their relative

Table 2.4
Japanese Population
California*

Year	Number (1,000)	Percent
1870	#	0
1880	#	0
1890	1	.1
1900	10	.7
1910	41	1.7
1920	72	2.1
1930	98	1.7
1940	94	1.4
1950	85	.8
1960	160	1.0
1970	214	1.1

*Census Bureau, Volume IIs and Special Reports.

#Indicates fewer than 1,000.

size declined, reflecting the exclusion laws. More recently, the relative size of the Japanese population has been increasing, but very gradually. It has not even regained its former "high."

San Francisco was the major port of entry for Asian immigrants and, not surprisingly, became the initial hub of Asian life. According to data collected from yearbooks published by various Japanese American organizations, in 1904 about one-fourth of the entire Japanese population of California resided in San Francisco.

After the initial period of settlement, the Japanese population began shifting southward to Los Angeles, then a relatively small, uncosmopolitan city. With estimates made by John Modell's *The Japanese of Los Angeles*, the percentage of all mainland Japanese living in Los Angeles County can be calculated.[63] Japanese were never more than 2.1% of the Los Angeles population. In short, the Japanese were (and still are) a tiny minority even in the area of their greatest concentration.

Economic Impact

During the early period of Japanese immigration, many worked on the railroads. In 1906, about one-third of all Japanese men were so employed, mostly as laborers but a few as shop workers. From that peak, railroad employment declined to 10,000 in 1909, and to 4,300 by 1920. The railroad never had the impact on the Japanese that it had on the Chinese, although as a by-product of railroad work, a few Japanese found themselves stranded in the interior of the country and there established small ethnic colonies. Also in this early period, Japanese worked as domestics, or "school boys" as they were called. Some were really students, but the name was also a euphemism for servant, cook, waiter, and general helper. In 1909, one study reported that between 12,000 and 15,000 Japanese worked in domestic services.[64]

Neither domestic service nor the railroad attracted the Japanese for very long. Soon they began gravitating towards farm work. In their book, Wilson and Hosokawa state that "it is difficult to overemphasize the importance of agriculture in the history of the Japanese in the United States."[65] According to one estimate, in 1910 30,000 Japanese were working in agriculture. This number, if accurate, represents three-fourths of all Japanese on the mainland. If only approximate, the number still indicates the importance that agriculture had assumed among the Japanese.[66]

The vast majority were field hands working under a "padrone" system, common to immigrant farm labor everywhere. Under this system a Japanese entrepreneur, called a *Dano-san*, would organize a gang of Japanese laborers and contract with farmers to have the gang work the fields. Depending on the *Dano-san*;, the size of these gangs varied from six to 100 or more. A *Dano-san* was necessary because few laborers spoke English, and all were enmeshed in Japanese culture. The *Dano-san* system provided workers the comforts of their culture while enabling them to work in an alien one. The system also served a latent function: it produced cohesive work units, or quasiunions. The *Dano-san* often held out for better wages and sometimes refused to work for certain farmers.

From farm labor, the Japanese quickly moved into farming itself. A common route was to truck farm (rent land), and from there, to become farm owners. Only a few farmers became extremely wealthy but most could make a living. The following figures, although not systematic, do provide an appreciation of the Japanese movement into agriculture:

1900: 39 Japanese farmers with less than five acres per farm.

1909: 13,723 Japanese farmers hold 16,449 acres and lease 6,000 more acres. Japanese crops valued at $6.2 million.

1910: Japanese own 17,035 acres and lease 17,762 acres. The 1910 Japanese holding amounted to 2% of all California farmlands.

1919: Japanese crops valued at $67 million. Japanese farmers (including truck farmers) produce 10% of all California produce at a time when the Japanese were less than 2% of the California population.

The Japanese also moved into tuna fishing. In 1915–1916, 13% of all tuna fishermen were Japanese; by 1920, it was 29% and by 1923, 50%. As early as 1913, Terminal Island, a community located near the canneries in Los Angeles Harbor, had become a company town of Japanese fishermen and their families. The Japanese introduced poling, a method for catching tuna with minimal damage to the fish.

In Southern California, gardens and lawns require upkeep all year around, and professional gardeners are common. Although the job requires minimal capital (pick-up truck, lawnmowers, and tools), it does demand long hours of hard work along with the initiative to establish a route of customers. Japanese soon dominated the gardening business, so much so that the stereotypical gardener became Japanese. Japanese also dominated an occupation which most urbanites have never heard of: chick sexing. As the job title implies, a chick sexor determines the gender of chicks. However strange it may sound, the task requires a special skill, which the Japanese monopolized. So complete was the monopoly that in some farm communites the myth arose that only the Japanese knew the secret of sexing chicks.[67]

Despite the small number, the Japanese ran into a whirlwind of hostility almost from their first arrival. If we arbitrarily use 1900 as the year when the Japanese population reached a significant size, then it took anti-Japanese forces only seven years to triumph at the national level.

Anti-Japanese Laws and Treaties

The Japanese were attacked almost from the very moment they arrived. As early as 1893, San Francisco attempted to segregate Japanese children into separate schools. Undoubtedly one reason was timing. Wilson and Hosokawa describe anti-Japanese hostility as the "tail of the anti-Chinese kite."[68] Labor's position on the Japanese was much the same as its previous anti-Chinese position. Fearing the possibility of low-waged Japanese workers, labor called for a ban on immigration. In 1900, labor unions sponsored a major anti-Japanese rally, abetted by San Francisco politicians. According to William Petersen:

> The main speaker was James D. Phelan, then mayor of San Francisco and later United States Senator from California, who until his death in 1930 endlessly iterated the same theme: 'The Japanese are starting the same tide of immigration which we thought we had checked twenty years ago. . . . The Chinese and Japanese are not bona fide citizens. They are not the stuff of which American citizens can be made.'[69]

The annexation of Hawaii that year fanned anti-Japanist fears even more. Hawaiian Japanese could now move to the mainland. Also that year, a case of bubonic plague was discovered in San Francisco. Mayor Phelan promptly proclaimed an epidemic, blaming the Chinese and Japanese. He ordered them quarantined even though his accusation was not supported by medical fact.

By the time the Japanese began immigrating in larger numbers, labor was better organized, more firmly established, and more experienced than it had been in the past. Samuel Gompers, a hero of the labor movement, was an outspoken opponent of open immigration, and was especially vitriolic towards the Japanese. He authored a pamphlet bearing a title which aptly summarized his views: "Meat Versus

Rice, American Manhood Against Asiatic Coolieism, Which Shall Survive?" And according to Petersen, "When Japanese poet and socialist, Sen Katayama, visited the United States in 1904, Gompers called him 'this presumptuous Jap' out of whose 'leprous mouth' come 'mongrel utterances'"[70]

In the following two years, a spate of anti-Japanese events occurred. In February, the *San Francisco Chronicle* opened an anti-Japanese campaign with a nine-column article arguing for exclusion. One reason mentioned was a fear that Japanese soldiers discharged from service in the Russo-Japanese war would immigrate to California and become a secret army awaiting orders to rise up and take over the country. Evidently the *Chronicle* viewed the anti-Japanese issue as a way to outdistance its arch competitor, the *Examiner*. In addition, one of the *Chronicle*'s owners, Harry deYoung, hoped to ride the issue into a Senate seat. Other newspapers also took part in raising anti-Japanese sentiment.

In March 1905, an anti-Japanese resolution was introduced in the California legislature. Among other things, it called upon California's congressional representatives to seek an exclusion bill. The resolution passed without a dissenting vote. The issue of Japanese children in the public schools was prominently mentioned during the debate.

The Japanese and Korean Exclusion League was formed in May 1905 under the auspices of labor. Upper-class elites also supported the league, which promptly began lobbying California's congressional delegation to introduce a Japanese exclusion bill. In October, the Exclusion League petitioned the San Francisco School Board to segregate all Mongolian children. Rumors of a possible war with Japan began floating about.

In April 1906, the San Francisco earthquake struck, and it was the Japanese area that was hard hit. With no choice but to find new residences, they began moving into white districts. Over the next few months, the mood turned violent, and several Japanese were attacked by gangs of young white males. The police did not take effective action.

In October, all Japanese and Korean children in San Francisco were ordered to attend the so-called Chinese school. At issue were 93 Japanese students. When the Japanese government objected, President Roosevelt sent a personal envoy to investigate the situation.[71] That March, Roosevelt barred Japanese immigration to the mainland from Hawaii, Canada, and Mexico.

Throughout that year and the early part of the next, the United States exchanged secret notes with the Japanese government. The substance of these notes formed the Gentlemen's Agreement. Under its terms, Japan halted further immigration to the United States. However, parents, children, and wives of Japanese already residing in the United States could join their families. The proviso regarding wives later became an issue.[72]

The agreement did not end the anti-Japanism in California. The Japanese presence in agriculture was being viewed with alarm, and soon became a major issue. In 1913, California passed the Alien Land Law. Persons not eligible to become naturalized citizens could not own farm land or lease it for more than three years. Japanese immigrants, being ineligible for citizenship by federal law, were prevented from owning their own farms. Seven years later, an initiative appeared before California voters asking them to affirm the Alien Land Law. The statewide vote was three-to-one (668,000 to 222,000) in favor of tighter restrictions. The initiative passed in every county of the state, and according to Modell's study of Los Angeles, it was particularly popular in lower socioeconomic areas.[73]

Enforcement of the land law was delayed while the Supreme Court took the case under advisement. In the interim, the uproar over picture brides was occurring. Anti-Japanists claimed brides violated the Gentlemen's Agreement (in fact, the agreement itself permitted brides). Sensitive to the issue, the Japanese government prohibited further immigration to the United States. In 1922, the Supreme Court affirmed that Japanese could not be naturalized citizens. And in 1923 the Supreme Court upheld the Alien Land Law.

One can debate the effect of the land laws. Many *Issei* put their farmlands in the names of their *Nisei* children, who were citizens by birth. Occasionally, sympathetic whites acted as a dummy holding company on behalf of Japanese farmers. Because of these legal devices, the alien land laws never had the effect hoped for by those who supported them. Nevertheless, Japanese farm holdings did stop increasing at their former rate (of course, the rate might have tapered off anyway).

During the Great Depression, Anti-Japanism receded into the background. Exclusion laws, land laws, occupational segregation, and residential segregation were all in place. World War II reignited anti-Japanism, and the first to feel the brunt were those Japanese Americans living on the West Coast. In the first days after Pearl Harbor, many were rounded up and interrogated, and some were sent to prison on vague suspicions of being "enemy aliens." None were ever convicted of any charges. In the early months of 1942, the entire Japanese population on the West Coast was ordered to report to various mustering stations; 110,000 men, women, and children were herded off to incarceration camps located throughout the western states. None of the 110,000 were ever charged with a crime, much less convicted. The story of the incarceration is itself a long one and details are not germane here, except to note that it represented the ultimate triumph of anti-Japanese forces.

Japanese Stereotype

During the nineteenth century, the Japanese were viewed positively. In 1892, a San Francisco newspaper described the Japanese as a

> . . . brave race, and much cleaner in their personal habits than the Chinese. Every steamer from Yokohama brings a full cargo of the pleasant little people from the Mikado's realm. They are picturesque people, as well as pleasant. They are polite, courteous, smiling and nobody ever has occasion to kick or cuff them, or even to upbraid them . . . . But they are taking work away from our boys and girls and from our men and women.[74]

Author Wallace Irwin made a career out of writing about Japanese immigrants. His stories were widely serialized in magazines and published as novels. His first Japanese protagonist was Hashimura Togo, an immigrant working as a domestic. In *Letters of a Japanese Schoolboy* (1909), Irwin portrays Togo as a Japanese country bumpkin. For example, when Togo arrives in America, he is met by his cousin and the two engage in the following conversation:

> 'How about Hon. Washington and Hon. Lincoln to copy for famous career?' [Togo asks]. His cousin replies: 'Hon. Washington could not tell a lie, while Hon. Lincoln was celebrated for gleeful anecdotes.' There Lincoln was most ablest man of them two. Also because of early struggle of career he was noble example for all Japanese Schoolboys enjoying poverty for American education.[75]

Irwin's portrayals became increasingly hostile. Twelve years later he published *Seed of the Sun*. In it, he describes the Japanese section of Bly, a small agricultural town in northern California:

> Here in Bly you will find nothing of the fairyland charm, the quaintness of composition, the age-old prettiness which we have learned to associate with Japan . . . . Brown, slanty-eyed men in baggy overalls, rough sweaters, and swampers' boots, muddy from the irrigation ditches, come slouching in towards the general store. In and out of the local garage small tinnish automobiles are charging noisily all day long. Little brown men sit at the wheel and gossip of grease

cups and gear shifts in the language of Nippon . . . . At the sight of a man the women bend their bodies stiffly from the waist up, accompanying the gesture with folding of the hands and a lowering of the eyes. In Bly, California, the male is lord.[76]

The same year (1921), Peter Kyne wrote a popular anti-Japanese novel, *Pride of Palomar*, about the Japanese push into California agriculture. In one scene the protagonist is motoring through the California countryside while he discusses the situation with a naive young lady from the East.

[The protagonist:] 'In common with all other Californians with manhood enough to resent imposition, I resent all Japanese.'

[The woman:] 'Is it true, then, that there is a real Japanese problem out here?'

'Why, I thought everybody knew that,' he replied a trifle reproachfully. 'As the outpost of the Occidental civilization, we've been battling Oriental aggression for forty years' . . . .

'This is entirely an agricultural section,' he explained. 'There are not labor-unions here. But,' he added bitterly, 'you could throw a stone in the air and be moderately safe on the small end of a bet that the stone would land on a Jap farmer' . . . .

'The lower standards of living of the Oriental enable him to pay much higher prices for land than a white man can.'

'But,' she persisted, 'these aliens have a legal right to own and lease land in this state, have they not?'

'Unfortunately, through the treachery of white lawyers, they have devised means to comply with the letter of the law denying them the right to own land, while evading the spirit of that law. Corporations with white dummy directors purchased by alien Japs in the names of their infants in arms who happen to have been born in this county,' he shrugged. . . .

'We know from experience that the class of Japs who have a strangle-hold on California are not gentlemen but coolies, and never respect an agreement that they can break if, in the breaking, they are financially benefitted.'

'Well,' the girl queried, a little subdued by his vehemence, 'how has the law worked out?'

'Fine—for the Japs. The Japanese population of California has doubled in five years; the area of fertile lands under their domination has increased a thousandfold, until eighty-five percent of the vegetables raised in this state are controlled by Japs. They are not a dull people, and they know how to make that control yield rich dividends—at the expense of the white race.'[77]

In this passage, the anti-Japanese stereotype is fully developed: they were devious, selfish, cunning, turned entirely inward to their own culture, eagerly awaiting their chance to overrun the country. Their positive traits, intelligence and diligence, only made them a greater menace.

Filipino Americans

The United States acquired control of the Philippines as a result of the Spanish American War. Soon after, by deliberate policy, an American imprint on the Islands was clearly visible. Two factors particularly affected immigration. English became the second (in some instances the first) language of the country. And the Pensionado Plan encouraged Filipino college students to study in the United States. The idea behind the plan was for these students to return home inculcated with American knowledge and values, which would further the Americanization of the Islands. In 1903, 100 students were selected out of 20,000 applicants. They matriculated at schools throughout the United States and most returned to take high positions in the Philippine government. By 1938, 14,000 Filipinos had used the plan.

Other than Pensionados, the major portion of the Filipino immigration went to Hawaii. Of the 113,000 Filipinos who immigrated between 1909 and 1913, an estimated 55,000 settled in Hawaii, 39,000 returned home, and 18,600 reimmigrated to the mainland, primarily California. With Japanese immigration halted by the Gentlemen's Agreement, Filipinos moved in to fill the demands for cheap labor. They were mostly male (the sex ratio was 14 males for each female), young (about one-half were between 22 and 29 years old), and single (20% were married but only 12% brought their wives with them). Unlike the Pensionados, they were poorly educated and fluent in neither English nor in Spanish. Like so many other immigrants, they were sojourning. Perhaps one-half returned to the Philippines.[78]

Data are spotty, but the following tables show the Filipino population for selected years.

Table 2.5
Filipino Population
California*

Year	Number (1,000)	Percent
1940	31	.4
1950	40	.4
1960	67	.4
1970	135	.7

*Census Bureau, Special Reports.

In 1940, the Filipino population of California was approximately 30,000; by 1960, it had more than doubled; and by 1970, it had doubled again. This high growth rate does not mean, however, that Filipinos are very numerous. They are but a small proportion of the total California population—less than 1%. Their relative size is even smaller than the Japanese, but that does not mean that Filipinos had no impact.

Economic Impact

Like the Chinese and Japanese, Filipinos were ineligible for citizenship and therefore could not engage in many professions or in politics. Although their right to purchase farm land under the Alien Land Laws was ambiguous, few tried to become land owners. Most labored in the fields.

Filipino farm workers were organized into a *Padrone system*. To win contracts, Filipino *Padrones* often settled for lower wages than the Japanese. Quite often, Filipinos managed to underbid Mexican laborers who contracted on an individual basis. When the Great Depression struck, farm wages began tumbling. For example, in 1929, asparagus workers (of whom many were Filipino) earned $4.14 per day. By 1934, they earned $3.30 per day. Faltering wages made the California fields a hotbed of labor activity. Prior to the Great Depression, major unions had not tried to organize farm workers. During the Great Depression they tried repeatedly to organize, and Filipino laborers figured in those activities. In 1934, Filipino workers struck the Salinas fields but the existence of two rival Filipino unions undermined this attempt. Despite another attempt in 1936, the Filipino union eventually failed.

Significant numbers of Filipinos found work in Alaska canneries. During the 1930s, 15% of cannery workers were Filipino, often California farm laborers seeking out-of-season jobs. Filipinos also served as crewmen in the Merchant Marine. Approximately 8,000 were so employed in 1930. In 1936, however, the Merchant Marine Act declared that 90% of a ship's crew had to be U. S. citizens, thus drastically reducing the number of Filipinos in the Merchant Marine. The United States Navy also used Filipinos as crewmen and recruited them in the Philippines. Throughout the 1930s, 4,000 Filipinos served, but by strict Navy policy and custom, they could only be stewards (mess boys who waited on officers).

Anti-Filipino Laws and Treaties

In California, Filipinos encountered the antimiscegenation law forbidding whites to marry blacks or Mongolians. The category that

Filipinos fell into was never clear. Local clerks determined the applicability of the law in any given case, and often refused to issue marriage licenses to Filipino-white couples. By 1933, California courts had
ruled that Filipinos did not fall under the antimiscegenation law. Filipinos were not Mongolians, the court reasoned, but Malayan. The
state legislature promptly closed this loophole by including Malayans
in the list of races not permitted to marry whites. The law was eventually ruled unconstitutional, but not until 15 years later.

Filipinos lived in a sort of legal limbo. Under the Cooper Act of
1902 they were defined:

> . . . as citizens of the Philippine Islands and, as such, entitled to the
> protection of the United States Government but not to United States
> citizenship. They owed allegiance to the United States; they were
> free to exercise all the privileges of any American citizen, except the
> right to vote, become naturalized citizens, join the U. S. Armed Forces,
> establish a commercial business, own real estate, hold public or
> private office at any level. . . .

This list of exceptions greatly limited the privileges of citizenship.
Filipinos travelled on United States passports, however, and could
freely enter and leave the mainland.

The ambiguous status of Filipino immigrants was not helped much
by Congress's 1906 action which provided that persons owing alle-
giance to the United States could, under some circumstances which
were vaguely specified, petition for citizenship. In 1917, Congress
further stipulated that Filipinos were nationals. They were not eligible
for citizenship, but neither were they aliens. A year later, Congress
also stipulated that Filipinos (as well as Puerto Ricans) who served
three years in the Navy or Marines could petition for citizenship. This
fact helps explain the popularity of the Navy's enlistment program.

The Tydings-McDuffie Act of 1934 somewhat clarified the ambiguous political status of Filipinos. It established a quota of 50 immigrants per year (Hawaii excepted) and provided a ten-year transition
period for the Philippines to become an independent country. Because
of World War II, independence did not take place until 1946.

The next year, Congress passed the Repatriation Act. Filipino
immigrants could receive free passage home, but once there they fell
under the 50 immigrants per year quota. Regardless of how poor
conditions were in the United States, apparently most Filipinos felt
conditions were worse in the Philippines. Only 7,400 persons
repatriated.

When World War II broke out, so did clashes between Japanese
and Filipino Americans. While the violence was short-lived and not

extensive, it does illustrate the depth of the ill-feeling between the two groups. Strangely, at first Filipinos were not allowed to join the United States military. That was changed in early 1942, and an all-Filipino battalion with white officers was formed. After the war, President Truman declared the Philippines an independent country. At the same time, Filipinos living in the United States were declared eligible for citizenship. In accordance with the 1924 Act, the Philippines had a 105-persons per year immigration quota.

Anti-Filipino Violence

Racial violence dogged Filipinos. In 1929, Exter (a California farm community) held a carnival attended by several Filipino farm workers. Motivated in part by fear of economic competition with Filipinos, whites began baiting and throwing stones at Filipinos, especially those accompanied by white women. A Filipino man stabbed a white man, and violence broke out. A mob of 300 whites attacked a farm which employed Filipinos. A barn was burned. The Filipinos fled.

The next year in Watsonville, a group of Filipino workers rented a dance hall and hired white women as escorts. For several days, white vigilantes demonstrated and one evening attacked the dance hall. Whites next attacked farms where Filipino laborers were living. One Filipino was killed and several were beaten. In 1933, 53 vigilantes drove 21 Filipinos from their homes. In 1934 in Modesto, vigilantes drove Filipinos from the town.

Two factors contributed to these violent acts. One was the fear that Filipino laborers might bid down white wages, as in fact, they did. At the time of the violence, Filipinos in Modesto were harvesting grapes at 90 cents per ton while whites were asking and receiving $1.50 to $1.70 per ton. The other motivating factor, which incensed white vigilantes perhaps more than wages, was interracial sex. Filipino men openly associated with white women, dating them, living with them, and hiring them as dance partners. Filipino men, dressed as nattily as possible, often appeared in public with white women. In this respect, and for no obvious sociological reason, Filipino males seemed less shy than Chinese and Japanese males.

Filipino Stereotype

Filipinos were labelled undesirable and unassimilable, suited to stoop labor and little else. Farmers believed that Filipinos made good asparagus workers because they were short and could easily bend over to reach the plants. They further believed that because they were dark skinned, Filipinos did not feel the sun, and that Filipinos were impervious to the fine peat dust which hangs over asparagus fields, causing wheezing and itching skin.

Unlike the Japanese, who were grudgingly thought to be cunning, or the Chinese, whose past accomplishments were admired, Filipinos were stereotyped as primitive. This belief probably began in 1904 at the St. Louis World's Fair, where the Filipino exhibits displayed the villages of the less developed areas of the Islands. Brett Melendy suggests the following:

> A viewpoint that gained statewide acceptance was made by Northern Monterey County Justice of the Peace D. W. Rohrback who charged the Filipinos with being disease carriers, destroying the American wage scale, and attempting to allure young American and Mexican girls. The Judge asserted that Filipinos, migrating from a very primitive society, were able to live fifteen in one room and sustain themselves on only rice and fish. In short, they corroded American standards of labor and morality.[80]

The report of the Commonwealth Club of California provides another example of the anti-Filipino stereotype. The report found Filipinos to be belligerent, a nuisance to public health, poorly educated, and unassimilable. Furthermore, the report said, they were morally unsuitable for American life. They often consorted with white women while wasting their wages on living extravagantly and gambling.[81]

The arguments of genetic degeneracy were also invoked. C. M. Goethere, a prominent Californian and a leader in discrimination against Asians, wrote thus:

> The Filipino tends to interbreed with near-moron white girls. The resulting hybrid is almost invariably undesirable. The ever increasing brood of children of Filipino coolie fathers and low-grade white mothers may in time constitute a serious social burden.[82]

Vietnamese Americans

Because the federal government did not separately tabulate Vietnamese until 1966, the most basic questions, such as how many Vietnamese have lived in the United States, cannot be adequately answered. Clearly, though, the majority of Vietnamese came as refugees. When

Saigon fell in April 1975, some 200,000 people fled the country. Approximately 130,000 refugees settled in the United States. Of that number, 20% were racially Chinese and were a minority group within Vietnam.[83] Whether these people consider themselves Vietnamese, Chinese, or Chinese-Vietnamese is not known. How the Chinese-Vietnamese and the Vietnamese-Vietnamese get along is not known either. Nor is it known how Chinese-Vietnamese classified themselves on the 1980 census. Conceivably, they could have listed their race as Chinese and been completely accurate. (The same possibility applies to Chinese-Filipinos.)

Unlike in the past, the federal government actively supported Vietnamese immigration. President Ford established an intergovernmental task force to supervise the program and authorized the Justice Department to bypass certain legal requirements and "red tape." Immigrants first lived in temporary camps abroad, and then moved to one of four camps in the United States. While the camps were hardly luxurious, they did provide the basic necessities of life. The government tried to socialize refugees into American culture via classroom and other training. Organizations, individuals, and states could sponsor immigrants by guaranteeing food, shelter, and assistance in finding employment.

The government followed a policy of dispersing immigrants throughout the country, attempting to place them in states with 3,000 or fewer Vietnamese. The rationale was that local resistance would be less if the number were smaller. For that reason, every state in the Union received at least a few refugees.

Once established, refugees could relocate as they pleased. It is widely believed that many moved to Southern California. Of all Vietnamese refugees, 27% were living in that state as of 1978. Today, a section of the Los Angeles metropolitan area is a well-established Vietnamese enclave, "Little Saigon."

Because the Vietnamese came as the result of unique political circumstances, they do not fit the pattern of past Asian immigration. A more balanced sex ratio is evident: 55% are male. Moreover, 78% are members of male-headed households. (The Vietnamese family unit, it should be noted, includes the extended family.)[84] The Vietnamese are also highly educated. Twenty percent of those 18 years or older have had some college education. Unlike the Vietnamese population of prewar Vietnam, where 10% were Catholic, 40% of the refugees are Catholic. And 75% of the refugees were born in the North and had fled South during the Vietnamese Civil War. All in all, the picture that emerges is that of a people who are educated, were relatively affluent in former times, and are urban, white-collar, and members of families. Politically, they are anticommunist and pro-United States.

Vietnamese have, with the aid of their sponsors, been successful in finding some kinds of employment: 94% of heads of households are employed, while 50% of females hold a part- or full-time job. Despite their employment, though, about one-third of Vietnamese require supplemental aid, suggesting that their jobs do not pay particularly well. A substantial number of Vietnamese have experienced downward mobility. According to government estimates, 68% of the heads of households had white-collar jobs in Vietnam but in the United States, only 39% of these people have the same level of job. Those who were blue-collar workers in Vietnam have experienced less downward mobility, but then compared to white-collar workers, they had less of a distance to fall.[85]

The historical antecedents of Vietnamese Americans are far different from those of the other Asian groups being considered here. Their socioeconomic and family backgrounds, the political situation, and the fact that they came in one massive swoop under federal auspices make them unique among immigrants to this country.

Summary and Conclusions

The history of each group is at the same time both specific and general. Each group encountered a unique set of social circumstances. The situation of the Californios would never be replicated by another group. The role of the Chinese in the gold fields could not be duplicated. The "timing" of Japanese immigration—on the heels of Chinese exclusion—was a coincidence. The war with Spain and its effect on Filipino immigration was unique. Just as unique was the Vietnam war and its effect on Vietnamese immigration. In each case, a particular set of historical forces combined to produce an outcome which will not occur again because those forces will never be replicated.[86]

If this reasoning is correct, then history is simply the story of what happened in the past. Of course, one should not denigrate the story. As will become evident in later chapters, the story often helps explain statistical outcomes. And if nothing else, the story conveys a sense of reality and understanding that numbers sometimes lack.

On the other hand, there may be a pattern to what happened in the past, and if there is, then history can serve as data. What events have in common becomes the basis for generalization, prediction, and explanation. Unfortunately, one cannot always find a pattern. And even if one does, others may disagree. The problems of any empirical research—validity and reliability—bedevil historial analysis as well. Here, rather than being sidetracked into a methodological debate which may not have an ultimate resolution, I offer the following commonalities:

- The size of the minority group had little to do with the intensity and scope of the majority reaction.
- The specific ethnicity or race of the group had little to do with the intensity and scope of the majority reaction.
- Antiminority forces prevailed. They succeeded in establishing a legal infrastructure that held the minorities in subordinate positions. In some cases, economic restrictions were interwoven with the legal restrictions.
- Violence accompanied the building of the infrastructure.
- Pejorative stereotypes developed. These were used to justify hostile actions against the minority. It is one of the ironies of ethnic relations that a group that does not succeed socioeconomically is blamed for being lazy and stupid, while a group that does succeed inspires envy and hostility.

Saxton's analysis of the anti-Chinese movement contains interesting sociological implications that, when generalized, help explain the commonalities just listed. He summarizes his argument as follows:

> A more or less free labor force was being pressed into competition with indentured labor [the Chinese]. On the other hand, the main defenders of Chinese importation were to be found among those who benefitted from the employment of contract gang labor. To this point, the division was quite simply economic. The economic division, however, coincided with a preexisting dichotomy of ideological and organizational patterns that stemmed from Jacksonian politics of the antebellum East.[87]

According to this argument, two factors triggered the anti-Chinese movement. One was the existence of economic competition between whites and Chinese. The other was the preexisting definition of an ethnically-racially defined category of "others." Let us consider each of these points.

When the Chinese were immigrating to California in large numbers, their presence produced a tripartite conflict between minority worker, majority worker, and majority employer. White labor generally opposed Chinese immigration, although the upward job push the Chinese gave to whites, and the Chinese willingness to perform jobs whites did not want, modulated white opposition to some extent. In the long run, though, neither modulating force prevented the Chinese from being defined as competitors with white labor. Thus, labor became one part to the conflict, and the Chinese became the other. The third party consisted of those who gained from immigration—mainly employers. They defended liberal immigration policies as an economic necessity, although that did not necessarily mean they considered immigrants on an equal social plane with whites. Just the opposite, because the Chinese were perceived as inferior, employers could exploit them with a clear conscience. That the interests of labor eventually prevailed over the interest of employers indicates the political balance between those two groups. Under other circumstances, employers might have prevailed. If, for example, the need for mass gang labor had continued through the early part of the twentieth century, those favoring liberal immigration might have had their way.

The early white population of California was composed mostly of immigrants from other parts of the United States. They brought with them social definitions of race. First developed to accommodate blacks, the definition was easily modified to accommodate Chinese. Whether the definition derived from Jacksonian politics (as Saxton argues) or from the broader cultural milieu of the time, more important is the derived implication. Even if inchoate, social definitions of racial groups existed, and those definitions placed nonwhites below whites. Miller's study of the anti-Chinese stereotype bolsters this argument, for he found that a clear and pejorative Chinese stereotype quickly developed.[88]

Generalization. The same points—competition with labor and a social definition of inferiority—apply to other groups.. Consider the Japanese. Employers found them hard-working and relatively cheap agricultural workers; therefore, the Japanese were welcomed. However, when the Japanese began expanding from manual labor to farming and fishing, they antagonized white economic interests. As with the Chinese, the tripartite conflict between minority labor, white labor, and employers was formed. And as with the Chinese, the interests of labor eventually won out. As a by-product of the Japanese exclusion, Korean exclusion also took place. Filipinos, although never very many in number, were likewise competing with white farm labor in certain agricultural areas. Because Filipinos immigrated from an American protectorate, they were in a unique and ambiguous legal position, which was eventually clarified when Filipinos were, for all practical purposes, excluded too. Mexican immigrants, both legal and illegal, had long provided employers with a source of cheap labor. While benefitting employers, Chicano labor threatened white labor and the tripartite conflict formed again. Blacks may have been a partial exception to this process. For some unknown reason, but going back to the early nineteenth century, blacks became a predominantly urban population and so never formed an agricultural labor pool. Though diffused throughout several urban labor markets, blacks did compete with white laborers. To the extent that they did, the tripartite conflict mentioned before applied to them as well.

The foregoing argument resembles various sociological theories. The overarching emphasis on competition between groups suggests conflict theory, the emphasis on economics suggests materialism, the specific relations between ethnic groups and other ethnic groups, and between ethnic groups and employers, suggest theories of the split-labor market, perfect market, and dual-labor market. While some attempt ought to be made to tie these theoretical strands together, that task is better left to the conclusion of this monograph, after the statistical data have been presented.

3

Demographic Potential

emography is the study of population and includes such topics as fertility, mortality, and migration. The discipline deals in statistics, equations, graphs, and data tables, which is probably why we seldom think of demography when contemplating the nature of human existence. Such quantitative data are not the stuff of drama, but the stuff of precise calculation, strict reasoning, and scientific explanation. Moreover, demography is abstract. Interest centers on the pattern and predictability of an aggregate rather than on the idiosyncrasies of an individual. To the demographer, the individual is one data point in a study that might have millions of data points.

While the methods of demography may strike the nondemographer as coldly quantitative, the motivation behind it is anything but that. "The first reason for studying demography," William Petersen writes, "is to attain an appreciably better understanding of the world in which we live."[1] Demography is also important for formal humanistic reasons. The French approach to history known as the *Annales* School—arguably the most influential school of the day—relies heavily on the idea of demographic cause. Historian Robert Darnton summarizes the school as follows:

> . . . one can distinguish levels in the past; that the third level (culture) somehow derives from the first two (economics and demography, and social structure); and that third-level phenomena can be understood in the same way as those on the deeper levels (by means of statistical analysis, the play of structure and conjuncture, and considerations of long-term change rather than of events).[2]

This short quotation cannot do justice to the full-scale philosophy underlying the *Annales* School, but it does emphasize the importance placed on trends and on the demographic underpinnings of history. It thus helps to correct the tendency to view society solely in terms of individuals and events rather than in terms of groups and broader

59

entities. This point is important when studying race relations, for as argued previously, an ethnic group exists *sui generis*.

An ethnic group also exists in a demographic framework. The size of the group partially depends on the size of the broader society. A group may be small in a large society, or large in a small one; and the potential of a large group is different from a small one, or at least that is a reasonable hypothesis. I call the possible impact of a group's demography *demographic potential*: the demographic characteristics of an ethnic group which positively or negatively contribute to its socioeconomic attainment.

Some demographic characteristics work to the group's advantage, facilitating rapid gains in socioeconomic status and little prejudice, while other characteristics work against the group. While hardly new ideas, specifying which characteristics affect which groups and how is not a mundane task. It is fraught with a great many logical and methodological difficulties.

Plan of the Chapter

In this chapter, some basic demographic characteristics of the white and nonwhite populations of California in 1980 are presented. The presentation may be regarded as partially exploratory, if by that one means delving into the data in search of tentative hypotheses. The presentation may also be regarded as partially descriptive: devoted to drawing a demographic picture of the groups. Or it may be regarded as partially confirmatory because a limited test of the relation between demographic and income characteristics is undertaken. However regarded, though, the concept of demographic potential gives focus to the task. The chapter has the following sections:

- ethnic composition of the California population;
- population pyramid for each ethnic group;
- sex composition of each ethnic group;
- age structure of each ethnic group;
- job squeeze;
- demographic potential and ethnic group income; and
- conclusions.

Ethnic Composition of the California Population

A most basic demographic issue concerns the size of ethnic groups. How one defines an ethnic group obviously will have a bearing on its size. A loosely defined group will be larger than a tightly defined group if all other things are equal. The 1980 census used a rather loose definition: self-identification. Respondents classified themselves according to whichever race they felt appropriate. For Asians, this procedure probably did not pose a major problem (except possibly for persons of mixed ethnic backgrounds).

The Census Bureau places Mexicans and other Hispanics in the white racial category, but provides a separate indicator for Hispanic origins. To account for this, I removed persons of Hispanic origin from the white category, and further, counted as Mexican only those persons who listed their origin as Mexican and their race as white. The final racial category, *other*, contains everyone not classified in the foregoing manner. Throughout the discussion, the "other" category—being a hodgepodge without sociological interpretation—is seldom reported or discussed, except when specific circumstances dictate otherwise (such as ensuring that percentages sum to 100%). The data are shown on the table.

Whites (more precisely, non-Hispanic whites) constitute the largest group, a finding of absolutely no surprise. Although the largest group, the figure shown is smaller than the one usually seen because the Census Bureau includes Hispanics in its count of whites. Mexican Americans are the second largest group, but considerably smaller than whites. Blacks form the third largest group, about one-half the size of the Mexican population. After blacks, the remaining groups are minuscule. Of Asians, Filipinos are the largest, but still less than 2% of the California population. Closely behind them are the Chinese and Japanese at slightly more than 1% of the population, and Koreans and Vietnamese at about .5%. All other groups combined, the residual category of other, make up some 6% of the California population.

The tininess of the Asian-American populations may come as a surprise to some. One could easily believe from the media that Asian-Americans are much more numerous, as they are often the subject of special reports and commentaries. This is certainly true of the

Table 3.1
Ethnic Composition of California
(1980)

Percent of California Population

W	M	B	F	C	J	K	V	Other	Total
66.3	15.5	7.7	1.5	1.4	1.1	.5	.4	5.6	100.0%

B-Black; C-Chinese; F-Filipino; J-Japanese; K-Korean;
M-Mexican; V-Vietnamese; W-White

Japanese. Hardly a day goes by without some news story referring to expansion of Japanese businesses in this country. Much of the recent immigration from Japan consists of short-term visitors and inter-mediate-term residents. These people are not Japanese Americans according to the definition here being used, yet few people carefully distinguish between them and Japanese Americans. Residential seg-regation further contributes to the misimpression. Films, photo-graphs, and television shots showing the teeming life and the crowded streets of Chinatown, or rows and rows of store signs written in Asian script, make the Asian population appear large, but that appearance is wrong, as the findings show.

Simple size is probably the most fundamental demographic char-acteristic of an ethnic group, but also very fundamental are age and sex composition. These characteristics are so basic, in fact, that demographers have developed special graphical tools for analysing them: population pyramids.

Population Pyramids

A *population pyramid* is a special graph used to display the sex and age composition of a population or group. The pyramid has two parts, with data for males on the left and data for females on the right. The horizontal bars of the pyramid represent specific age categories, usu-ally at five-year intervals because agencies customarily report data in that manner. This study, however, uses ten-year intervals. The broader intervals better highlight the overall shape of the population pyramid, and that shape is the focus of the discussion. To help make compar-isons between groups, each horizontal bar on the pyramid represents the percent of the group accounted for by that particular category of sex and age. When transformed this way, the graphs are technically called *percent population pyramids*. Also, to further aid intergroup comparison, the base of the pyramids always ranges from 15% on the left to 15% on the right.

Population pyramids not only describe a group, special types of pyramids serve as hypothetical models, ideal types, or standards against which existing groups can be compared. If we assume that births, deaths, and migration do not change, then *prototype* pyramids can be constructed, and the demographic future of a group may be pre-dicted by comparing its actual pyramid to the prototype. These assumptions are only partially valid, of course, and the predictions may or may not come true in reality. Three common prototypes are shown in Figures 3.1–3.3.

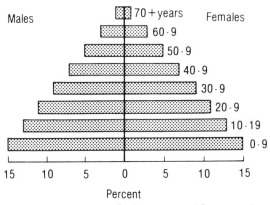

Figure 3.1: Prototype Population Pyramid Expansive

The first prototype is the *expansive pyramid*. It has a broad base and systematically tapers to a point. This shape indicates a group with many young people and relatively few aged. The group is growing. The second prototype is the *stationary pyramid*. It has a midportion narrower than its base or top. This indicates slow or zero population growth. The third, the *constrictive pyramid*, has a narrow base, bulging midportion, and moderately tapering top, indicating the group does not have enough young people to replenish itself over the long run. Although one might construct other prototypes, these three—which are the most common ones—should serve present purposes. We may compare them to the actual population pyramids for each of the groups under study (Figures 3.4–3.11).

Comparing the pyramids for each ethnic group to the prototypes, the following can be noted:

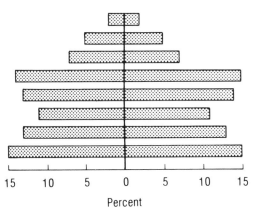

Figure 3.2: Prototype Population Pyramid Stationary

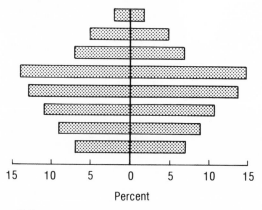

Figure 3.3: Prototype Population Pyramid Constrictive

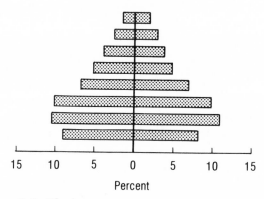

Figure 3.4: Blacks

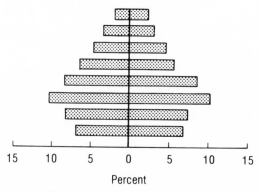

Figure 3.5: Chinese

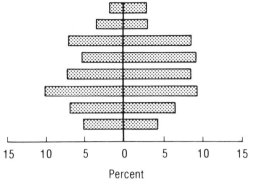

Figure 3.6: Japanese

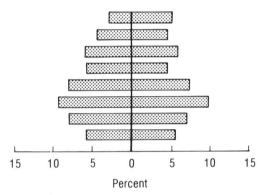

Figure 3.7: White

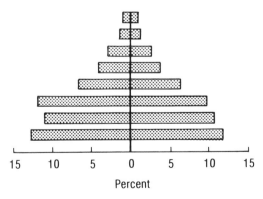

Figure 3.8: Mexican

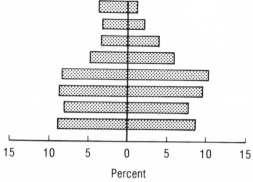

Figure 3.9: Filipino

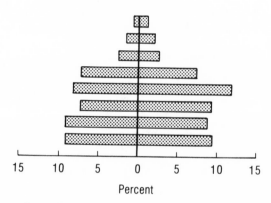

Figure 3.10: Korean

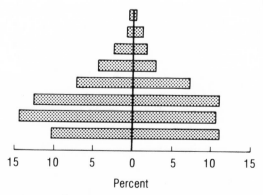

Figure 3.11: Vietnamese

• The pyramids for blacks, Chinese, Japanese, and whites resemble the constrictive prototype. They have bases that are narrower than their midsections, and then they taper to a peak. This means the number of young people, especially children (say, aged nine or younger) is so small that the population cannot be maintained in the long run.

• In contrast to those pyramids, the Mexican American pyramid is expansive. It has a wide base and an ever-narrowing top portion, indicating that there are more young persons in the population than older ones. The Chicano population should grow at a high rate.

• The pyramids for the remaining groups (Filipinos, Koreans, and Vietnamese) have bases and midsections of approximately the same size, and then they quickly taper off. They are neither clearly expansive nor clearly constrictive, falling somewhere between those two extremes. If anything, they resemble the stationary prototype more than the others, but that resemblance is not strong.

There are several demographic advantages to being a constrictive population. Such a group will not have a high number of young dependents in the near future, which frees resources from child rearing to direct consumption and economic endeavors. The freeing occurs directly with money. It also occurs indirectly. Time ordinarily devoted to child rearing can be used for other activities. With regard to women, it may considerably ease their participation in the work force. A constrictive population will also have a relatively small cohort of children passing into the active population, and young workers will encounter less competition in finding jobs. Finally, a constrictive population is usually older than an expansive population. And an older population, because it has relatively few dependent children and many mature active persons, will have a high earning potential.

A quick caveat is required here. Today's young children are the offspring of today's fecund population (usually taken to be women aged 15 through 44). Fertility patterns can change, and sometimes quickly. Even if that seems unlikely given current economic and social conditions, it could happen. More difficult to predict, but more important, is future fertility. When the current cohorts of children mature, they make far different fertility choices than their parents did, choices which might radically alter the shape of the pyramid. Moreover, migration can have an overwhelming influence, and no one knows what future migration will be. Those forces that propel people to leave their homelands for the United States might change; the attractiveness of this country might diminish; American immigration laws might change. Thus, while the current shape of the pyramid suggests the long-run demographic future of the group, that shape by no means guarantees the future.

The short run is more predictable because birth, death, and migration are less likely to change in the near future, and if they do change, they have less time to produce an effect. So in the absence of contradictory data, the current pyramid does provide a basis for making short-term estimates. Briefly, ethnic groups with expansive pyramids will grow and ethnic groups with constrictive pyramids will shrink.

Sex Composition

If males and females died at the same rates, and if there were no migration, then the proportion of males and females in a group would always be equal to the proportions found at birth. Such a situation is purely hypothetical, of course. In most Western societies, females outlive males, and an imbalanced proportion results. The imbalance will be especially pronounced for groups that have undergone selective migration or which have suffered catastrophic losses due to war or disaster.

Sex composition is measured by the *sex ratio*, or the number of males per 100 females. The following table displays these ratios.

The Vietnamese and Chicano populations have more males than females, which is unusual. In the case of the Vietnamese, the circumstances of their immigration may be the explanation. These people suddenly fled a war tortured nation when South Vietnam fell. Surely, males were in a better position to flee. They were more mobile than females, possibly more motivated because of political and military involvements, and more important, had more opportunities. For instance, as the end neared, many military personnel commandeered aircraft and ships and left. Females were not in positions to do that.

The Mexican American population also has more males than females. This too may be due to selective migration. The immigrant flow from Mexico was (and is) composed mainly of males seeking work. The in-flow of illegal immigrants is predominantly male also, but because they do not fill out census questionnaires, one cannot calculate their influence on the sex ratio.

Table 3.2
Sex Ratios*

K	J	B	F	W	C	M	V
84	86	96	97	97	99	105	108

*Number of males per 100 females

B-Black; C-Chinese; F-Filipino; J-Japanese; K-Korean;
M-Mexican; V-Vietnamese; W-White

Among Chinese Americans, the sex ratio is almost perfectly balanced (99 males per 100 females). This represents a major historical change. For many years the Chinese sex ratio was highly imbalanced and demographers thought the Chinese population might eventually disappear because the paucity of Chinese women limited natural growth while the exclusion laws prevented replenishment from abroad.[3] Now, the ratio approaches parity and that fear seems unjustified.

Like the Chinese, Filipinos were originally an overwhelmingly male population due to the selective immigration of male laborers. As recently as 1970 in California, there were 124 male Filipinos for every 100 females.[4] Today, however, the census count reveals a different situation. The Filipino sex ratio of 97, very similar to the white ratio, reflects the impact of the liberalized immigration laws.

The white sex ratio does not seem exceptional given the age of the white population and the constrictive shape of their pyramid. The black sex ratio is slightly lower, although essentially the same statement applies to it. Differential mortality is a possible reason for the slightly higher deficit of black males. Black infants die at twice the rate of whites, and infant mortality disproportionately strikes males.

In some ways, the most interesting cases are the Japanese and Koreans. They have the lowest ratios among the eight groups, despite the historical preponderance of males in their populations. Picture brides helped equalize the sex ratio (a system in which neither the Chinese nor Filipinos participated), and the natural growth of the second and third generations also helped. Today, the ratios have reversed. There are only 84 Korean males for every 100 Korean women. The Japanese ratio is slightly higher (86). Explaining these radical shifts in sex composition on the basis of natural growth or post-1965 immigration is difficult. Why should so many more females be born than males? Or why should so many females be currently immigrating? Another explanation seems more satisfactory: after World War II and the Korean War, but prior to 1965, immigration from Japan and Korea consisted overwhelmingly of war brides.[5] This meant that many more Korean and Japanese women entered the country than men, thus weighting the sex ratios towards females.

Age Composition

One of the most important indicators of a group's demographic potential is its age structure. A group with a low mean age, one composed of many youths and children, has a different demographic trajectory than a group with a high mean age. Both groups require resources

from society but of vastly different kinds. Socialization—family structures, peer group support, formal education, job training—is the most
basic requirement for a young group. Its future lies ahead of it and
its contributions to society will be made later. The opposite applies
to an older group. The broadest indicator of group age is the mean.
These are shown in Table 3.3.

We can see from the table that the groups substantially vary in
their ages. Whites and Japanese have the highest mean (36 years) while
Mexicans and Vietnamese have the lowest means (24 and 23 years);
the range between extremes, 12 to 13 years, is substantial. The Vietnamese and Mexican populations are in their mid-twenties, an age
when people have typically just finished college, are entering the work
force, and are starting their families. In contrast, whites and Japanese
are in their mid-thirties, an age when their families are well established and their career patterns marked out. Whites and Japanese are
about to settle down while Vietnamese and Chicanos are just getting
established.

The mean is a summary measure, indicating an overall age level,
and it is a good basis for making general statements. More detailed
statements require more detailed measures. This requirement becomes
clear when one considers the age grading of society.

Age Grading

Like all societies, American society is age graded. We accept, hardly
without thinking about it, that certain behaviors should coincide with
certain age categories. Children can cry and scream in public but
adults may not. Adults may curse while children may not. The elderly
may be forgiven for being forgetful, and so may children, but not the
middle aged. In addition we accept that power should be distributed
by age. Children have virtually none; the aged have very litte; and the
middle aged have the most. The middle aged also bear the respon-
sibility for rearing children and for supporting the aged, if necessary.

Age grading can have a major impact on an ethnic group. The
sizes of the various age strata within a population affect power and
wealth. A group with few young people can divert resources from

Table 3.3
Mean Ages

W	J	C	F	B	K	M	V
36	36	32	30	29	28	24	23

B-Black; C-Chinese; F-Filipino; J-Japanese; K-Korean;
M-Mexican; V-Vietnamese; W-White

child raising to savings, to business enterprises, to better housing, or to an overall increase in the level of material comfort. At the other end of the age continuum are groups with large elderly populations. American culture proclaims that the golden years should be (ideally) a time of leisure and withdrawal from work and from many social obligations. The aged have already contributed to society and may be partially or completely independent financially. The aged, therefore, require less formal education but, due to declining physical robustness, may require more health care.

Age Categories

The population pyramids have already shown the overall age structure of each ethnic group. Now we need to look at specific age strata and the relations between them. Each group has been divided into three categories: (1) children or the dependent young, (2) the aged, and (3) the active. The active category consists of everyone not in the first two categories. Taken together, children and the aged constitute a dependent population while the active populations bear the "burden" (that may not be precisely the right word) of supporting that "dependency" (that may not be the right word either, but demographers customarily use it).

Stipulating the precise age at which each category ends and begins necessarily involves some arbitrariness. Age 16 was chosen as the upper limit for the child category. Hence, anyone younger than that is presumably a dependent, a full-time student, or a preschooler.

The active population consists of persons 17 through 64 years of age. Many persons in this category, particularly younger ones, might be full-time students. Others might not be in school but still engaged in nonwork activities. Perhaps we should think of this category as the group's combined actual and potential labor carrying capacity, actual because most in the age bracket are working and potential because most of the others could work if circumstances and choices were otherwise.[6] Anyone 65 or older was considered aged. Nowadays some analysts distinguish between the "old" and the "very old" (which begins at around age 75). While the argument that the very old face different problems than the merely old makes sense, it is not an issue addressed here. Present purposes will be served by following the more traditional cutoff age. These data are shown for each ethnic group.

Examining the table, several points can be made.

- Of the eight groups, Japanese Americans have the largest proportion—three out of four—in the active category. They also

Table 3.4
Age Composition

Age Category:	J	C	W	K	F	B	V	M
Active (17-64)	75	68	67	65	63	62	60	57
Children (16 or younger)	18	24	21	32	29	32	38	40
Aged (64 or older)	7	8	12	3	8	6	2	3
Total Percent	100	100	100	100	100	100	100	100

B-Black; C-Chinese; F-Filipino; J-Japanese; K-Korean;
M-Mexican; V-Vietnamese; W-White

have the smallest proportion of children and a moderate proportion of aged.

- Chinese have the second largest active population (68%). Almost one-quarter of the Chinese population are children, while 8% are aged.
- Whites have an almost identical percentage in the active category, a relatively small percentage in the child category, and the largest percentage in the aged category.
- The Korean population ranks next in size of active population. The proportion of children is approximately one-third while the aged category is relatively small.
- The active population among Filipinos is slightly smaller than that of Koreans; the aged category is comparatively large, however, as is the proportion of children.
- The size of the active black population is virtually the same as that of Filipinos; approximately one-third of blacks are children but only a moderate proportion are aged.
- Like Koreans and blacks, about one-third of the Vietnamese population consists of children. The active proportion is slightly below that of blacks, and the aged category is the smallest among the groups.
- Of all groups, the Mexican American population has the smallest active population and the largest proportion of children. It also has one of the smallest proportions in the aged category.

While one could continue describing the data in this manner, it would be tedious. A single index would facilitate the discussion, and fortunately, such an index exists. Because the three age categories must total 100%, if one category is large, either or both of the other categories must be smaller, and conversely so. The *dependency ratio* summarizes the relationships between the three categories. It tells the number of dependents (children plus aged) per 100 active persons.

As the table shows, the Japanese American population has the lowest dependency ratio of any group being considered. There are 34 dependents per 100 active persons. A substantial gap exists between the Japanese ratio and the next highest ratio, that for the Chinese. There are 47 dependent Chinese for every 100 active persons. Following the Chinese are whites and Koreans. Beginning with Filipinos, the dependency ratio reaches 60; the black ratio is also approximately 60. Among the Vietnamese, there are 68 dependents for every 100 active persons, and among Chicanos, there are 75 dependents for every 100 active persons.

Groups with high dependency ratios have relatively small numbers of active persons supporting large numbers of dependents—"few hands to feed many mouths"—a situation unfavorable to the accumulation of wealth and leisure. In contrast, groups with low ratios have "many hands for few mouths," which eases the burden on the active population. Additionally, with low ratios each dependent may receive a larger proportion of group resources because resources are divided among fewer dependents. From this demographic viewpoint, then, one can conclude that Japanese and Chinese are the most favored populations, that whites, Koreans, Filipinos and blacks are neither particularly favored nor particularly handicapped, and that Vietnamese and Chicanos are the least favored.

Fertility

High fertility is one consequence or cause (the direction is not always clear) of having large numbers of young people in a population. Compared to an older group, a young group usually has higher fertility, which results in a low mean age. It may be too obvious to require

Table 3.5
Dependency Ratios*

J	C	W	K	F	B	V	M
34	47	51	54	60	61	68	75

*Number of persons 16 or younger and 65 or older per 100 persons aged 17 through 64 years.

B-Black; C-Chinese; F-Filipino; J-Japanese; K-Korean;
M-Mexican; V-Vietnamese; W-White

saying, but high fertility also requires a sufficient number of fecund women in the population.

The *child-woman ratio* is here used to measure fertility. This is the number of children aged four or younger per 100 fecund women (assumed to be women aged 15 through 44 years). The ratio can be calculated from the age and sex composition of the population. Other information, such as that contained on birth and death certificates, is not required. Admittedly, the child-woman ratio is not the best fertility measure, but it is sufficiently precise to order the data for present purposes. The ratios are shown on Table 3.6.

The Japanese have the lowest fertility of any group: 17 children per 100 fecund women. Koreans follow with 24 children per 100 fecund women. While low Japanese fertility could be anticipated from their high mean age, that is not true of Koreans. They are neither particularly young, nor particularly aged. It may be that immigration from Korea is highly selective of adults, or it may be that Koreans value small family sizes, or it may be attributed to some other factor. At present, Korean fertility is a puzzle.

Whites and Chinese have the next highest ratios, followed by Filipinos. There is a small jump to the black ratio (34); the Vietnamese ratio (37) follows. A substantial jump occurs with Chicanos, who have the highest ratio by far: 53 children per 100 fecund women. While high Mexican fertility comes as no surprise—the youth of the Mexican population and past writings suggest it—the magnitude is noteworthy. For example, the Chicano ratio is almost one-and-one-half-times higher than the next highest ratio (Vietnamese), and some three-times higher than the lowest ratio (Japanese).

The child-woman ratio has much the same importance as the dependency ratio. A population with high fertility must allocate much time, effort and money to childbearing and child rearing while a population with low fertility can allocate its resources to other activities. In that sense, high fertility hinders socioeconomic attainment. By this logic, Japanese and, to a lesser degree, Koreans are in a favored positions and whites, Chinese and Filipinos are in an intermediate

Table 3.6
Child-Woman Ratios*

J	K	W	C	F	B	V	M
17	24	25	27	31	34	37	53

*Number of children 4 or younger per 100 women aged 15 through 44 years.

B-Black; C-Chinese; F-Filipino; J-Japanese; K-Korean;
M-Mexican; V-Vietnamese; W-White

position. In the least favored positions are blacks, Chicanos, and Vietnamese.

Because anything to do with children and parenthood touch sacred American cultural values, some qualifications are required. The argument does not mean children are a strictly economic commodity and important only because they require scarce resources, but the argument does mean there is a rational component to childbearing. People consciously or quasiconsciously make fertility choices, and those choices have a consequence for the group and for society even if individuals are unaware of it. Some demographers add a more ideological dimension to the fertility decision. They argue that in very specific circumstances, a minority will choose high fertility in order to gain a political advantage, the basic premise being that as the group grows larger, its power increases. That may or may not be the empirical case.[7]

Job Squeeze

The dependency ratio just discussed relates the active and dependent populations, using age categories within the active population itself. Because the age span is long (aged 17 through 64 years), demographers sometimes divide the active population into two categories: young and mature. The relation between the two categories has an important consequence: it produces the *job squeeze.*

Considers first the general case of the job squeeze and society as a whole. Compared to younger workers, older workers usually have more seniority, more experience, more on-the-job training, and in many cases, are in positions protected by union and civil service rules. When many older persons are in the work force, therefore, younger workers face extremely stiff competition in acquiring jobs and, when they do gain a foothold, in moving up the ladder. The situation becomes even more difficult if many young workers are competing for a limited number of jobs. In contrast, when there are relatively few older workers and relatively few young entrants, competition is lessened, and youths find the employment outlook brighter and wages higher.

A simple ratio compares youths (aged 17 through 29 years) with mature persons (aged 30 through 64 years). When multiplied by 100, the index shows the number of youths per 100 mature persons. This can be called the *job squeeze ratio*.[8] These data are shown in Table 3.7.

In the active Japanese population, there are 48 youths for every 100 mature persons, which is the lowest ratio of any group. The

Table 3.7
Job Squeeze Ratios*

J	K	W	F	C	B	M	V
48	52	57	58	62	78	102	116

*Number of persons aged 17 through 29 per 100 persons aged 30 through 64 years.

B-Black; C-Chinese; F-Filipino; J-Japanese; K-Korean;
M-Mexican; V-Vietnamese; W-White

Korean population follows closely (ratio of 52), then whites (57), Filipinos (58), and Chinese (62). With the black population, the job squeeze ratio begins to climb (78); and with the Mexican population, the ratio jumps markedly: there are 102 youths for every 100 mature Chicanos. Among Vietnamese, the ratio climbs still higher: 116 youths for every 100 mature persons. As these statistics document, the groups vary widely along this measure—the highest ratio is over twice the lowest ratio, a fact suggesting that if the job squeeze affects income, then some groups will fare much betters than others.

When assessing the effect of the job squeeze on income, account must be taken of where ethnic group members seek employment. If group members work within the ethnic economy itself, then the group's squeeze ratio is relevant. If members seek employment in the broader society, then the ratio prevailing there is relevant. Unfortunately, no one knows the proportion of each ethnic group working within the group, and the proportion working in nonethnic jobs. However, for sake of argument, let me create two brief scenarios. (1) Assume that every member worked within his or her own group. In this case Japanese and Koreans hold the most favored positions, having the lowest job squeeze ratios, and Chicanos and Vietnamese hold the least favored positions with ratios exceeding 100. Blacks also have a fairly high squeeze ratio, while the remaining groups fall in the midrange. (2) Assume a radically different situation in which every young ethnic worker is assimilated and seeks employment in the white job market while every mature ethnic worker is not assimilated and remains in the ethnic job market. Under those circumstances, ethnic youths contribute to the white job squeeze ratio, changing it from the current level of 57 to 85, an increase of almost 50%. If one further assumed that the white job market has absolutely no discrimination, the entry of ethnic youths would drive down wages as competition for positions increased. Only if the number of jobs increased commensurately, would wages not be bid down.

Unquestionably, neither scenario describes reality, but the broad implication is that demographic structure affects group attainment, and that the effect will occur apart from racial prejudice and dis-crimination. The narrower implication is that age composition within the active population can make a great difference to income, an empirical issue to which the analysis now turns.

Demographic Potential and Income

Demographic potential means that certain features of a group's demography predispose the group toward socioeconomic achieve-ment. That is a hypothesis; can it be confirmed empirically? Do groups with higher demographic potential have a higher socioeconomic attainment than groups with lower potential?

In a general way, the answers are already known. Japanese are often publicized for their economic advancement. To illustrate, *Time* recently reported that Japanese Americans have the highest median family income of any ethnic group in the United States, and in addi-tion, their family income exceeded that of whites.[9] A study of Asians, Chicanos, and blacks in California concluded that the Japanese might not even be a minority.[10] Concerning demographically less favored groups, Mexican Americans rank low on socioeconomic measures. The typical Mexican family has an annual income of $12,800; 35% of Mexican families have incomes of less than $10,000.[11] Accounts of the Vietnamese usually stress the economic hardships they face and the large percentage who depend on welfare.[12] Still, despite the general confirmation of the premise, more precise data would be desirable. It is not at all clear if the premise applies equally to all groups, espe-cially those with intermediate rankings.

To achieve more precision, an income measure was calculated. The sum of income from all sources was divided by the group's size to yield per capita income. That figure was then transformed to its natural logarithm equivalent, a common practice. The Pearsonian correlation (symbolized r) between per capita income thus trans-formed and several demographic characteristics was computed. The correlation summarizes the strength of a relation, but because there are only eight groups, the scatterplot associated with each correlation provides better information (Figures 3.12–3.16).

Inspection of the scatterplots shows the following:

- The weakest statistical relationship is between the sex ratio and per capita income ($r = -.62$). Examining the figure shows the scatter of the data points about the regression line, indicating a relatively weak relation.

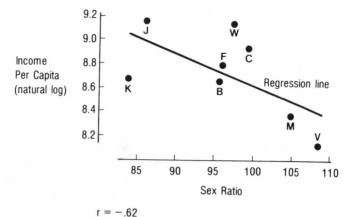

r = −.62

Figure 3.12: Income and Sex Ratio

- As expected, per capital income and the dependency ratio proves to be inversely and highly related; the higher the dependency ratio, the lower the per capita income ($r = −.85$), while the probability of erroneously concluding that this correlation is valid when in fact the true correlation is zero, is less than one in 100 (that is, $p < .01$). In light of what was discussed regarding dependency, the inverse relation is reasonable. Examining the scatterplot reveals a tight fit of data points about the regression line.
- The relation between per capita income and the child-woman ratio turns out to be strong. As fertility increases, income decreases. The correlation is moderately high to high by soci-

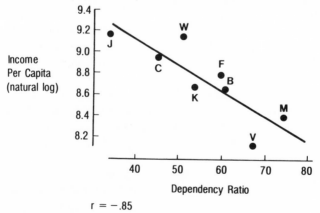

r = −.85

Figure 3.13: Income and Dependency Ratio

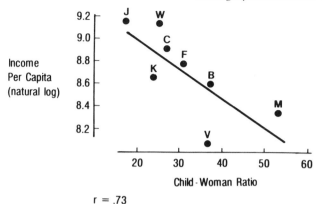

r = .73

Figure 3.14: Income and Fertility

ological standards (r = −.75, p < .01). Nothing about the scatterplot appears exceptional. The points simply follow the regression line but without too much scatter.

- An inverse relation exists between per capita income and the job squeeze ratio (r = −.89, p < .01). The scattergram shows a tight clustering of data points, with the possible exception of Koreans. A group with that low a job squeeze ratio should have a higher income. A possible reason for the relatively low Korean income may be the time of most Korean immigration. Not until fairly recently did the Korean population expand, leading to the growth of "Little Seoul" in Los Angeles and other mostly Korean districts. As new immigrants, Koreans might encounter problems of assimilation and acculturation which offset the fairly

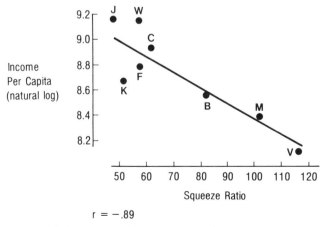

r = −.89

Figure 3.15: Income and Squeeze Ratio

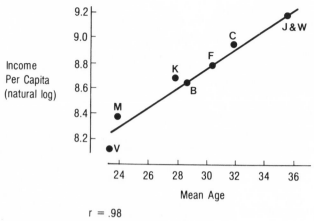

r = .98

Figure 3.16: Income and Age

favorable demographic composition of their active population. If that is true, though, it should also apply to the Vietnamese, another recently arriving group. The point on the graph representing the Vietnamese falls almost directly on the regression line. All we can say at this juncture is that the Korean finding is not easily explained, even after the fact.

- An extremely strong relation is found between per capita income and mean age of the ethnic group ($r = .98$; $p < .01$). As the scatterplot shows, virtually all data points fall on the regression line. Three slight exceptions prevent the relation from being virtually perfect: Koreans and Mexicans whose incomes are somewhat high for their mean age, and Vietnamese whose income is somewhat low.

Given the statistical strength of the relation between income and age, one should reconsider why it is so important. The relation makes no sense at the extreme. Income will not keep rising as mean age increases to, say, 85 years or more, but of course, that is a hypothetical extreme. More realistically, within the middle range of mean ages, the relation does make sociological sense. The relation between income and the job squeeze ratio implies that as people mature, they accumulate seniority, experience, and training, rising in rank to higher paying, more secure positions. Thus for the group as a whole, maturity is accompanied by higher earnings.

Other group factors indirectly bear on the relationship. The income measure was calculated on a per capita basis, so the size of the group, as well as the size of the children and aged sectors, were taken into account. This occurred in two ways. First, given a fixed sum of income, the larger the group, the smaller the per capita income. Second, given a fixed group size, the larger the dependent populations, the smaller the active population. Data on the dependency ratio show that a large dependent population means a large proportion of children, which lowers the mean age of the group. In turn, a young group will have many dependent children requiring support, while an older group will have many active persons contributing to total income.

Although there were good theoretical rationales for anticipating the relation between per capita income and mean age, the size of the correlation was still surprising. One can only wonder if the relation can be replicated by fresh data on other groups, but satisfying that curiosity must await future research.

Conclusions

The data suggest the following major conclusions.

- Of the seven minorities (that is, excluding whites) Japanese Americans are the most demographically favored group. They are a constrictive population and have the smallest dependency ratio, smallest squeeze ratio, lowest fertility, and highest mean age.
- The demographically least favored groups are Mexican Americans and Vietnamese Americans. They are the youngest, have the highest dependency ratios, the highest squeeze ratios, and highest fertility. Moreover, they are expansive populations. Blacks are the third least favored group.
- The remaining ethnic groups (Chinese, Filipino, and Korean) fall between these extremes with no clear ordering among them.

The analysis was conducted upon each demographic factor separately, but the demographic potential of a group results from all the demographic forces acting upon it in concert. If we could parcel out the independent contribution of each factor we could then rank the factors as to importance. However, with only eight groups, multivariate analysis was not possible. (Later chapters do use multivariate analysis but on individual level data.)

Taken as a set, the findings provide hints about the future of these ethnic groups and indicate how much of the future is contained within the demographic structure of the group itself. This conclusion may run contrary to what many wish to believe.

It is comforting to believe that ethnic groups control their fate by working hard and making the most of the opportunities afforded them, for such thoughts fit with the American dream, the Protestant Work Ethic, and the idea of an open democratic society. Less comforting is the thought that prejudice and discrimination determine what happens to minorities. Because of the political implications, this aspect of ethnic relations has drawn the most attention, from the media and from professional social scientists. Surely, discrimination is hateful, but in a strange sort of way, it is also a comforting argument. It implies that something can be done about the situation. The political system can be altered, the value system of society redirected, and so the fate of the minority is, in principle, changeable.

Perhaps least comforting is the thought that impersonal, blind, unalterable forces determine ethnic fate, and that we are powerless to change the situation. At this point, discomfort with the notion of demographic potential may arise, for the concept seems to imply helplessness and hopelessness in the face of demographic currents. But that is untrue. Just because a group is demographically favored does not mean the group will necessarily succeed, nor does it mean that an unfavored group always will fail. The concept in no way precludes awareness, sacrifice, democracy, and political actions. The concept only asserts that demographic forces play an important role, one which has not been sufficiently emphasized in the past.

4

Assimilation:
Descriptive Emphasis

I f all people were the same, assimilation would not be a concern, but they are not, and from this ludicrously obvious, simple, and profound fact derives the basic issue of ethnic relations: assimilation. Merely recognizing that people are different, and that those differences are an issue, is a first step, a basis for the beginnings of an inquiry. It is insufficient, though, as it raises more issues than it resolves. In particular, these come immediately to mind: (1) Why do so many people choose to interact on the basis of their ethnic differences rather than on what they have in common? (2) Why are some differences important while other differences are not?

These issues lie beyond the scope of this investigation; the data do not speak to them. The data do, however, permit us to examine a closely related issue. We know that certain ethnic differences have, for many reasons, been deemed socially significant, and some of them can be examined. The procedures are straightforward, although not without their technical complications. The result is a series of findings which allow us to compare the groups to each other.

These comparisons are intended to describe the state of assimilation currently characterizing the groups under study. To this end, only those variables thought to be especially relevant to assimilation are analyzed, and further to this end, the comparisons are kept deliberately simple—simple in the sense that they involve only one variable at a time. (Complex comparisons more suitable for explanation are presented in later chapters.)

Plan of the Chapter

The chapter consists of the following:

- Socioeconomic assimilation, including:
  - occupation;

* education; and
* income.
* Loosing past ties and gaining new ones, including:
  * time of immigration;
  * citizenship;
  * language spoken at home; and
  * language.
* Conclusions.

Socioeconomic Assimilation

As any introductory sociology textbook discusses, socioeconomic status can be measured by different methods, and depending on the method, the results will differ.[1] This chapter uses the *objective method*. The specific indicators are the ones most usual in this type of research: occupation, education, and income. These indicators are convenient because the Census Bureau routinely collects the data but, as will be amplified below, some care must be exercised when interpreting them.

Occupation

The number of occupations in the United States exceeds 40,000, obviously too many to analyze separately. Although reducing the number to seven might be going to the opposite extreme, that is a common practice. Census Bureau codes permit one to classify occupation into seven categories which roughly parallel occupational prestige.[2] Managerial and professional workers rank highest while operators, fabricators, and laborers rank lowest. Between these extremes the rankings are less clear and should not be interpreted too closely as prestige rankings.

The data shown on Table 4.1 are for persons at least 16 years of age and who are employed in the civilian labor force. Some numbers in the columns of the table are printed in boldface to indicate a category in which the minority percentage is higher than the corresponding white percentage. If a pattern is present, then the boldface provides a visual clue to it.

Looking at the table, one can observe that for Mexicans, a clear pattern of boldface numbers is present. The Mexican percentage in lower-ranking occupations, beginning with service, is consistently higher than the white percentage, and correspondingly, the Mexican percentage in higher-ranking occupations is consistently lower than the white percentage. In other words, Chicanos are overrepresented

Table 4.1
Occupations
(California, 1980)*

Occupation	B	C	F	J	K	M	V	W
Managerial	7	12	7	11	12	4	6	12
Professional	9	**16**	11	**16**	10	4	8	14
Technical, sales, administrative support	33	35	**37**	35	31	20	30	35
Service	**21**	**16**	**16**	12	**14**	**16**	13	13
Farming, forestry, fishing	2	1	**5**	**7**	2	**10**	2	2
Precision production, crafts, repair	9	7	10	8	10	**14**	**15**	12
Operators, fabricators, laborers	**19**	**13**	**14**	11	**21**	**32**	**26**	12
Totals	100	100	100	100	100	100	100	100

*Includes persons 16 years or older in the civilian labor force.

N.B. Boldface type indicates that the minority percentage in this category is higher than the white percentage.

B-Black; C-Chinese; F-Filipino; J-Japanese; K-Korean;
M-Mexican; V-Vietnamese; W-White

in lower-ranking occupations and underrepresented in higher-ranking occupations. So clear a pattern describes no other ethnic group, although less clearly defined patterns are present. One can observe that, except for the Japanese, all minority percentages are higher than the white percentage in the Operators, fabricators, laborers category, and no minority percentage is higher than the white percentage in the Managerial category, although some are identical or very close. Aside from these cases, no consistent direction of effect appears in the data.

This is an important conclusion. One can reasonably hypothesize that discrimination produces the *systematic* overrepresentation of minorities in lower occupations, but the data indicated that Mexican Americans are the only group supporting this hypothesis. Although other groups are overrepresented in some lower-ranking categories, they are not *systematically* relegated to lower-ranking occupations.

A larger percentage of each group, except Chicanos, works in the category of Technical, sales, administrative support than in any other category. This category alone accounts for some one-third of all workers, and even for Chicanos, it accounts for one-fifth. While many minorities are overrepresented in the lowest-ranking occupations, there are some exceptions. The Japanese percentage is slightly lower than the white percentage, while the Chinese and Filipino percentages are not too much greater. At the other end of the occupation continuum, managerial jobs, the Chinese, Japanese, and Koreans are identical or very near the white percentage.

Index of Dissimilarity. With eight groups and seven occupational categories, a cell-by-cell analysis requires 56 comparisons. To illustrate, Japanese and whites have the same percentages in the category of Technical, sales, administrative support. That indicates high assimilation. However, the Japanese percentage in the Farming, forestry, fishing category is higher than the white percentage, indicating low assimilation. Differences such as these make assessing the level of overall assimilation difficult. Although mental allowances for the differences could be made to arrive at a net level, a single number summary would be more objective, more parsimonious, and less tedious. The index of dissimilarity is such a number.[3] If an ethnic group were completely assimilated occupationally, then the ethnic percentage in each occupation would be proportional to the ethnic percentage in the population (or sample) being studied. Under those circumstances, the index of dissimilarity would be zero, meaning no differentiation (or complete assimilation) existed. To the extent that differentiation (nonassimilation) exists, to that extent the index will not be zero, up to a maximum of 100%. This interpretation of the index is consistent with the operational definition of assimilation as the extent to which one group differs from another along a specified distribution.[4] For instance, in a comparison of the Japanese occupational distribution with the white distribution, an index value of seven indicates that 7% of whites would have to switch occupational categories to reduce the index value to zero. Or, because the index itself provides no information about direction of effect, 7% of Japanese would have to switch. Direction can only be found by studying the raw percentages themselves. If direction is present, then the distributions will "crossover": one group will be consistently overrepresented in the lower (or upper) portion of the distribution. The pattern of boldfaced number shown on Table 4.1 indicates whether direction is present or not. Looking back at the table, only for Chicanos is a clear pattern visible (which will be discussed momentarily).

Unlike the problem of direction, the problem of categorization does not lend itself to so facile a solution. An index based on five categories will not, in general, be identical to an index based on 15 categories even if the same variable and people are being compared. Even with the same number of categories, broad groupings will produce a different index value than narrow groupings, and the occupational categories are broad. Consequently, some ethnic groups may be concentrated in the lower ranking occupations within the broader categories while the other groups are concentrated in the higher occupations. If that is true, then an index based on broad categories will produce a different value than one based on narrow categories.

While being discussed with reference to occupation and the index of dissimilarity, the same issues must be faced whenever respondents are classified along any variable. The issues are more conceptual than statistical. What are the conceptual category boundaries for occupation? Would anything be gained by classifying persons into narrow occupations such as fruit picker, vine pruner, legal aid? With reference to educational categories, would it be better to classify people into categories such as Grade One, Grade One and One-Half, Grade Two, Grade Two and One-Half, and so on? Or would it be better to use categories such as grammar school, high school, college? I can offer no resolution to these issues other than to say that purpose determines categorization, and that for showing general relationships, broad categories are more useful than narrow ones. With those points in mind, one might examine the indexes of occupational differentiation shown on Table 4.2.

Values for Filipinos, Chinese, Koreans, and Japanese are less than 10%. Values are higher for Vietnamese and blacks, and much higher still for Mexican Americans. Approximately one out of three Chicanos would have changed occupations in order to reduce the amount of differentiation to zero.

The index values are numbers telling the amount of differentiation. They do not tell whether the amount represents high, moderate, or low assimilation. To decide that, we must turn to other criteria. One criterion is probability. Unfortunately, probability provides no help with the data at hand. For all the index values shown, the null hypothesis that the true index value is zero is easily rejected.[5] (The same is true for the indexes of educational and income differentiation shown later.) Without an adequate statistical standard, we will have to rely on qualitative criteria.

Table 4.2
Occupational Differentiation*

Percentage

F	C	K	J	V	B	M
5	6	6	7	14	15	34

*Index of dissimilarity.

B-Black; C-Chinese; F-Filipino; J-Japanese; K-Korean;
M-Mexican; V-Vietnamese; W-White

We can ask, At what point should one say "only"? Should one say Filipinos are "only" 5% differentiated from whites? Or that the Vietnamese are "only" 14% differentiated? Or Chicanos are "only" 34% differentiated? Obviously, no definitive answer exists; it all depends on one's judgment. In my judgment, a difference of ten percentage points seems important. Therefore, I reserve "only" for that amount. While the criterion is arbitrary, it is not capricious and it does have the
virtue of being public. In the end, readers must make their own decisions.

According to the 10%-criterion, one can say Filipinos, Chinese, Koreans, and Japanese are only 7% or less differentiated from whites along the distribution of occupation. The values for Vietnamese and blacks are more than two-times that, and for Chicanos, five- to six-times that. One may, therefore, conclude that Vietnamese, blacks, and especially Mexicans, are highly differentiated from whites. This result is no surprise. The evidence already examined suggests that Japanese, Chinese, and Koreans are only slightly differentiated from whites, but the evidence does not suggest the low Filipino index. Apparently, the influx of Filipino immigrants since the Hart Cellar Act has not followed the pattern found before World War II. Occupationally at least, they now tend to resemble the majority. Regarding Vietnamese and blacks, while they are between the extremes, they are much closer to Chinese and Japanese than to Mexican Americans.

Class of Worker. People pursue their occupations in a variety of ways. They can work in the public or private sectors, or they can be self-employed. These possibilities are formalized with a variable called "class of worker," technically referring to the type of ownership of employing organizations.

For ethnic relations, class of worker has a particular importance. Work is among the most fundamental activities in any society. In large part, groups differ in affluence because they have different work patterns. When a group can find substantial employment in equalitarian organizations, upward mobility is enhanced. For instance, many blacks were attracted to California by the belief that government work was open to them.[6] Asian prosperity is due to their self-employment in small ethnic enterprises, or so it is widely believed. This belief was (and still is) accompanied by the belief that Asians use large numbers of unpaid family workers to keep operating costs low. Indeed, the image of wives and children working as indentured laborers had a prominent place in the attacks on both Asian immigrants and those from Mediterranean countries.[7] By tabulating class of worker, some hints as to these and other possibilities can be gleaned.

Table 4.3
Class of Worker*

Class of Worker	B	C	F	J	K	V	M	W
Private salary and wages	67	72	**77**	69	72	**80**	**83**	73
Federal government worker	**9**	**5**	**8**	**4**	2	3	3	3
State government worker	**5**	**5**	3	**5**	2	3	3	4
Local government worker	**15**	7	8	9	4	8	7	9
Self employed, not incorporated	3	8	3	**10**	**15**	4	3	8
Self employed, incorporated	1	2	1	2	**3**	1	1	2
Unpaid family worker	0	1	0	1	**2**	1	0	1
Totals	100	100	100	100	100	100	100	100

Includes persons 16 years or older in the civilian labor force.
N.B. Boldface type indicates that the minority percentage in this category is higher than the white percentage.

B-Black; C-Chinese; F-Filipino; J-Japanese; K-Korean;
M-Mexican; V-Vietnamese; W-White

The large majority of each group works for private salaries and wages, that is, for a privately owned organization. The values vary from 67% of blacks to 80% or more of Vietnamese and Mexicans. While these findings do not necessarily invalidate beliefs about self-employment among Asians and government employment among blacks, the findings do indicate that private organizations provide the single largest source of employment for every group.

For blacks, employment by federal, state, and local governments provides the second largest category of employment. Combined, government work accounts for 29% of black employment. Blacks are the only minority group to have entered government service in disproportionately large numbers. While blacks have been attracted to government work, they have found local government to be the most attractive.

The self-employed (not incorporated) category has a disproportionately high percentage of Japanese and Koreans. This category is highly heterogeneous, including mom-and-pop stores as well as large enterprises and professional practices. Nevertheless, the data support the impression that some Asian groups have opted for self-employment in unusually high numbers. At the same time, the same data warn against too quickly generalizing from one Asian group to a next. Note that neither Filipinos nor Vietnamese have a higher self-employed percentage than whites. Regarding Chinese, the commonly seen pictures of Chinatown shops and the seemingly ubiquitous Chinese restaurants, may be producing a false impression. No more Chinese are self-employed than whites. The other self-employed category includes only incorporated businesses, and accounts for a small proportion of each group.[8]

When considering data on self-employment, one should bear in mind the nature of survey taking. By and large, only the successful self-employed are tabulated. Persons who started their own businesses and failed are not counted. Consequently, some care must be taken in interpreting the figures. Different groups may have approximately the same start-up rates but fail for different reasons.

Supposedly, a factor leading to success with small businesses is the unpaid family worker. They are the children, wives, and other relatives of the head of a family business. For blacks and Chicanos, the percentage of unpaid family workers is zero (after rounding), and the highest percentage is only 2% (Koreans). Contrary to the impression and arguments made before, Asians do not constitute particularly high proportions of unpaid family workers, nor does any other group.

The final point about these data concerns the similarity of the percentages. They are fairly homogeneous across the table, as indicated by an absence of a distinctive pattern of boldfaced numbers. Indexes of differentiation verify this impression (Table 4.4).

Chinese and Japanese are thought to be groups which have made substantial gains in socioeconomic standing, and these data are consistent with that thought. Both groups are extremely close to whites (approximately 4% differentiated). Blacks are an exception to the generally low—10% or less—indexes shown on the table. They are 13% differentiated from whites. While not an unimportant amount, it is still a rather moderate value given that the maximum is 100%. The dominant impression one gathers from the table is that, overall, the minority groups resemble whites.

Table 4.4
Class of Worker Differentiation*

Percentage

C	J	K	V	F	M	B
3	4	9	7	9	10	13

*Index of dissimilarity.

B-Black; C-Chinese; F-Filipino; J-Japanese; K-Korean;
M-Mexican; V-Vietnamese; W-White

Education

Before looking at the data on education, a problem must be addressed: how much sense does it make to compare ethnic groups with regard to education? Is a Vietnamese respondent who completed twelve years of school in prewar Vietnam comparable to a black respondent who completed twelve years of school in Watts? One might argue that because each respondent was educated in a system that presupposed a different culture, their educations are completely different. Although that argument might be valid, it lies outside the ken of the current data set. And even if different data were available, equating education across two vastly different cultures would still be difficult or, perhaps, impossible. The same difficulty even arises when comparing native-born persons. How meaningful is comparing the educations of blacks and whites, for instance? The white suburb obviously differs from the black ghetto, and, because educational systems draw resources from their communities and are imbedded in the community culture, the systems will inevitably differ. Equating educational quality between American school systems is not easy either.

There are mitigating considerations, though. The distinction between lower, intermediate, and higher education is followed almost everywhere, if for no other reason than age grading. In most educational systems, the student must perform satisfactorily at one level before passing to the next level, a requirement that acts as a partial corrective to educational quality. And that American colleges can assess the credentials of domestic and foreign applicants further suggests a modicum of commonality exists between different educational systems. When all of these factors are taken into consideration, the situation does not seem so bleak and one should not be overly pessimistic. As long as the foregoing problems are recognized and "mental" reservations made, comparisons can, and are, routinely made.

Shown below are the median number of school years completed for persons 25 and older. This criterion is the standard one, and is based on the assumption that by age 25, most people have completed their formal schooling. Note that the data are for the highest school year completed.

As the display shows, on the average Mexicans have completed the fewest number of school years. Their median level, 11 years, is equivalent to ninth grade. Blacks, Vietnamese, and whites have all completed 14 years (equivalent to completing the twelfth grade), while Chinese and Japanese have completed 15 years (freshman year of college). Filipinos and Koreans have the highest median education: 16 years (sophomore year of college). The relatively high Asian medians are consistent with what is believed about those groups. "That education

Table 4.5
Median Education*

M	B	V	W	C	J	F	K
11	14	14	14	15	15	16	16

*School years completed, persons aged 25 or older.

B-Black; C-Chinese; F-Filipino; J-Japanese; K-Korean;
M-Mexican; V-Vietnamese; W-White

is highly valued not only among Chinese but also among other Asian American groups is a generally accepted fact,"[9] one researcher has written. Even the Vietnamese, a recent group, are on an educational par with whites.

The most interesting findings concern blacks and Mexicans. Contrary to what one might suspect from news reports and impressions lingering from older research, nowadays blacks in California are not a widely undereducated mass. The typical black now has the same educational attainment as the typical white, suggesting that trends toward educational assimilation have had far-reaching results.[10] The data also emphasize the lagging position of Chicanos. They are far behind every other group. A factor behind this lag might be immigration. Groups with high median education, such as Koreans and Filipinos, may be from the upper sectors of their societies while Chicanos may be from the lower sectors of Mexican society. Whatever the reasons, though, these data hint at the possibility that Mexican Americans are becoming California's underclass.

Medians show overall levels. The following percentage table shows more detail. As with some of the other tables, the boldfaced numbers denote a category in which the minority percentage is higher than the white percentage.

Three percent or less of blacks, Filipinos, Japanese, Koreans, and whites are in the lowest educational category (kindergarten or less). In contrast, 5% to 8% of Chinese, Vietnamese, and Mexicans are in that category. In every instance the minority percentage in this category is larger than the white percentage. While the numbers are not large in absolute terms, neither are they trivial when one considers how low a level of education that is. For most practical purposes, it is equivalent to no education at all.

The table further shows that 39% of Chicanos have completed only elementary school, as have 19% of Vietnamese. The percentages are lower for blacks, Chinese, and Filipinos, and lowest for Japanese, Koreans, and whites. That blacks have the highest percentage completing high school is worth nothing.[11]

Table 4.6
Education*

Percentage

Education Level	B	C	F	J	K	V	M	W
Kindergarden or less	1	8	1	1	3	5	6	0
Elementary school (grades 1–8)	**13**	**15**	**15**	6	9	**19**	**39**	8
High school (grades 9–12)	**48**	25	27	41	33	38	39	45
College (1–4 years)	32	33	**42**	**39**	**45**	32	14	35
Post college (5+ years)	6	**19**	**15**	**13**	10	6	2	12
Totals	100	100	100	100	100	100	100	100

*Highest school year completed, persons aged 25 or older.

N.B. Boldface type indicates that the minority percentage in this category is higher than the white percentage.

B-Black; C-Chinese; F-Filipino; J-Japanese; K-Korean;
M-Mexican; V-Vietnamese; W-White

Operationally, higher education is the percentage completing at least one to four years of college. By this definition, Koreans rank highest and Filipinos second highest. Mexicans rank lowest. Postcollege is defined as completing five or more years of college and, as the table shows, Chinese rank higher than any other group.

The blacks' data should be studied more closely. The findings showed that relatively more blacks have completed elementary school than whites, slightly more blacks have completed high school than whites, and almost as many blacks have completed one to four years of college as whites. Only in the postcollege category do blacks rank substantially below whites. One can therefore conclude that educationally, blacks are now very close to, or exceed, white levels. Of course, this statement does not take into account quality of education, but even so, the increases in black education are impressive.

The index of differentiation can also be calculated on the education data (and the same qualifications regarding category number and width should be kept in mind).

The amount of educational differentiation between Japanese and whites is only 5%, lowest among the groups. Reviewing the pattern of boldfaced numbers on the previous table, one can see that the Japanese percentages in the two highest categories exceed the white percentage, indicating that the reason for the low index is that

Table 4.7
Educational Differentiation*

Percentage

J	B	K	V	F	C	M
5	9	14	16	18	21	36

*Index of dissimilarity

B-Black; C-Chinese; F-Filipino; J-Japanese; K-Korean;
M-Mexican; V-Vietnamese; W-White

Japanese are overpresented at college levels. The differentiation between blacks and whites is also low, only 9%, but unlike the Japanese case, this comes about because the black percentages in the lower educational categories exceed the white percentages, but then crossover in the higher categories. At the other extreme, Chicanos are the most differentiated educationally, 36%, because they are overrepresented in the lower categories and underrepresented in higher ones; so are the Vietnamese, but not to the same extent. The high index for Chinese and Filipinos may counter common impressions. However, note on Table 4.6 that the Chinese are overrepresented in the highest category and in the two lowest categories while Filipinos are overrepresented in the two highest categories and in the two lowest categories. These are not clear crossover patterns, and they indicate a reason for the index values: Chinese and Filipinos are educationally differentiated because they have attained high levels of education and because they have not.

Income

Of the three socioeconomic measures being considered, income is the most easily compared across groups because it is measured by a standard unit: U.S. dollars. Nevertheless, complete comparability is not guaranteed because the purchasing power of the dollar varies from group to group. Persons living in a concentrated ethnic ghetto have a different standard and cost of living than persons living in high-rise apartments or outlying areas. Analysts sometimes can make statistical adjustments for these differences, but unfortunately, the necessary indexes are not available for all the groups under study, so purchasing power must be subjectively taken into account when drawing conclusions.

Table 4.8 shows median income from all sources except welfare, for persons aged 15 years and older. Welfare was excluded because it is a payment received for, in a sense, not having much income. To include it would thus make poorer groups appear to have more income, hence making them more assimilated than they are.

Vietnamese and Chicanos have the lowest median incomes, as one can see on the table, and past writings would lead us to expect that. Koreans are next. Given their educational attainment, one might expect their income to be higher, but this is not the case. Blacks and Filipinos have the same median incomes and are followed by the Chinese. Japanese and whites have the highest median incomes of all. While the differences between each median and the adjacent medians are not especially large, the range between the highest and lowest median is substantial: $5,000 per year.

Because they have the highest median education, one might suppose that Filipinos and Koreans would have the highest median income and that Chicanos, because they have the lowest education, would have the lowest income. The latter is true, but the former is not. Even this simple observation shows the lack of correlation between educational attainment and income attainment. Evidently, there is more going on than these simple statistics can elucidate (Chapter 7 returns to this issue).

Table 4.9 shows income divided into levels. For the Vietnamese, the frequencies in the higher categories are too small to calculate a reliable percentage, although figures are shown for purposes of completeness.

Unlike the tables for education and occupation, a clear pattern exists for income. The distribution of boldfaced numbers indicate that the minorities are consistently overrepresented in income categories up to the $15,000 category, with two exceptions. The Filipino percentage in the lowest category is the same as the white percentage, and the Japanese percentages in that and the next highest category are the same or lower than the white percentages. These exceptions are small, however, and even with them, the high density of boldfaced numbers over the lower income categories is clearly visible.

Table 4.8
Median Incomes*

($1,000)

M	V	K	B	F	C	J	W
9	9	10	11	11	12	14	14

*Income from all sources except welfare, persons aged 15 or older.

B-Black; C-Chinese; F-Filipino; J-Japanese; K-Korean;
M-Mexican; V-Vietnamese; W-White

Table 4.9
Annual Incomes*

Income Category	B	C	F	J	K	M	V	W
$4,999 or less	**17**	**15**	**14**	**12**	**19**	**22**	**23**	14
$5,000–$9,999	**25**	**22**	**28**	**19**	**28**	**33**	**30**	19
$10,000–$14,999	**23**	**20**	**27**	**20**	**20**	**22**	**25**	18
$15,000–$19,999	**16**	**15**	**15**	**16**	13	12	12	14
$20,000–$24,999	11	11	9	13	9	7	7	13
$25,000–$29,999	4	6	3	**8**	3	2	2	7
$30,000–$39,999	2	5	2	7	4	2	1	7
$40,000–$49,999	1	3	1	2	2	0	0	3
$50,000 or more	1	3	1	3	2	0	0	5
Totals	100	100	100	100	100	100	100	100

*Income from all sources except welfare, persons aged 15 or older.

N.B. Boldface type indicates that the minority percentage in this category is higher than the white percentage.

B-Black; C-Chinese; F-Filipino; J-Japanese; K-Korean;
M-Mexican; V-Vietnamese; W-White

The $15,000 category is the transition point. In that category the percentages for blacks, Chinese, Filipino, and Japanese are higher than the white percentage and the percentages for the remaining groups are lower. Above $15,000, only one boldfaced number appears (Japanese). At higher income levels, minorities are underrepresented.

Even though the pattern of overrepresentation and underrepresentation stands out, one should not overlook the within group distribution. The majority of every group falls in the lower three income categories, varying from one-half of whites to three-fourths of Vietnamese and Chicanos. Conversely, although relatively few persons are in the upper income category, more whites are there than any other group. To illustrate, 5% of whites are in the $50,000 or more category compared to no Chicanos or Vietnamese. When it comes to the highest incomes, whites predominate.

As with the data on occupation and education, the index of differentiation was computed. They are shown in Table 4.10.

That Japanese are only 5% differentiated from whites seems reasonable in light of previous data and discussion. Moreover, as Table 4.9 illustrated, the Japanese and white distributions do not crossover. The Chinese are only slightly more differentiated than the Japanese, but their index value has a clear crossover. Chinese are overrepresented at lower income levels and underrepresented at higher ones, and so income parity is being achieved through closing the gap at all income levels. Somewhat unanticipated is the differentiation for Koreans and blacks. While various predictions could be made as to the

Table 4.10
Income Differentiation*

Percentage

J	C	K	B	F	M	V
5	7	15	15	19	22	26

*Index of dissimilarity.

B-Black; C-Chinese; F-Filipino; J-Japanese; K-Korean;
M-Mexican; V-Vietnamese; W-White

relative rankings of the two groups, Koreans are as income-assimilated as blacks. The most highly differentiated groups are Filipinos, Chicanos, and especially the Vietnamese. In all cases, the income distributions crossover, indicating that the minorities are disproportionately concentrated in the low-income categories.

An overall socioeconomic picture seems to be forming. Asians are identical or are close to whites in terms of education and occupation, but fall behind in income. The one exception is the Japanese, who have the highest median income of any group (although proportionately more whites are still in the highest income category). The Vietnamese are in a peculiar position. Educationally and occupationally, they resemble other Asians but have not been able to achieve much income parity. Blacks are generally intermediate and Chicanos are the most highly differentiated group in California.

This picture is a description based on socioeconomic measures and it is only loosely tied to any body of theory. It is, nevertheless, broadly consistent with both past writings and what one would suspect from the historical background of the groups. More detailed clues as to why this picture exists comes from examining other dimensions of assimilation.

Losing Past Ties and Gaining New Ones

Observers familiar with a specific ethnic group can usually distinguish a second or later generation member from new arrivals even without hearing them speak. The newly arrived display the unconscious tags of their former culture. They may hold different facial expressions, walk in a different gait, or use different gestures. The intraethnic group expression, FOB, refers to the distinctiveness of recent immigrants. Data at hand do not permit inquiry into such behavior, but certain available measures can be interpreted as indexes of assimilation. As long as the index is correlated with the underlying conceptual variable, knowing the index will provide information we otherwise would not have.

Time of Immigration

Assuming that early immigrants are more assimilated than later immigrants, the time of immigration acts as rough surrogate for the possibility of cultural assimilation. Admittedly, an immigrant group can reside in a country for a long period without assimilating, sometimes through self-conscious choice, such as the Amish. Groups like the Amish, however, are rather uncommon. Even if immigrants are indifferent to assimilation, the longer they have been in the United States, the more assimilated they become due to "cultural osmosis": they interact with the host society in thousands of little, casual, unplanned, everyday ways—through radio, television, newspapers, street signs, clerks, salespersons—and unwittingly become somewhat assimilated. To a degree, assimilation cannot be avoided without strong, conscious efforts, and probably not even then.

To make the data more compact, the year of immigration was divided into two time periods: early (1969 or before) and recent (1970 or later). 1969 was chosen as the dividing line because the Hart Cellar Act revising immigration laws became fully operational in that year.

These results (Table 4.11) affirm what one might suspect: that blacks and whites are overwhelmingly native born. The table also shows that most Japanese and Mexicans are native born, a finding which may come as a surprise. In contrast to these comparatively high rates, approximately one-third or less of Chinese, Filipinos,

Table 4.11
Time of Immigration*

Percentage

Time of Immigration	V	K	F	C	M	J	W	B
Born in U.S.	8	16	31	38	65	70	94	98
Recent immigration (1970 or later)	91	72	46	37	22	13	1	1
Early immigration (1969 or earlier)	1	12	23	25	13	17	5	1
Totals	100	100	100	100	100	100	100	100

B-Black; C-Chinese; F-Filipino; J-Japanese; K-Korean;
M-Mexican; V-Vietnamese; W-White

Koreans, and Vietnamese were born in the United States. The Vietnamese and Korean percentages are especially small.

Among both Vietnamese and blacks, only minuscule proportions immigrated before the Hart Cellar Act went into full effect. The percentage of early white immigrants is not large either. Recent immigration is a different matter. Koreans and especially Vietnamese are overwhelmingly recent immigrants, and so their impact on American society is just beginning. In contrast, the Japanese are the Asian group with the lowest percentage of recent immigrants. This statistic may run contrary to the belief that Japanese businessmen and their families are arriving in large number, but it is consistent with the statistical fact that most Japanese in the United States are native born.

The values for blacks and whites were expected, but note the black percentage is somewhat higher than the white percentage. Carrying out the logic of opportunity for assimilation just enunciated, whites may be less assimilated than blacks, which in hindsight may make some sense. After all, blacks have been in this country about as long as whites, and therefore could be considered equally as indigenous. Although I am not sure at what point a group loses its designation as "immigrant," in light of the high percentage of American-born Japanese and Mexicans, they probably should not be considered so; they are now indigenous Americans.

Citizenship

Native-born Americans have citizenship as a birth right, and most seldom think about it. Immigrants face a much different situation. They cannot take citizenship for granted because it requires a conscious decision and a lengthy legal process. Citizenship symbolically represents joining American society, and it implies permanent settlement in the United States, which will become the home of one's offspring. Acquiring citizenship has an emotional meaning too. Some people cry at the ceremony. Many frame their citizenship papers and display them on the wall. For these reasons, naturalization represents a further step or commitment to assimilation.

The naturalization rates shown on Table 4.12 are only for foreign-born persons because only they have the option of applying for citizenship.

Just a small percent of Vietnamese are naturalized. Undoubtedly, the recency of their immigration lies behind this statistic. Sheer time is required to meet residence requirements for citizenship and to become sufficiently acquainted with the English language, history, and other topics necessary to pass the citizenship examination. Time is also required to settle, learn the culture, and become committed to a place in American society. Internal migration has aggravated the

Table 4.12
Naturalization Rate

Percentage*

V	M	K	J	C	F	B	W
7	19	26	37	39	45	51	58

*Percent of foreign born.

B-Black; C-Chinese; F-Filipino; J-Japanese; K-Korean;
M-Mexican; V-Vietnamese; W-White

problem. Initially dispersed throughout the United States, substantial numbers of Vietnamese have migrated to Southern California.

Considering that Mexicans have a long California history, their naturalization rate may seem low. However, with California so close to Mexico, many Chicano immigrants may harbor realistic hopes of returning in the near future. Then, too, the huge Mexican barrios and the large Mexican population make interactions with broader Anglo society less necessary, and hence all things Anglo less salient, including citizenship.

The naturalization rates among Koreans, Japanese, Chinese, and Filipinos are higher than the Mexican rate. A major difference between them and Chicanos is group size. While these Asian groups are large enough to support ethnically toned neighborhoods, they are not so large as to saturate a widespread area. The qualitative differences between ethnic areas can be substantial, although hard to describe in words. One only has to walk through Los Angeles's barrio and then through the areas surrounding Chinatown, Little Tokyo, or Little Seoul to appreciate these differences. The latter areas seem like ethnic shopping centers and tourist traps. The barrio seems like a country unto itself.

The comparatively high naturalization rate among Filipinos might be due to historical roots. Coming from a country once ruled by the United States where the English language is common, Filipinos are undoubtedly familiar with American culture and hence are more open to acquiring citizenship. The naturalization rates among blacks and whites are higher still, but the number of foreign born among those groups is so small that the rates may not be too meaningful (I included them for purposes of completeness).

Language

So important is language that some social scientists believe it shapes our very thoughts. While that may or may not be true, language is a key to assimilation. Without language proficiency, immigrants cannot communicate with the host society, either interpersonally or formally. Neither can they acquire the socialization that comes through television, newspapers, radio, and scores of other sources such as billboards, shop signs, and the like. Immigrant subculture is replete with stories of persons who for years, unable to read English, got around the city by looking for the pictures on billboards; and one day when the billboard was taken down, they were lost.

Language is also political. The issue of who has the right to speak which language has led to bloodshed (for example, Belgium) and political acrimony (for example, Quebec). At the urging of Mexican American groups, Spanish has been introduced in many Southwestern schools as a second language, a trend that Secretary of Education William Bennett called a "failed path" because, in his opinion, it retards assimilation.[12] Some states have formally adopted English as the official language, a move opposed by interest groups who claim it is a forerunner to officially sanctioned discrimination.[13] While political issues obviously cannot be resolved here, they do point to the importance of language with regard to assimilation.

The Census Bureau reports two questions on language. One asks about the ability to speak English, the other asks about the language normally spoken at home (excluding persons aged 3 or younger).

Language Spoken at Home. Data on language spoken at home are shown in Table 4.13.

For blacks and whites, since neither group is composed of very many immigrants, only a small percentage speak a language other than English at home. As the table emphasizes, a large gap exists between them and the Japanese, among whom somewhat less than one-half speak a language other than English (presumably Japanese) at home. A large gap also exists between Japanese and Filipinos. While in many places in the Philippines English is common (for example, Manila has English radio stations), almost three-fourths of Filipino Americans do not use English at home. This finding is somewhat

Table 4.13
Language

Percentage*

B	W	J	F	M	C	K	V
4	6	46	71	76	82	86	96

*Percent speaking languages other than English at home.

B-Black; C-Chinese; F-Filipino; J-Japanese; K-Korean;
M-Mexican; V-Vietnamese; W-White

inconsistent with the high rate of Filipino naturalization. Yet, if assimilation is a multivariate phenomenon, some factors may determine both naturalization and English usage while other factors determine just one or just the other. For instance, using the native tongue may be a matter of aesthetic rather than political choice. Some immigrants say they miss their language and like to speak it when among themselves.[14] It can also be a matter of convenience. The measure refers to the home, and there speaking the native language may be easier than struggling with a foreign one. This would be particularly true when interacting with immigrant parents and grandparents. These same considerations help account for the high percentages found for Chicanos, Chinese, Koreans, and Vietnamese.

English-Speaking Ability

Developing proficiency in English may be difficult, even for the native born. It involves several factors: place of birth, ability, length of time in the United States, availability of schooling, necessity, motivation, and others. Although Census Bureau data cannot reveal the contribution of such factors, the Bureau does inquire about ability to speak English. Whoever fills out the questionnaire is asked to rate him or herself and others in the household. Judges used the following categories:

Very well:	no difficulty in speaking English
Well:	minor problems
Not well:	seriously limited
Not at all:	spoke no English

The data reflect the opinion of a nonsocial scientist (the householder) rather than systematically trained observers. That must introduce biases, but of an unknown kind and to an unknown extent. These methodological considerations suggest that the data are a crude measure of English proficiency, but still, they may be instructive.

There are also some conceptual considerations with the measure. Filipinos, and some blacks and whites, have immigrated from bilingual societies, making English ability an ambiguous indicator of assimilation. To take a hypothetical extreme, would English facility indicate the assimilation of Canadian immigrants to the United States? A much different issue—the controversy surrounding black English—also bears on the interpretation of the data. Is black English a correct language or is it a deviation from proper English? And how meaningful is it to compare black English to other forms of English? The same question can be raised regarding English spoken by Chicanos, Filipinos, and other ethnic group. Their versions of English may be just as correct as the "Queen's English," but nevertheless their abilities may be denigrated. I raise these issues because they introduce ambiguity. I can only assume that enough commonality exists to make intergroup comparisons meaningful. The following data are only for bilingual persons; native speakers are excluded. Based on the assumption that one can interact well enough even without speaking English excellently, the following table shows the combined categories of *very well* and *well*.

The values on Table 4.14 vary from more than 90% for Filipinos, blacks, and whites to 54% for Vietnamese. If one accepts that proficiency in English indexes assimilation, then Filipinos are the most assimilated Asian group. Given the bilingual culture of the Philippines, this seems reasonable. Following this same logic for Asian groups from non-English-speaking societies, the Japanese are the most assimilated—more than three-fourths speak English well or very well. Chinese and Koreans are less assimilated, but not too much less than the Japanese. Even among the Vietnamese, the group with the most recent immigration history, somewhat more than one-half are proficient in English.

Those are the findings, but what they indicate for assimilation is not totally clear. In many cases, immigrants do not have to be very proficient in English. A good example is the famous Mexican baseball player, Fernando Valenzuela of the Los Angeles Dodgers, who was born and raised in Mexico. According to an interview in a popular sports magazine, "Why hasn't Valenzuela completely crossed the language bridge? The answer is simple: he hasn't had to, in large part because of his good fortune of living in a city with a Spanish heritage."[15] So widespread is Spanish in certain sections of the Los Angeles barrio that some shopkeepers place a sign in the window proclaiming, "AQUI, SE HABLA ENGLISH" (English spoken here).[16] A similar process could be occurring among Chinese, Koreans, and Vietnamese. In heavily

Table 4.14
Ability to Speak English

Percentage*

V	K	M	C	J	F	B	W
54	64	68	69	76	91	93	93

*Percent of nonnative English speakers, with a well or "very well" proficiency.

B-Black; C-Chinese; F-Filipino; J-Japanese; K-Korean;
M-Mexican; V-Vietnamese; W-White

ethnic neighborhoods, the native language is common on billboards and shop signs. Clerks, bank tellers, barbers, insurance agents, accountants, doctors, lawyers, and almost everyone else, can speak at least a smattering of the language. Local radio stations and some television channels broadcast ethnic language programs. Thus, the necessity to acquire English proficiency is greatly reduced.

Conclusion

The major findings are summarized as follows.

- By and large, Japanese Americans are no longer socioeconomically differentiated from whites. On all three indicators of socioeconomic status, Japanese were very near white levels, and sometimes surpassed them. For example, the Japanese proportions in the categories of managerial professional workers were slightly higher than the white proportion. Japanese median income was the same. Additionally, 70% of Japanese were born in the United States, and are therefore citizens and native speakers by birth. While assimilation has progressed apace for the Japanese, that does not mean all prejudice has vanished. Racial epithets are still heard. The term "Jap" is so common it often passes unnoticed as a derogatory term, as any Japanese American can attest.[17]
- Nearly the same proportion of Chinese as whites are in managerial, professional, and technical occupations. Median Chinese education is the same as the Japanese median, but median Chinese income is significantly (by $2,000) lower than the white median. This last figure means that Chinese have not been successful in translating their educations and occupations into income. The high proportion of Chinese who are not native born coupled with the moderately high proportion who cannot speak English very well, may be the reason for their low incomes.
- Vietnamese and Mexicans present a surprisingly similar statistical picture. The Vietnamese population contains an exceptionally high proportion of immigrants, and both groups have low rates of naturalization. Large numbers of both groups speak English poorly or not all, and both are concentrated in the lower brackets of occupation. Both groups have low incomes. While Vietnamese have about as much education as whites and blacks, Chicanos do not. Unlike the Japanese, these groups are surely minorities in the sense of being less assimilated and having less socioeconomic attainment than the majority.

- Vietnamese appear to be the group least likely to assimilate in the near future. The recency and trauma of their immigration, their low rates of citizenship, and the handicap of language all stand in the way of rapid assimilation. Favoring assimilation is their comparatively high education and the fact that they cannot reasonably hope to return to Vietnam in the near future. Regardless of whether anyone likes it, the Vietnamese are here to stay.
- Filipinos used to be a mostly male, poor, uneducated, and unassimilated group. Now, regardless of immigration status, almost all speak good English and approximately one-third are native born. The level of Filipino education is higher than the white level, yet relatively fewer Filipinos than whites are in the managerial category while median Filipino income is lower than the white median. Obviously some factor other than education and language ability lies behind the socioeconomic position of Filipinos.

  While currently behind whites, other data suggest that Filipinos are the group most likely to make quick strides toward fuller assimilation. Their citizenship rate suggests they have a commitment to the United States, and their proficiency in English means that language will not be a major impediment.
- The educational distribution of blacks is almost identical to the white distribution; the medians are identical. Yet the proportion of blacks in higher occupational categories is below the white level, as is black income. While the black-white educational gap has closed, gaps in occupations and incomes remain.

When comparing ethnic groups, there is a tendency to claim that one group has suffered more than another and that this suffering explains the relative positions of the groups. Such an explanation is easily read into ethnic histories, and I do not dispute it. I would, however, add that there must be more to the explanation than that. When interpreted broadly, the data just reviewed suggests the importance of causal forces deriving from the structure of society and from the structure of the groups, possibilities that the next few chapters explore.

5

Assimilation and Residential Segregation

T he urban landscape is a checkerboard of neighborhoods, some
of which are exceedingly black, or exceedingly Chicano, or
exceedingly Asian, or poor, or rich. Compaction, compression,
concentration, segregation, and ghettoization—all describe the social
mosaic of a city. From the beginning of formal sociology, this uneven
distribution of people over space has been the subject of voluminous
academic research, much of it motivated by political and ideological
concerns. Obviously, neither the politics nor the research have caused
residential segregation to disappear, nor is segregation likely to disappear in the near future.

While not wishing to sound unduly pessimistic or apologetic, one
should remember that ghettoization has existed for centuries. Rome
had a "Christian section" and many medieval cities had "Jewish quar-
ters" (from which the modern term *ghetto* derives). If anything, history
suggests that ghettoization will be an integral part of the urban landscape for many years to come. Of course, the historical fact of the
matter does not make it ethically right or inevitable, but the long
history does imply that strong, persistent, generalized, and complex
social forces underlie residential segregation. Coming to grips with
this issue ideologically and scientifically is not an easy task.

Plan of the Chapter

This chapter consists of the following:

- Chicago School, as a general framework or background;
- methodology and meaning of ghettoization;
- Findings;
- Ethnic group size and ghettoization;
- Findings;

- Socioeconomic status and ghettoization;
- Findings; and
- Comments and conclusions.

Definition. Before proceeding, a note on terminology. I use the terms *ghetto, barrio* and *residential segregation* synonymously. I also use *residential integration* as the opposite of residential segregation.

Perspective for Interpreting Ghettoization: The Chicago School

In broad outline, researchers have offered two general frameworks for explaining ghettoization. The first views ghettoization as the outcome of prejudice and discrimination. The majority disdains the ethnic group and will not live near them. Hence, the ethnic group becomes segregated. Because the law now mandates open housing, blatant discriminatory practices are not as common as they once were, but more subtle device, such as "steering" by real estate agents, can achieve the same end.[1] Whatever the means, though, the theoretical point remains that the causal force behind ghettoization is majority antipathy for the minority.

Prejudice represents but one way of explaining ghettoization. Another way, the basic one adopted herein, recognizes the importance of prejudice but goes beyond it to examine structural forces as well. Previous researchers have identified several forces, and their work constitutes a long tradition. They interpreted ghettoization as the group's adaptation to its environment, a view that is sometimes called human ecology, or more generically, the Chicago School. In brief, the Chicago School argument can be summarized this way:

(1) Metropolitan life attracts diverse peoples.

(2) This creates problems of interdependence coupled with problems of racial and ethnic hostilities.

(3) Separate groups come to reside in separate areas of the city for several reasons.

    (a) Initially poor immigrants to the city, either from abroad or from rural areas, gravitate towards the older, run down sections of the city, usually near the central business district. Over time, these people rise in socioeconomic status and leave the core for other neighborhoods. Such neighborhoods are usually to be found near the urban periphery.

    (b) The process applies mainly to white immigrants. Non-whites cannot easily leave the areas of initial settlement.

One reason is race hostility, another is low socioeconomic status. Even if ethnic prejudice were nonexistent, non-whites could not afford to move, which is another way of saying they cannot successfully compete with whites for desirable housing and locations. Hence, areas inhabited primarily by a single ethnic group come into existence. We call these ghettos, ethnic enclaves, or segregated neighborhoods.

(4) Compacting various ethnic functions in one locale increases the economic efficiencies of communication, distribution, and transportation. For instance, having the ethnic market located in one section of the city, the ethnic club located across town, the ethnic church located in another section, and ethnic residences located in still another section would make little ecological sense. (These advantages generalize beyond the ghetto; they apply to diverse institutions. The ghettoization of financial districts, garment districts, university districts, and central business districts, suggests as much.) Socially, compaction makes for greater ethnicity, as group members interact with other members, speaking the language, eating ethnic foods, following ethnic customs.

(5) These areas develop institutions geared to the unique cultural and social requirements of the ethnic group. A group may voluntarily congregate to attain mutual support and to carry out their lifestyles in the privacy of their own group. An extreme example are separatists, such as the Amish, who attempt to restrict all interactions with the majority by isolating themselves physically. Less extreme, but perhaps as effective, are groups such as Hassidic Jews who manage to remain ethnically isolated while living in New York City.

The ghetto, in short, becomes a community which represents the group's adaptation to society.

To judge from their theoretical writings, the Chicago School was primarily interested in the ghetto's structure and relation to the environment. Their empirical research, however, suggests otherwise. In another context but with present relevance, Milla Alihan noted that despite theoretical predilection, Chicago School researchers actually performed general sociological studies on persons living in ghettoized areas. They took the ghetto as given, and proceeded to analyze such topics as delinquent gangs, taxi dancers, and ethnic groups.[2] Many other researchers, whether formally a part of Chicago School or not, have followed their lead. For instance, in a much-praised work, Elliot Liebow gives a highly detailed and insightful glimpse into black street life.[3] He was interested in the individual, and took the ghetto environment as a given. Had these individuals been living elsewhere, then that locale would have been taken as given. There is certainly nothing wrong with the approach, and as long as Chicago School researchers (and others) focused on individuals, the question of statistically measuring ghettoization never arose. However, when researchers began analyzing urban areas with aggregated data, analysis shifted from individuals in ghettos to ghettos as *areal* units.[4]

With this shift in unit of analysis, the link between individual and ghettoization became tenuous. What is true at the level of an area unit might not be true at the individual level, yet the individual often remained the focus of theoretical interest.[5] This presents a lacuna. As long as data represent one level of analysis and theoretical interest is at another, a mismatch exists. Either the data must be brought into conformity with the interest (or vice versa), or it must be assumed that the data reflect the individual. This assumption might be valid, but in most cases there is no way of definitely ascertaining that.

The ideas of the Chicago School have been introduced as a framework and intellectual-historical backdrop for the theoretical arguments to be presented later. A detailed critique of the ideas lies far beyond the scope of this work. More immediate is the question of how much ghettoization exists with regard to each group under study. Although a limited concern, it can be addressed with the current data. To do that, however, requires some comments on methodology and measurement because both are closely linked to the conceptual meaning of ghettoization.

Methodology and the Meaning of Ghettoization

Measurement

In this section of the chapter, the measure of segregation will be the index of dissimilarity (ID), the same index used before.[6] Simply put, the value of the ID indicates the percentage of one group that would have to change census tracts in order to be equally distributed across the city. This value can vary from 0%, or absolutely no segregation, to 100%, or total segregation.[7]

I find this interpretation satisfactory, but limitations should be acknowledged. The interpretation says nothing about exchanging residences with whites, a process which would have to occur if some all-powerful force implemented residential integration by fiat. Nor does the ID take into account what level of segregation would exist if people chose their residential locations on the basis of chance alone.

For these reasons, some authors feel the ID should be abandoned.[8] On the other hand, it can be argued that no one is about to impose mass residential integration by fiat, nor are whites about to exchange residences with nonwhites, nor are people about to randomly select their places of residence. I therefore draw a conditional conclusion: there is no absolutely correct criterion for all purposes.

Other aspects of the ID warrant mention. It does not directly measure spatial concentration. Consider two contrasting situations: (1) Every other block in the city is populated only by blacks. This distribution is uneven, and certainly most observers would agree that it constitutes a form of segregation. (2) Every black lives in a few contiguous blocks in the city. This distribution is compacted and uneven. It, too, is a form of segregation. However, the ID does not distinguish between the two forms. Fortunately, this does not create a major problem. In their pioneering monograph on urban segregation, Karl and Alma Taeuber assert, "Unevenness without clustering is, however, hypothetical and not to be found in U. S. cities."[9] A 1970 study of all large metropolitan areas in the United States corroborates the Taeubers's assertion. Delimiting on maps the sections of the city in which a majority of blacks lived, the compactness and contiguity of these areas were immediately and obviously apparent even on the most superficial inspection.[10] Although both studies were done with older data (1960 and 1970), major changes in the conclusion seem unlikely. Residential patterns change, but not very quickly.

More problematic is the applicability of the conclusion to groups other than blacks. The existence of well-defined ethnic areas, such as Chinatown, Little Tokyo, and the East Side (a Los Angeles barrio) suggests unevenness, contiguity, and compaction go hand-in-hand, but without comparative data, one cannot be absolutely certain.

Concerning the expected value of the index, that depends on the ethnic proportion of the urban area, a dependency which leads some critics to say that comparisons between cities with different proportions are unjustified. However, one can argue just the reverse: if an index of segregation did not allow for the minority proportion, it would not be proper to compare cities. How much sense does it make to compare segregation levels under the assumption that every city has the same minority percentage?[11]

Finally, one should recognize that if different ethnic groups live in the same neighborhoods, which is a kind of residential integration, that will not be reflected in the index. This computational point raises a persistent, nagging problem: what does it mean to say a tract is residentially integrated? Consider several possibilities:

- The tract contains only the majority group—which is pure segregation.
- The tract contains only one minority group, say blacks—which is also pure segregation.
- The tract contains both whites and Asians, but no Mexicans or blacks—which is a kind of integration and segregation combined.
- The tract contains Mexicans and blacks, but no whites or Asians— which is also a kind of integration and segregation combined.

While more combinations can be created, these are enough to make the point that residential integration can refer to different ethnic mixes, and which mix one studies will vary by purpose. In this research, the issue being addressed is the integration of each ethnic group *vis-a-vis* whites. Rightly or wrongly, white-minority integration is, in fact, the mix that has historically been the center of moral and political storms, with much violence committed because of it. For that reason, it is the mix being studied now.[12]

Units of Analysis

For present purposes, an *urban area* is operationally defined as the 21 Standard Metropolitan Statistical Areas (1980 SMSAs) in California. An SMSA consists of a large urban nucleus plus the nearby communities which have a high degree of economic and social integration with the nucleus. Once the Census Bureau determines that the criteria of social and economic integration are met, the entire county (or counties) is included in the SMSA designation. More loosely speaking, an SMSA is what most people mean by a large metropolitan area.

The Census Bureau subdivides each SMSA into *tracts:* areas intended to be relatively homogenous with respect to population characteristics, economic status, and living conditions. Tracts usually contain between 2,500 and 8,000 residents and correspond to a neighborhood, again loosely speaking. The ID was calculated on census tracts averaged across the total SMSAs. Census tracts are undoubtedly the most frequently used areal unit for studying residential segregation, and by using them again, present outcomes can be compared with other findings.

Small tracts—those with fewer than 500 residents or 50 dwelling units—were excluded for two reasons. First, they are usually located in atypical areas of the metropolis, most often at the very fringes with much open land and few residents. Second, being based on so few people, estimates of segregation levels might be unstable.

In general, tract data are not highly detailed and for race classifications, the Census Bureau reported only the raw count of persons. This limits what can be done, but even so, indexes of residential segregation could be calculated for the seven ethnic groups separately (later, broader ethnic groupings and a different index will be used for studying the influence of socioeconomic variables on segregation).

There is a relation between the way segregation is measured, with the ID, and the areal unit upon which it is based.[13] The larger the unit, the less the segregation. To see this, consider blacks and whites residing in a hypothetical city. If the entire city is the unit of analysis, then segregation will be zero; everyone—both blacks and whites— lives within it, but that is not what one typically means by residential integration. At the other hypothetical extreme, if dwelling units are the unit of analysis, then segregation will be nearly 100% even if black dwelling units are randomly located throughout the city. That is because blacks and white rarely share the same dwelling unit, but one would probably not call that residential segregation. Although the effect of tract size should not be ignored, some evidence suggests the effect is not overly strong.[14] It is also possible that big SMSAs will have higher index values than small ones simply as a function of size, because big SMSAs have more tracts, and the greater the number of tracts, the higher the index—all things being equal, of course. Research, however, suggests that is not a major problem.[15]

Considering all the problems just discussed, one might wonder why use the ID at all. The reason is simple and compelling. Since the Taeubers' major study on black segregation in 1965, the ID has been the measure most often presented, and over time, researchers have become familiar with both its limitations and its interpretation.[16] Because accumulation of knowledge is a foundation for scientific advancement, this represents a simple but significant advantage. As long as the limitations are borne in mind—and empirically their impact is not as large as the length of the discussion might imply—they should not cause one to come to a misleading conclusion.

Levels of Ghettoization

Bearing all of this in mind, the Table 5.1 shows the ID by ethnic group and metropolitan area.

One can see a considerable amount of variation across SMSAs. The means vary from a low of 46% to a high of 76% while the standard deviations vary from 8% to 13%. Of the seven groups, the Vietnamese are most often the most highly segregated (although in many cases

Table 5.1
Indexes of Dissimilarity (Ghettoization)
For Seven Ethnic Groups

Dissimilarity Between Whites
And

Metropolitan Area	B	C	F	J	K	M	V
Anaheim	50	48	50	35	54	53	62
Bakersfield	64	60	69	58	79*	56	81*
Chico	61	64*	72*	58*	98*	50	88*
Fresno	62	48	54	43	80*	45	80*
Los Angeles	79	56	55	54	56	53	69
Modesto	57	57	44*	50*	74*	44	79*
Oxnard	53	54	60	45	64	59	79
Redding	56	86*	85*	63*	97*	45	50*
Riverside	54	58	54	45	61	43	78
Sacramento	56	60	50	47	60	50	76
Salinas	66	40	45	41	56	57	74
San Diego	62	50	62	39	63	50	67
San Francisco	71	57	58	42	61	52	75
San Jose	49	36	56	29	50	53	63
Santa Barbara	42	56	58	33	66	46	72
Santa Cruz	39	52	58	47	57*	62	89*
Santa Rosa	45	64	47	42	69*	43	85*
Stockton	62	53	55	41	75*	43	79
Vallejo	52	45	58	41	69	33	72*
Visalia	62	62	66	65	85*	39	93*
Yuba City	52	64*	52	41	76*	36	86*
Mean	57	56	58	46	69	48	76
Standard deviation	10	10	10	9	13	8	10

*Based on fewer than 500 persons.

B-Black; C-Chinese; F-Filipino; J-Japanese; K-Korean;
M-Mexican; V-Vietnamese; W-White

the number of Vietnamese is so small that the resulting values may not be very stable).

In the past, values for black segregation typically exceeded 80% to 90%, and so the values on the table might be considered moderate or even low. Whether they would be low relative to some ideological standard is a different issue, of course. The Japanese, in this regard, are the least segregated group with a value of 46%.

These data are surprising. Contrary to the impressions presented by the popular media, neither blacks nor Chicanos are the most ghettoized ethnic group. The misimpression may be the result of the historical fame (perhaps *infamy* is a better word) of certain ghettos. The Watts ghetto was the site of the 1965 Watts Riot, a riot usually taken as the starting point of the urban-racial crisis of the 1960s. The Chicano barrio of Los Angeles became famous even before that. The Zoot Suit Riots of World War II focussed heavy attention on that Mexican American community. Another cause of the misimpression is the "invisibility" of the Asian ghetto. For some reason, the Asian ghetto is not defined as a social problem, or if a problem, a mild one. This benign image may be due to the reputation those places have for being exotic islands of Asian culture, open to the public. For many Anglos, "eating Chinese" and browsing through the gift shops of Chinatown is the closest contact they have with Asian life, and the contacts are pleasant, hardly connoting a social issue. But whatever image one might have about whichever group, the data make one point clear: residential segregation is the norm.

This conclusion naturally raises the question of why? The straightforward answer is money and it lies embedded in the Chicago School's notion of residential zones radiating outward from the urban core. Wealthy groups can afford to disperse, poor groups cannot, and accordingly, the less income a group has, the more segregated it should be. This simple hypothesis can be assessed by relating segregation to income. These data are shown on the following graph (Figure 5.1). The dark bars represent the ID and clear bars represent group income in 1979.[17] So that the two measures can be compared along the same scale, income was standardized to the same mean and standard deviation as the ID. This statistical procedure facilitates comparison; it has no substantive implications.

We can see on the graph that the Japanese are the least segregated and have the highest income while Vietnamese are the most segregated group and have the lowest income. These cases—which are at the extremes—lend credence to the idea that increases in income are associated with decreases in segregation. However, the middle range cases imply a different conclusion. Mexicans are only slightly more segregated than Japanese, yet Mexican income is substantially below the Japanese level; Koreans are more segregated than Filipinos and have a lower income; Chinese have a higher income than blacks but are about as segregated. Thus, over the entire range of ethnic groups, these data demonstrate only slight support for the hypothesis. Except at the extremes, income seems to make little difference.

The topic of income and segregation will be addressed again in the broader context of socioeconomic standing, but for lack of data, the definitions of the groups will have to change. At this point, examining the influence of group size on ghettoization is more convenient.

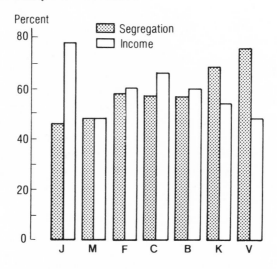

* Index of dissimilarity; income standardized

Figure 5.1: Mean Segregation and Mean Income

Ghettoization and Group Size

Because it is such a basic demographic characteristic, minority group size is a crucial variable for explaining ghettoization. The theoretical basis relating the two variables was laid out about 20 years ago.[18] Wrote Hubert Blalock in 1967,

> One of the most frequent 'common sense' generalizations made in the field of minority-group relations concerns the relationship between discrimination and the relative size of the minority. In so far as they are known, the facts are by no means simple to explain, however.[19]

Blalock reasoned as follows: (1) Larger minority groups pose a greater threat to the majority than smaller groups. (2) The majority responds to the threat with discrimination and prejudice. (3) Hence, larger groups will be more discriminated against than smaller groups. (4) Carrying this "common-sense" notion beyond common sense, he further reasoned that the relationship between relative size and discrimination would be nonlinear. A visual representation of this argument based on fictitious data for ten urban areas is shown on Figure 5.2.

Assume that only whites and blacks reside in these hypothetical cities, that the measure of inequality is the ID, and that minority

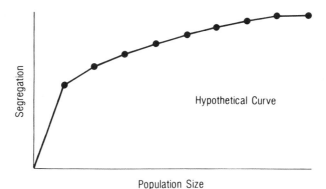

Population Size

Figure 5.2: Relation Between Population Size and Residential Segregation

population size is the percentage of the urban area that is black. Given these circumstances, the curve is negatively accelerated: it gradually slopes upward and begins to quickly level off. As the black percentage increases, the level of ghettoization increases but at a decreasing rate until at some point, changes in the black percentage have only negligible impact on ghettoization. Once ghettoization reaches 100%, or very near to that, increasing the relative size of the black population cannot increase ghettoization. Although this reasoning might seem highly mathematical, it has sociological underpinnings. Another way to study this relation is to consider a change in minority group size of ten percentage points. The effect of the change will depend on the minority's current size. Going from 0% to 10% is much different than going from 35% to 45%. In the former case, the dominant majority would perceive the threat as great, while in the latter case, because the minority group is already relatively large, becoming somewhat larger would not change the majority's perception of the situation very much.

Evidence has generally confirmed the relation between minority percentage and majority-minority inequality. For example, one study found that for metropolitan areas in the Southwest, the larger the Mexican American percentage, the lower the Mexican American income level. The same was true for blacks. These findings were not unanticipated, for the study opened with a conclusion from a literature review: "Researchers have found that, virtually without exception, the larger the relative size of a minority, the greater the majority-minority disparities in income."[20]

The posited relation between group size and discrimination may be formally expressed as a regression model:

$$Y = B \log X$$

where Y represents a measure of discrimination, X is relative group size, and B, the standardized regression coefficient, is a constant calculated from the data. When relative size is transformed with logarithms to render the equation linear, standard regression procedures may be used to calculate B.

This model rests upon an extensive theoretical base. Blalock's reasoning can be specified along three lines, as follows:

(1) *Cultural Threat.* If the majority views their status (position in the infrastructure) as insecure and susceptible to being dislodged by the minority, then a relatively large minority would be more threatening than a small one. Such threats might come on the political front, where the minority might out-vote the majority, or on the social front, where the minority might impose its culture on the majority, or possibly on the psychological front, where the perception of minority dominance might be untenable to the majority (a perception underlying the often heard statements: "They're taking over" and "I don't mind them as long as we aren't outnumbered"). Perceiving themselves as threatened, the majority responds with discrimination, prejudice, and inequality. These mechanisms hold the minority at bay, block their power, and halt their cultural hegemony. In practice, these mechanisms become interwoven, and separating them for research purposes is not always possible.

(2) *Community.* Up to this point, ethnic group size has meant relative size (the group as a proportion of the total), but for some purposes, absolute size is the proper measure, as for instance, when considering the ethnic population to be a marketplace or a pool of social support. An ethnic newspaper draws its readership overwhelmingly from the ethnic population, and the greater that number, the greater the potential audience. Social interactions between ethnic members strengthen the sense of community and cultural cohesiveness, and the greater the number, the larger this web of affiliations. In neither of these or similar instances, is the size of the majority at issue, for that number does not bear upon the effects of absolute minority size.

(3) *Economic Competition.* Inequality can result from infrastructural competition. Both the ecological perspective and cultural materialism suggest that possibility.[21] The larger the size of the minority (up to some point), the more the minority comes into competition with the

majority. Jobs are an obvious point of contention. Assuming fewer good jobs exist than applicants, discrimination helps reserve them for the majority, leaving the undesirable jobs for the minority. Blalock writes:

> The larger the relative size of the minority, however, the more minority individuals there should be in direct or potential competition with a given individual in the dominant group. As the minority percentage increases, therefore, we would expect to find increasing discriminatory behavior.[22]

Both the economic competition and cultural threat arguments assume that the majority is motivated to discriminate and further that the majority has sufficient power to impose discrimination. Power and prejudice are translated into action through myriad incidents and behaviors in which individuals engage. They are also translated into action through organizational and societal actions. Through policies, laws, procedures, and customs, discrimination becomes an integral part of the infrastructure, whether consciously intended or not. The arguments further assume a correspondence between discrimination and existing structural inequalities. However, because direct measures of prejudice are seldom available on a large-scale comparative basis, one must rely on measurable inequalities and infer that discrimination produced them.[23]

A Model and an Evaluation of It

Three hypotheses have been identified to account for ghettoization: (1) discrimination as a function of majority responses to perceived cultural threat, indexed by the relative size of the minority; (2) the communal aspects of ghettoization, indexed by the absolute size of the minority; and (3) the relative economic power of the majority and minority, indexed by a measure yet specified. In order to compare these three hypotheses and, at the same time, render them more explicit, they can be incorporated into a conventional regression model as follows:

$$Y_{ij} = B1_{ij}\, X1_{ij} + B2_{ij}\, X2_{ij} + B3_{ij}\, X3_{ij}$$

where the subscript i is the SMSA, j is the ethnic group, Y is ghettoization, $X1$ is relative group size, $X2$ is absolute group size, and $X3$ is a measure of relative economic power. The *B*s are standardized regression coefficients (*betas*) and indicate the relative importance of each variable controlling for all other variables in the equation. Based on this equation, the following hypotheses can be offered:

(1) If the reasoning about community is correct, then absolute minority size should be associated with ghettoization.

(2) If the reasoning about cultural threat is correct, then relative minority size should be associated with ghettoization.

(3) If the reasoning about economic competition is correct, then that measure should be associated with ghettoization.

(4) If more than one variable has an effect, that would imply more than one causal force is at work. Under the assumption of multiple causation being used herein, there is no reason that should not be the case.

Procedures

Independent Variables. For the independent variables, the operational definitions are fairly routine:

(1) Absolute minority population size is the number of the minority in the SMSA.

(2) Relative minority population size is the minority proportion of the sum of the given minority plus whites. Other minorities are not included in the proportion to keep the comparison between the given minority and the majority.

(3) Relative economic status is the ratio of white mean income to minority mean income. Means are based on income from all sources except welfare for all persons in the labor force.[24] If the income ratio exceeds one, that indicates whites have more economic status than the minority; if the ratio is less than one, the reverse is indicated; and if the ratio is exactly one, the groups have equal status.

Absolute minority size has been transformed with logarithms. Even though preliminary analysis showed that the transformation made almost no difference to the outcome, a log scale for absolute size is convenient. The same analysis also showed log transformations of relative size and of the income ratios made the models slightly worse. Consequently, those two measures were not transformed in the analysis.

Dependent Variable. In this section, the Coleman Index will be used to measure residential segregation.[25] Using blacks and whites as illustration, this measure may be interpreted as follows: for each tract in which a given number of blacks live, a given proportion of whites is found. Multiplying the two values produces the number of "expected" whites residing in the tract with blacks. The index will be zero when all whites live in tracts by themselves.[26] One can verbally describe the index as the proportion of whites in the tract of the average black. Note that rather than the positive effect discussed by Blalock, here the direction of the effect is negative. The change results from the nature of the Coleman index; it is not a substantive change in the logic of the hypotheses.

As mentioned before, conventional regression analysis was applied, and sometimes one hears a rule of thumb saying that there should be at least ten units of analysis for each independent variable in the equation. By that rule, the present equation should be based on at least 30 SMSAs, but in fact, it is based on 21 or fewer cases. Because the number of SMSAs cannot be increased, the obvious alternative was to reduce the number of independent variables. Rather than do that, however, I preferred "stretching" the "rule" a bit.

Confidence in the regression analysis was bolstered by, in addition to the usual statistical outcomes, the visual evidence from partial regression plots. These graphs express the relation between each independent variable and the dependent measure controlling all other independent variables and are useful guides, especially when the number of cases is relatively small.[27] That is because the plots highlight leverage points or, in this application, SMSAs exerting a disproportionately large influence on the slope of the line. However, only one leverage point was identified: Los Angeles in the equation for Japanese Americans. This is so minor an exception to the general pattern which prevailed across a total of 63 graphs that it is not shown. It is, moreover, explicable in light of the early and continued concentration of Japanese in the Los Angeles area.[28]

Findings Regarding the Coleman Index

Results are shown on Table 5.2. The table displays some descriptive statistics and the terms of the full model. Mean income was not available for all groups, hence the different sample sizes. Descriptively, one can see that the Coleman index is lowest for blacks and Mexicans, and highest for Japanese and Koreans. While one might be tempted to directly compare the Coleman index to the ID, such a comparison would not be meaningful. The Coleman index does not directly incorporate the effect of ethnic group size, whereas the ID does.[29]

The table also shows that for each group, the model explains a substantial proportion of the variance in the Coleman index. For all

Table 5.2
Descriptive Statistics and Regression Analysis
of the Coleman Index (SMSAs, 1980)

Ethnic Group	Descriptive Statistics Coleman Index			Regression Model Income Ratio	Absolute Size	Relative Size	Fit
	Mean	SD	N	B1	B2	B3	R²
Black	.77	.20	19	.03	-.07	-.86*	.84
Chinese	.95	.06	20	-.11	-.18	-.81*	.90
Filipino	.92	.07	18	-.15	.05	-.75*	.56
Japanese	.97	.03	20	.09	-.35	-.49	.61
Korean	.98	.02	15	-.08	-.10	-.85*	.81
Mexican	.78	.10	20	-.03	-.23*	-.79*	.88
Vietnamese	.92	.21	15	-.10	-.61*	-.31	.78

SD: standard deviation.
N: number of SMSAs.
B: standardized regression coefficients.
R²: proportion explained variance.
* Statistically significant at or beyond the .05 level of probability.

equations, the squared multiple correlation coefficients (R^2s) are statistically significant and, by sociological standards, moderate to very large. One can conclude, therefore, that the model fits the data for each group.

That conclusion, however, does not mean every term in every model has an important effect. In order to assess a specific variable, one must examine the standardized regression coefficients (Bs). The regression coefficients for the income ratio are near zero, and none are statistically significant. Apparently, economic competition has no effect on segregation. Regarding absolute minority size, only the Vietnamese and Mexican findings support the hypothesis, but regarding relative minority size, most coefficients are large and statistically significant (the Vietnamese and Japanese exceptions will be discussed momentarily). These results are in accord with Blalock's argument linking relative minority group size to majority exclusion. Larger groups, it would seem, constitute more of a threat and so are more segregated.

Given the overall clarity of the results, reducing the model by removing absolute size and the income ratio seemed appropriate. When this was done, the following model was produced:

$$Y_{ij} = - B_{ij} \log X3$$

where $X3$ is the logarithm of relative group size. This is Blalock's model specified for the Coleman index (that is, a negative coefficient is hypothesized). It contains only relative size, transformed with logarithms. To evaluate the transformation, two versions of the model were fitted: one log transformed, the other nontransformed (Table 5.3). We can compare the fit of the two models with the standardized regression coefficients (with one independent variable in an equation and ignoring the sign, B is equal to the square root of R^2). In every equation but one, the log transformation either fits the data less well than the nontransformed version or is only very slightly superior. For Vietnamese, the one exception, the log transformation produces a substantially better fit, improving from a nonsignificant and small coefficient to a large and significant one. This effect is probably related to the skew of the distribution. Most California Vietnamese live in Los Angeles; very few live elsewhere. For example, in Redding (a northern California SMSA) the Census Bureau counted no Vietnamese at all.

Excluding the Vietnamese equation, one can say that the nontransformed model fits the data very well. The explained variances ranged from 56% to 88%, and all were statistically significant. Inspection of scatterplots suggested the relationships were typically linear, although for the Chinese equation, one city, San Francisco, was an outlier. Figure 5.3 shows this.

The pattern indicates that if San Francisco were removed from the analysis, the slope of the line would be much less pronounced, and when removed, the explained variance fell from 88% to 69%. San Francisco is important in the equation, an importance following from the city's historical background. From early on, San Francisco was

Table 5.3
Reduced Model for the Coleman Index
Log and Nonlog Versions by Ethnic Group
(SMSAs, 1980)

	Log Transformed	Not Log Transformed
	B	B
Black	-.87	-.92
Chinese	-.77	-.94
Filipino	-.79	-.78
Japanese	-.65	-.75
Korean	-.67	-.90
Mexican	-.92	-.92
Vietnamese	-.86	-.14*

B: Standardized regression coefficient.
* Statistically not significant at the .05 level of probability.

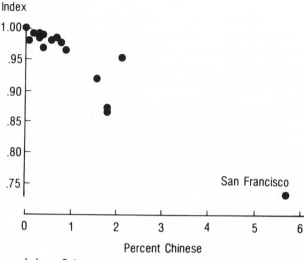

Index: Coleman index. Percent Chinese; percent of whites plus Chinese, 21 SMSA's

Figure 5.3: Chinese Segregation and Percent Chinese

the major center of Chinese life in the United States. Because seven ethnic groups were compared across 21 SMSAs, the two minor exceptions (Chinese and Vietnamese equations) do not change the main conclusion: relative size is related to ghettoization.

Discussion

Relative Size. To an extent, the strength of the relation between relative size and ghettoization might be expected on grounds of measurement alone. Recall that the Coleman index specifies the proportion of whites in the tract of the average minority. This proportion must in some way be a function of the proportion of whites in the metropolitan area (or, conversely, the proportion of the minority because the two proportions sum to one). If the proportion of whites in the typical minority tract is a direct function of the minority proportion, then the regression coefficient for the reduced model should be equal to one, which means that for every standard unit reduction in the minority proportion, the Coleman index changes by one standard unit. In other words, the proportion of whites for the average minority directly varies with the minority proportion—a situation which is, in a manner of speaking, fair. But if the coefficient is below one, that means the white proportion for the typical minority changes less than one unit. This can be thought of as unfair or as a form of segregation. The coefficients were below one, as Table 5.3 shows, indicating that segregation exists. In one way, this is obvious, but in another way, it is not. For Asians, especially those with reputations for being upwardly mobile and assimilation oriented, the existence of residential segregation might come as a surprise to many observers.

Absolute Minority Size. Absolute minority size and the Coleman index are not related. The statistical outcomes leave little doubt about that fact, but how can it be explained? One explanation centers on the possibility of methodological inadequacies. This possibility cannot be absolutely ruled out because direct measures of communal complexity and extensity were not available. Face validity seems high, however, and the measure has behaved as expected in other research, lending predictive validity to present use.[30]

When measuring population size itself, the Census Bureau counts people. Although direct, counts can be inaccurate. The poor and transient, for instance, are frequently undercounted. Nevertheless, undercounting cannot explain all the negative findings. It might explain a single group but not seven groups, particularly because some have high socioeconomic standing and are therefore not likely to be miscounted in the first place.

The raw count of persons was transformed with logarithms, a commonly used transformation appropriate on theoretical grounds.[31] This procedure does raise the possibility that logarithms are not the appropriate scale. If other transformations are more appropriate, the graphs should have indicated as much; that they did not lends some assurance about the correctness of the scaling.

If one accepts that the methodology was adequate, then the explanation for the negative findings must be sought in theory. The original hypotheses seemed to be grounded in adequate theory, but there may not have been sufficient specification. Ghettoization may occur when a very small ethnic population size is reached, after which ghettoization does not increase as a simple function of size. If that is true, then the seven groups may have already passed the threshold, and hence their levels of ghettoization no longer vary with their absolute sizes.

It might also be that ghetto infrastructure depends less on the ethnic group and more on the larger society than heretofore appreciated. The Chicano church, for instance, receives support from the church as a whole even though the congregation might consist of barrio residents. The restaurant industry would not be so important to the Chinese American economy were it not for non-Chinese clientele. Agriculture would not be so important to the Japanese American economy if it did not fit in with the nationwide demand for produce. Economic factors such as these, in turn, affect residential location: Chinese restaurants congregate in or near Chinese neighborhoods, the Los Angeles wholesale produce market is located near Little Tokyo and what were, for a long time, Japanese American residential areas. While these examples do not prove the thesis, they do suggest possibilities that might be studied in later research.

Relative Economic Status. As with absolute size, the statistical results are clear about the Coleman index and the ratio of mean incomes: they are not related. Although this finding might be due to inappropriate measures, alternatives do not readily come to mind. Dollars are dollars, and they are highly isomorphic with economic power. However, granting the measure appropriate does not mean that the scaling—the ratio between means—was necessarily appropriate. As a precaution, several scalings were tried: differences between means, log of the differences between means, log of the ratio between means, and the coefficient of variation. None improved the fit between model and data.

While the income ratio did not behave as expected when treated as an independent variable, as a dependent variable the ratio may respond in a theoretically anticipated fashion. Generalizing from the Blalock argument, relative minority size and the income ratio should be negatively associated: the larger the minority, the more the minority competes with the majority and the more the majority responds with efforts to keep the minority in check. As before, the outcomes of this process should be reflected in the relative economic status of groups. The simple correlations that follow provide statistical hints about the empirical facts of the matter, as shown on the accompanying table:

Table 5.4
Pearson Correlation between Relative Minority Size and the Ratio of White to Minority Mean Income

B	C	F	J	K	V	M
.15	-.06	.14	.15	-.36	.08	.05

B-Black; C-Chinese; F-Filipino; J-Japanese; K-Korean;
M-Mexican; V-Vietnamese; W-White

No correlation is statistically significant; all are small, some are negative, while others are positive. Without doubt, the income ratios are not correlated with relative group size. Because economic status has such a prominent place in ecological theory, cultural materialism, the Annales School, and the Chicago School, these negative findings are especially puzzling. More will be said about them in the concluding section of the chapter, but until then, two related hypotheses will be tested with census tract data.

Socioeconomic Status and Ethnic Status

Embedded in the writings of the Chicago School are two somewhat contradictory ideas. One is that socioeconomic status determines assimilation, including the kind represented by residential location. The other is the recognition that blacks (and by implication, other nonwhites), may not assimilate or upgrade to residences commensurate with their socioeconomic standing. Each possibility represents a testable hypothesis.

Socioeconomic Status

Robert Park stated the relationship between socioeconomic status and residential location as follows:

> Under the conditions imposed by city life in which individuals and groups of individuals, widely removed in sympathy and understanding, live together under conditions of interdependence, if not of intimacy, the conditions of social control are greatly altered and the difficulties increased.
> Where individuals of the same race or of the same vocation live together in segregated groups, neighborhood sentiment tends to fuse with racial antagonism and class interests.
> Physical and sentimental distances reinforce each other, and the influence of local distribution of the population participates with the influence of class and race in the evolution of the social organization. Every great city has its racial colonies, like the Chinatowns of San Francisco and New York. . . .[32]

The Chicago School employed a multivariate approach, maintaining that no single variable should be singled out as the most important, but then neither should the importance of socioeconomic status be underestimated. Without that variable, the radial distribution of ethnic groups from urban core to periphery would not be explicable.

Robert Park further wrote, in 1926, that, "The point is that change of occupation, personal success or failure—changes of economic and social status, in short—tend to be registered in changes of location."[33] Regarding Mexican Americans, Grebler and associates said, in 1965, that, "Thus it [residential location] provides a general indicator of the minority's status in different localities, an indicator of social as well as physical distance from the core group."[34] In 1981, a research piece concluded this: "Nonetheless, it seems clear that increasing social status has an important negative effect on ethnic segregation. . . ."[35] As these quotations imply, the argument remains current. Yet, despite what appears to be overwhelming common sense and common observation supporting the argument, its validity should not be taken for granted. Equally supported by common sense and common observation is an alternative argument: the so-called ethnic status hypothesis.

Ethnic Status

Ethnicity may determine residential location regardless of socioeconomic status. According to Milton Gordon, "The tendency toward ethnic communality, as we have demonstrated, is a powerful force in American life and is supported, once the ethnic subsociety is formed, by the principle of psychological inertia, comfortable social immersion, and vested interests."[36] Even if all socioeconomic barriers to integration suddenly vanished, segregation would not suddenly vanish. Quite apart from whether groups desire integration, the inertia of the extant community would deter it. Communities are composed of institutions, and these institutions have a deep-rooted history in the locale. Institutions are complexly interrelated: media interacts with business, politics, and the church; the church interacts with business; and politics interacts with the others, and so on. Thus, the whole intertwined mass has an inertia that must be overcome before large scale changes can occur.

Prejudice is another barrier that would not necessarily vanish along with vanishing differences in social class. Country clubs, athletic clubs, various fancies, and the like have long restricted ethnic groups regardless of the group's socioeconomic standing. For nonwhites, skin color is an added basis for discrimination. Park recognized that once settled near the urban core, blacks would have much more difficulty moving to outlying rings than would white ethnic groups.

The normal working of the real estate market further deters the disappearance of residential segregation. Because of the large monetary investment required, people shop for housing carefully and slowly. The legal requirements involved in transferring deeds and obtaining loans take several weeks or months to complete. Also playing a role is the symbolic significance of housing as part of the American dream. "[People] tend to connect that dream to certain kinds of houses—notably detached houses in the suburbs—and to the belief that those houses used to be available to anyone who worked hard enough," writes an architectural historian.[37] A house is the single largest investment most people ever make and represents a major accomplishment, both economically and symbolically. Hence, threats to housing trigger large-scale resistance—regardless of the facts, regardless of whether the threats are real or imagined.

Which hypothesis—socioeconomic or ethnic status—is correct? Findings are mixed. Several studies support the ethnic status argument while others support the socioeconomic status argument.[38] Differences in measurement, data, and the specific ethnic groups analyzed make comparisons difficult, compounding the confusion. Under these conditions, the conservative conclusion is not to come to a conclusion until further evidence can be gathered, a task to which this chapter now turns.

Procedures

The two hypotheses may be evaluated using census tract data. While a tract is a more micro-level unit than an SMSA and, presumably, more likely to demonstrate detailed relations, tract data are not without problems. The unit is relatively small and, to guard the confidentiality of respondents, the Census Bureau reports only limited tract data. These limitations include detailed cross classifications of variables such as race, income, education, and occupation. Without the cross-breaks, some facts simply cannot be known.[39]

The Census Bureau reports data on the catchall category "Hispanic," but they are not defined as a separate race and, therefore, cannot be identified separately from whites while maintaining information about socioeconomic standing.[40] Only four broad racial groupings are available for analyzing the socioeconomic status of tracts. One (native American) is not under study and the other (Asian) lumps all five Asian groups into one category. This aggregation has troublesome implications. For example, Japanese and Vietnamese must be treated identically insofar as income is concerned, yet we already know their incomes widely differ.

While these problems with the data are real, they do not preclude all analysis, and I proceeded on the hope that even limited empirical findings are better than none. As will be evident, the data provide a good deal of information.

For measuring socioeconomic status, two variables were used: school years completed and total family income in 1979. The education measure consisted of five categories and the income measure of nine categories.[41] Residential segregation was measured with the index of dissimilarity but unlike the previous application, the index was calculated within categories of socioeconomic status, a procedure which isolated the effect of status on segregation.[42] This was the main methodological motive for using these data. The calculation is most easily explained via a hypothetical example (Table 5.5).

Socioeconomic status has been divided into three categories, and within each, the index of dissimilarity was calculated. This controls socioeconomic status and allows one to compare index values across status categories. Using the procedures illustrated by the table, the index was calculated within categories of both education and income, and for both blacks versus whites and Asians versus whites. The calculations bear on the two hypotheses as follows:

(1) According to the socioeconomic status hypothesis, one would expect the ID to be highest in the lower-status group, intermediate in the middle group, and lowest in the upper-status group. This translates into a regression model:

$$Y_{ij} = B_{ij} X_{ij}$$

where i is a metropolitan area, j is an ethnic group, Y is the ID, B is the standardized slope of the regression line, and X is a socioeconomic category (education or income). Under the socioeconomic status hypothesis, the slope should be negative—residential segregation decreases as socioeconomic status increases. As far as I know, past researchers have not considered the precise form of the relation. In the absence of guidelines, I presume it is linear.

Table 5.5
Illustration of the Index of Dissimilarity by Socioeconomic Status
(Hypothetical Example)

Socioeconomic Status

	Lower		Middle		Upper	
Tract	Majority	Minority	Majority	Minority	Majority	Minority
A	100*	20	75	10	250	50
B	125	15	5	50	250	10
C	90	10	50	0	100	25
	ID:	12.8	ID:	79.5	ID:	29.8

* Frequencies in the cells.
ID: Index of dissimilarity calculated within each category of socioeconomic status.

(2) According to the ethnic status hypothesis, the ID should be the same for all categories of socioeconomic status. In other words, socioeconomic status makes no difference for residential segregation. That assumption does not change the regression model, but it does lead to the prediction that the standardized slopes are equal to zero—which is the same as saying that socioeconomic status and residential segregation are not related.

Findings Regarding the Index of Dissimilarity

The IDs, as calculated above, were regressed against the income categories and then regressed against the education categories for blacks and Asians separately. This was done for each SMSA (tract data for Yuba City were not available). If each SMSA and each group is thought of as constituting a test of the hypotheses, then the hypotheses were tested a total of 40 times. Table 5.6 displays the results.

Table 5.6
Fit of the Linear Model for the Index of Dissimilarity by Ethnic Group and SMSA, 1980

| | Income | | Education | |
| | Black | Asian | Black | Asian |
SMSA	B	B	B	B
Anaheim	.16	-.66*	-.33	-.45
Bakersfield	.28	-.78*	-.78	-.85
Chico	-.72*	-.11	-.72	-.93*
Fresno	.84*	-.57	-.27	-.90*
Los Angeles	.46	-.51	-.91*	-.60
Modesto	-.66*	.05	.24	-.40
Oxnard	.00	-.55	.18	-.56
Redding	.30	.20	.66	.12
Riverside	.24	-.69*	-.64	-.60
Sacramento	.81*	-.27	-.68	-.46
Salinas	.81*	.02	.02	-.22
San Diego	.84*	.03	-.61	-.49
San Francisco	.46	-.46	-.86	-.43
San Jose	.34	-.57	.20	-.47
Santa Barbara	.81*	.57	.83	.12
Santa Cruz	.55	-.45	.90*	-.14
Santa Rosa	.48	-.07	-.44	-.19
Stockton	.63	-.45	-.79	-.48
Vallejo	.52	.00	.18	.31
Visalia	.87*	-.38	.45	-.46

B: Standardized regression coefficient.
*   Statistically significant at or beyond the .05 level of probability.

Considering black income, one can see on the table that eight of the 20 equations have standardized regression coefficients that are statistically significant. However, of the eight, only two are negative as called for by the socioeconomic status hypothesis; the others are positive. The positive cases contradict the socioeconomic status hypothesis, but they do not support the ethnic status hypothesis because it predicts the regression coefficients to be zero.[43] If one considers statistically nonsignificant coefficients to be zero, which is the null hypothesis, then 12 equations support the ethnic status hypothesis. Turning to the data for Asian incomes, three equations have significant and negative regression slopes (Anaheim, Bakersfield, and Riverside) while the other 17 equations do not. With regard to education, support for the socioeconomic status hypothesis is found in only the black equation for Los Angeles and in the Asian equations for Chico and Fresno.

In sum, across 20 SMSAs, two ethnic groups, and two measures of socioeconomic status, a significant negative regression slope appeared only a few times, implying that residential segregation did not consistently decline with increasing socioeconomic status. Because the socioeconomic and ethnic status hypotheses were paired so that support for one implied lack of support for the other, one can conclude that the ethnic status hypothesis is supported.

An Alternative Model. While the preceding conclusions follow logically from the a priori construction of the arguments, information contained in the finely detailed data are being overlooked. Table 5.7 and Table 5.8 show the index of dissimilarity by socioeconomic status, ethnic group, and metropolitan area.

Indications that Asians are less segregated than blacks have already been seen. Perusing the tables, one can see this is true in almost all metropolitan areas across all socioeconomic categories. Exceptions have been indicated by an *e* on the table. Occasionally, Asians are more segregated than blacks within a specific income category in a specific SMSA, but considering strings of *e*s, only in Bakersfield, Riverside, and Vallejo are Asians consistently more segregated. The same, however, is not true when socioeconomic status is measured by education (Table 5.8). By that measure, Asians are almost always less segregated from whites than comparably educated blacks.

Also indicated on the two tables, by an *h*, are those instances in which the index value of a given category is higher than the value of the preceding lower category. Only the highest and lowest income categories were so marked. Examining the pattern of the *h*s, one can see that among blacks, in 17 SMSAs the highest income category is

Table 5.7
Index of Dissimilarity by SMSA and Income Category
for Blacks and Asians

SMSA	Inc	ID	ID
		B	**A**
Anaheim	1	88	70
	2	91h	75h
	3	86	72
	4	81	58
	5	81	57
	6	86	50
	7	82	41
	8	86	44
	9	90h	53h
Bakersfield	1	80	83e
	2	82h	88eh
	3	80	87e
	4	68	81e
	5	77	82e
	6	77	76e
	7	64	70e
	8	73	76e
	9	92h	72e
Chico	1	88	92e
	2	89h	97eh
	3	93	98e
	4	94	93
	5	95	83
	6	97	91
	7	97	89
	8	89	89
	9	50	95eh
Fresno	1	70	80e
	2	76h	77e
	3	80	82e
	4	71	53
	5	76	61
	6	76	60
	7	72	55
	8	87	56
	9	94h	60h
Los Angeles	1	83	64
	2	83	69h
	3	84	68
	4	81	57
	5	81	57
	6	82	55
	7	82	52
	8	83	53
	9	85h	59h

Table 5.7
Index of Dissimilarity by SMSA and Income Category
for Blacks and Asians (Continued)

SMSA	Inc	ID	ID
		B	A
Modesto	1	77	84e
	2	86h	83
	3	93	78
	4	80	74
	5	86	70
	6	86	64
	7	79	60
	8	90	77
	9	50	86eh
Oxnard	1	80	77
	2	85h	88eh
	3	78	84e
	4	74	64
	5	72	72
	6	72	66
	7	71	46
	8	74	53
	9	83h	67h
Redding	1	92	50
	2	95h	50
	3	50	96e
	4	98	88
	5	50	98e
	6	50	50
	7	95	95
	8	94	50
	9	99h	92h
Riverside	1	64	81e
	2	69h	89eh
	3	71	84e
	4	63	74e
	5	66	68e
	6	65	69e
	7	54	55e
	8	62	61
	9	77h	66h
Sacramento	1	64	74e
	2	65h	75eh
	3	68	72e
	4	63	62
	5	62	55
	6	66	53
	7	65	54
	8	69	57
	9	75h	70h

Table 5.7
Index of Dissimilarity by SMSA and Income Category
for Blacks and Asians (Continued)

SMSA	Inc	ID	ID
		B	**A**
Salinas	1	74	73
	2	72	66
	3	62	52
	4	63	47
	5	75	50
	6	78	47
	7	72	44
	8	82	56
	9	90h	66h
San Diego	1	72	67
	2	75h	71h
	3	69	66
	4	66	60
	5	69	60
	6	71	58
	7	74	57
	8	81	63
	9	86h	69h
San Francisco	1	78	65
	2	77	72
	3	76	66
	4	74	58
	5	76	56
	6	75	55
	7	74	53
	8	76	53
	9	82h	61h
San Jose	1	73	60
	2	76h	71h
	3	76	73
	4	63	50
	5	67	50
	6	65	44
	7	60	38
	8	72	40
	9	84h	50h
Santa Barbara	1	65	63
	2	64	69eh
	3	63	63
	4	52	51
	5	67	60
	6	64	65
	7	59	59
	8	77	77
	9	92h	74

Table 5.7
Index of Dissimilarity by SMSA and Income Category
for Blacks and Asians (Continued)

SMSA	Inc	ID B	ID A
Santa Cruz	1	87	90e
	2	92h	73
	3	90	91e
	4	88	74
	5	87	70
	6	93	59
	7	83	62
	8	90	66
	9	99h	73h
Santa Rosa	1	82	89e
	2	96	92h
	3	81	95e
	4	83	80
	5	83	76
	6	92	71
	7	85	66
	8	86	67
	9	96h	99eh
Stockton	1	70	67
	2	78h	73h
	3	75	67
	4	73	56
	5	77	55
	6	81	53
	7	71	49
	8	74	51
	9	88h	61h
Vallejo	1	69	67
	2	65	87eh
	3	65	70e
	4	61	58
	5	62	64e
	6	60	62e
	7	56	59e
	8	65	64
	9	81h	76h
Visalia	1	82	85e
	2	83h	94e
	3	89	84
	4	82	82
	5	87	83
	6	91	76
	7	87	67
	8	99	81
	9	99	81

Inc: Family income, 1979: $2,500; 6,250; 8,750; 12,500; 17,500; 22,500; 30,000; 42,500; 65,000+
ID: Index of dissimilarity.
B: Blacks.
A: Asians.
h: Index of this category higher than preceding category; for highest and lowest categories only.
e: Asian index higher than black index for this category.

Table 5.8
Index of Dissimilarity by SMSA and Education
Categories for Blacks and Asians, 1980

SMSA	Ed	B	Group A
Anaheim	1	82	50
	2	83h	52h
	3	68	37
	4	69	37
	5	73h	39h
Bakersfield	1	77	73
	2	74	78
	3	69	62
	4	66	58
	5	55	45
Chico	1	86	79
	2	95h	90h
	3	90	83
	4	94	65
	5	86	54
Fresno	1	74	49
	2	77h	58h
	3	63	45
	4	62	45
	5	68h	36
Los Angeles	1	83	54
	2	84	56h
	3	82	50
	4	79	48
	5	74	49h
Modesto	1	82	62
	2	79	58
	3	77	45
	4	62	45
	5	84h	45
Oxnard	1	68	65
	2	69h	61
	3	64	49
	4	65	46
	5	68h	44
Redding	1	95	86
	2	83	95e
	3	89	87
	4	95	93
	5	93	94eh
Riverside	1	67	65
	2	68h	65
	3	59	46
	4	55	49
	5	55	43

Table 5.8
Index of Dissimilarity by SMSA and Education
Categories for Blacks and Asians, 1980 (Continued)

SMSA	Ed	B	Group A
Sacramento	1	65	61
	2	63	54
	3	62	47
	4	58	48
	5	56	44
Salinas	1	64	49
	2	72h	45
	3	67	39
	4	71	41
	5	71	41
San Diego	1	76	56
	2	74	56
	3	67	49
	4	67	52
	5	63	50
San Francisco	1	77	56
	2	78h	52
	3	73	47
	4	70	46
	5	64	45
San Jose	1	63	45
	2	61	48h
	3	56	35
	4	56	37
	5	61h	37
Santa Barbara	1	56	53
	2	56	53
	3	56	41
	4	55	43
	5	62h	51h
Santa Cruz	1	76	48
	2	66	56h
	3	69	48
	4	68	41
	5	81h	52h
Santa Rosa	1	79	60
	2	81h	62h
	3	67	45
	4	68	45
	5	69h	53h
Stockton	1	74	59
	2	74	57
	3	68	45
	4	64	42
	5	59	43h

Table 5.8
Index of Dissimilarity by SMSA and Education
Categories for Blacks and Asians, 1980 (Continued)

SMSA	Ed	B	Group A
Vallejo	1	70	59
	2	63	56
	3	55	43
	4	55	51
	5	63h	57h
Visalia	1	74	68
	2	78h	65
	3	78	66
	4	85	64
	5	83	63

Education: School years completed: 4; 10; 12; 14; 19.
B: Blacks.
A;   Asians.
h: Index of this category higher than preceding category;
            for highest and lowest categories only.
e: Asian index higher than black index for this category.

more segregated than the second highest category; among Asians that is true in 16 SMSAs. A much less pronounced pattern is found for education: eight instances for blacks and eight for Asians. If the data are aggregated across the 20 SMSAs, the overall trend should be evident on the following graphs.

The graphs relate the midpoints of the income and education categories to the ID. For both socioeconomic measures, the general shape of the black curve mirrors the Asian curve, but the latter is consistently lower. The form of the relations is the same, but the levels differ.

Figure 5.4 shows that Asians are less segregated than blacks, except for the lowest categories. The figure also shows that among both blacks and Asians, the second lowest income category is more segregated than the lowest category, and the highest income category is more segregated than the second highest. Because education is a measure of socioeconomic status, one expects it to behave similarly to income; however, it does not (see Figure 5.5). The education curves are much simpler. Segregation does decline between the second and third categories, but before and after that point the curves are virtually flat.

If one concentrates attention on the income data because the pattern seems less clear, one can ask what the pattern implies theoretically? One implication is that beginning at approximately a $30,000

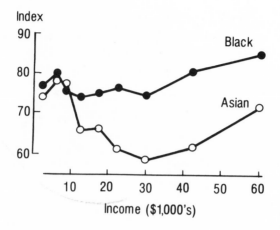

Index of dissimilarity. Income : Family income
Means for 20 SMSAs

Figure 5.4: Income and Residential Segregation

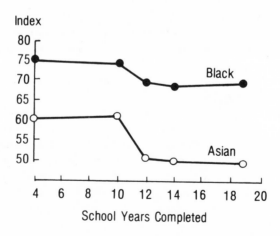

Index of dissimilarity: Means for 20 SMSAs

Figure 5.5: Education and Residential Segregation

annual income, as people become wealthier, they begin using their wealth to avoid integration, and at the highest income levels, people can easily afford to locate elsewhere. This possibility, it should be noted, applies to both majority and minority.

The pattern shown for the least wealthy further reinforces this interpretation. They are less segregated than the next highest income category, a pattern implying that they (the least wealthy) may not have the resources to avoid integration. Sociologists sometimes speak of voluntary segregation. This may be the obverse case: involuntary residential integration brought about by a lack of socioeconomic standing.

At the least wealthy end of the income spectrum, segregation translates into ghettoized areas, and at the other end, it translates into rich suburbs. The lower-to-middle range of the curve, however, has a less clear translation, in part because the Asian and black patterns diverge at that point. For blacks, the curve moves generally upward, but for Asians, it continues downward to the $30,000 point. The upward trend for blacks is consistent with the argument just made regarding the wealthy avoiding integration, but the downward trend for Asians is puzzling. Several explanations come to mind. It may be that people in this range of income wish to improve their housing even if it means living near Asians. It may be that these people have no attitudinal opposition to Asian integration, although why is unknown. And finally, it may be that in the lower-to-middle range of the curve people have sufficient income to afford better housing, but not enough income to indulge in the "luxury" of living in highly segregated neighborhoods.

In general, the curves on Figure 5.4 might be described as "wavy" or "oscillating": they show what analysts call a "cubic" relation. A cubic regression model can be fitted to the data, and should fit very well. Fitting the equation, though, is a somewhat narrow exercise, and a rather controversial one when done after seeing the results, as one just has. For those reasons, the findings on the cubic equation are reported in the chapter appendix.

Summary and Conclusions

The following is a brief summary of the major empirical conclusions:

- When the unit of analysis was the standard metropolitan area and the measure was the ID, Japanese Americans were the least segregated of the seven ethnic groups, although their level was still greater than 40%. Vietnamese were the most segregated, with a level slightly more than 75%. Residential segregation is a fact of urban life.

* When the unit of analysis was the SMSA, the ID and group mean income were not related except at the extremes.
* No evidence was found that linked relative economic status to segregation, or that linked absolute ethnic group size to segregation.
* Relative minority group size was associated with residential segregation in a simple nonlog form rather than the negatively accelerated, logarithmic form originally hypothesized. Historical considerations helped resolve a few minor exceptions to the preceding result.
* In general, the findings supported the broader argument that the majority perceives a larger minority as more threatening than a smaller one and responds by imposing inequality on the minority.
* When the unit of analysis was the census tract, no simple overall linear relation between socioeconomic status and residential segregation was found. In most metropolitan areas, the form of the curves was the same for the blacks and Asians, but Asian segregation levels were consistently lower than those of blacks. Among the less wealthy, the differences were minor. If segregation is a kind of imposed inequality, it is being imposed on both Asians and blacks in the same way, but to differing degrees.
* The preceding findings support the argument that noneconomic ethnic factors play a very important part in determining ghettoization. However, the relation between income and ghettoization may be more complex than initially thought. *Ad hoc* analysis suggested that the relation between the two variables might be cubic in form.

Most of the above hypotheses concerned socioeconomic status in one way or another, and most were not supported or were supported only for a few metropolitan areas. If methodological explanations for the findings are ruled out (possibilities addressed previously), then the largely negative results mean that one should reconsider the theoretical basis for believing that socioeconomic variables and residential segregation are related.

An alternate line of reasoning, one still based on economics but in a different way, changes the thrust of causation. Rather than treating minority competition as a threat, the alternative emphasizes majority gains from minority participation in the economy. Several

historical examples of this have already been presented: the Anglo majority benefited from the Chinese in the gold fields, and later from their labor on the railroads, and the Japanese, Filipinos, and Chicanos all worked (and many still work) the California fields, providing manpower which growers believe is indispensable.[44] Currently, Chinese merchants deal with Anglo businessmen, Japanese produce wholesalers routinely interact with white buyers from giant supermarket chains, black teachers instruct and supervise white children at school. Although participation in one economic sector sometimes leads to conflicts with other sectors (some labor unions have opposed minority participation), certain infrastructural forces nevertheless impel minority participation in the economy.

This means that during the day, mutually beneficial economic concerns draw minority and majority together, but at day's end, those same economic concerns cease to operate, and each group goes its own way home. No economic gains are to be had from living next door to the minority.[45]

Such reasoning has not been underscored enough. When the Chicago School and others argued that increased socioeconomic status leads to reduced interethnic antipathy, they were optimistically assuming that hostilities derived from rational economic concerns. Once those concerns were resolved, the basis for antipathy vanished, and so too did the antipathy. This argument has a certain appeal; it makes everything reasonable, rational, and most important, solvable. And in fact, it undoubtedly applies to some ethnic groups. It may not, however, apply to *all* groups with *equal* force along *all* dimensions of assimilation. And even if the original basis for antipathy was economic, the antipathy can linger long after the basis has disappeared. As the present data shows, even those nonwhites whose socioeconomic standing equals or exceeds the white level are segregated residentially.

There is yet another consideration. Recall that the highest income categories were often more segregated than the second highest categories. Although briefly mentioned before, the implication of these data require fleshing out. One can entertain the following:

(1) Often, one receives the impression that whites are running from the minority—the very terms white *flight* and *blockbusting* connote as much. So strong is this image that one seldom asks, "is the minority pursuing?" Perhaps not. Perhaps the minority prefers to avoid assimilation, perhaps not totally, but to some degree.

(2) In seeking to establish some middle level of assimilation, the minority encounters a problem. Robert Park claimed that assimilation was inevitable. It may or may not be inevitable, but it is difficult to

entirely avoid. Cultural saturation—radio, television, newspapers, jobs, schools, and a host of other contacts—force the dominant culture on the minority. Total, complete avoidance is impossible.

(3) However, even while recognizing the impossibility of total avoidance (if indeed, that is the goal), some semblance of ethnic integrity and identity can still be maintained. Devices such as language schools, ethnic-dominated churches, ethnic stores, ethnic professional associations, ethnic newspapers, and ghettoization all help keep ethnicity alive from generation to generation.

(4) Keeping ethnicity alive requires resources. For example, to establish an ethnic-language school one needs teachers, space, supplies, and pupils—in short, economic and social resources of all kinds. To shop at an ethnic store means that (a) the store must be there, but for the store to be there, (b) the ethnic group must have the resources and desire to support it.

The foregoing leads to a conclusion often neglected in past writings: high socioeconomic standing, and the resources which it implies, can be a basis for resisting assimilation and for maintaining an ethnic infrastructure and ethnic social identity. The effectiveness of language schools and other institutions in maintaining ethnic subculture might be questioned, of course. In the long run, cultural assimilation may be inevitable, as Park suggested.[46] But in the short run and regardless of achieving manifest goals (few ethnic-language schools are successful if success is measured by the fluency of the school's pupils), the latent goal of maintaining ethnic infrastructure and identity is furthered.

To what extent the foregoing scenario is played out in fact is unknown. It is, however, an idea worth exploring in future research.

Attitudinal support for integration seemingly runs counter to the lines of reasoning just pursued. Polls conducted by the National Opinion Research Center reveal that in 1984, 72% of white adults disagreed with the statement, "White people have the right to keep blacks out of their neighborhoods if they want to, and blacks should respect that right." At the same time, 51% knew of blacks living in their neighborhood. Considering the size of the black population, that percentage could represent a significant amount of integration.[47] (It could also represent one or a few black families whose presence in the neighborhood is well known because they are black.) Further indications of prointegration values are reflected in the outlawing of practices such as racial covenants on deeds, steering by realtors, and blue lining by lending institutions. Whether effective, that these laws even exist indicates some societal commitment to integration.

While attitudinal support is one kind of pro-assimilation force, behavior is another. What people believe or say may be quite different from what they do, a possibility long recognized.[48] Because the current study assumes that assimilation is a multivariate phenomenon, attitudinal support for integration is not incompatible with extant segregation. Considering the imperfect correlation between attitude and behavior, the emotional loadings attached to housing, the nature of real estate markets, and the inertia of change, an inconsistency between high verbal support for integration and actual segregation is not all that surprising.

Another factor affecting residential integration is the "potential for community." Some groups are more prone to segregation than others. I suspect this potential has not been studied simply because comparative research on ghettoization has not been done very much. Expanding the scope of research raises other possible explanations. Contrast the following possibilities:

(1) The first is a group with a weak basis for ethnic solidarity, as, for example, one composed mainly of unattached males from diverse locales in the country of origin, perhaps even with predisposing hostilities towards each other, with little experience in leadership and business, and with few extant institutions. Early Filipino immigration illustrates this type. Recalling their historical background, one can note that Filipinos came from different areas of the Philippines and brought with them preexisting antipathies. Taglogs were generally considered to be more gentile and "superior," while Illocanos were stereotyped as "country bumpkins." Overwhelmingly male and mobile, they had little opportunity to establish familial institutions. Overwhelmingly Catholic but not especially religious, the church did not have a major communal impact. Because the initial basis for community was low and made even lower by job mobility, the Filipino potential for community and, by implication, ghettoization, was comparatively low.

(2) The second is a group with high potential, as for example, one that immigrates as family units from similar and high socioeconomic backgrounds. Sharing much and having previous experience in organization and commerce, they would have a high potential for intraethnic solidarity, community, and ghettoization. The Vietnamese illustrate this. Surely, their story is one of disruption, disorganization, and violence, yet most managed to escape as a part of extended family networks and brought with them a family structure. Moreover, many came from middle- and upper-class backgrounds. They were educated, had experience in business, government, the military, and the

professions. Once the initial traumas of forced immigration had passed and life settled into a routine, the Vietnamese had a high capacity for community, which is another way of saying they had a high capacity for ghettoization. The quick emergence of Los Angeles's Little Saigon attests to this capacity.

Even while groups differ in this capacity, that does not mean all socioeconomic differences are irrelevant. There could be a significant interaction between the two variables: groups with high socioeconomic standing and high capacity for community will be more ghettoized than low-standing, low-capacity groups.

The last point is more speculative. Even if all socioeconomic and discriminatory considerations are held constant, ethnic groups may still be segregated. As sociologist Jack Douglas has wryly noted, we too easily forget that people sometimes do things because they like it, and an ethnic group may like its ethnicity.[49]

APPENDIX

Cubic Relation

The relation between residential segregation and socioeconomic status can be described as "cubic." Such a relation is easier to visualize than to verbalize and is therefore graphed for San Diego (Figure 5.6).

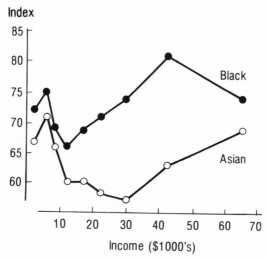

Figure 5.6: Illustrating a Cubic Relation: San Diego, 1980

The graph illustrates the "waves" of the curve, and further, that while Asians and blacks have similar segregation patterns, the amount of segregation is less for Asians. The San Diego data typify a cubic relation, but it is, of course, only one SMSA out of 20. The following equation gives the generic form of a cubic relation for three independent variables:

$$Y_{ij} = B1_{ij} \, Xl_{ij} + B2_{ij} \, X2_{ij}^{2} + B_{ij} \, X3_{ij}^{3}$$

where, i and j are ethnic group and metropolitan area respectively, X is income, and Y is the index of dissimilarity. This is a standard cubic regression. When this equation was solved for the 20 SMSAs being studied, it fitted very well, as the following table demonstrates.

Because the linear and cubic equations have different degrees of freedom, the table shows adjusted R^2s. The adjustment should be

Table 5.9
Fit of the Cubic and Linear Models Relating the Index of dissimilarity to Income and Education, Ethnic Group and SMSA, 1980

| | Black | | Asian | |
| | Cubic | Linear | Cubic | Linear |
Equation	R²adj	R²adj	R²adj	R²adj
SMSA				
Anaheim	.30	-.11	.83*	.35*
Bakersfield	.53	-.05	.58	.55*
Chico	.99*	.45*	-.01	-.13
Fresno	.62*	.67*	.55	.22
Los Angeles	.51	.10	.64*	.15
Modesto	.68*	.36*	.79*	-.14
Oxnard	.68*	-.14	.59	.20
Redding	.02	-.04	.07	-.10
Riverside	.54	-.08	.73*	.40*
Sacramento	.75*	.60*	.84*	-.06
Salinas	.54	.61*	.86*	-.14
San Diego	.89*	.66	.63*	-.14
San Francisco	.81*	.10	.62*	.09
San Jose	.60	-.01	.54	.23
Santa Barbara	.74*	.61*	.37	.22
Santa Cruz	.40	.21	.52	.09
Santa Rosa	-.11	.11	.86*	-.14
Stockton	.56	.31	.72*	.08
Vallejo	.92*	.16	.07	-.14
Visalia	.67*	.73*	.26	.02

R²adj: Coefficient of determination adjusted for the degrees of freedom.
*   Significant at or beyond the .05 level of probability.

regarded as descriptively useful whereas the probability levels reported on the table are based on the conventional F-test.[51] Unlike previous tables, standardized regression coefficients are not shown because they have little substantive meaning for present purposes.

Regarding blacks, the cubic equation fits the data in ten cases as judged by the criterion of statistical significance. By the same criterion, the cubic fit for Salinas is worse than the linear fit, but that is the only SMSA for which that is true. Whether statistically significant or not, the cubic equations have larger adjusted R^2s (although sometimes only slightly) than the linear equations, with the exception of Salinas and Santa Rosa. A similar pattern can be noted among Asians: ten equations fit the data, and the cubic adjusted R^2 usually exceeds the corresponding linear value.

At this point, some cautionary notes are in order. The cubic equation *should* fit well because the form of the curve was determined after reviewing the data. This procedure may strike some analysts as backwards—it does not test a hypothesis but merely reiterates something already known. Also, a technical characteristic of curve fitting should be recognized. As the number of categories in the independent variable approaches the number of independent variables, the curve must fit the data more and more perfectly. The income data have only nine categories, fewer than ideal but still a serviceable number. Moreover, all equations were based on the same number of categories, and because some equations fitted better than others, the fits cannot be attributed solely to the number of categories. In sum, after taking these caveats into account, the fact remains that the cubic equation aptly describes the data. Reasonable theoretical rationales for the cubic fit exist, but being an *ad hoc* interpretation and analysis, the issue must remain open.

6

Intermarriage

Intermarriage is the litmus test of assimilation, as scholars agree. Consider these statements. Donald Bogue: "One widely used index of the extent to which two populations have assimilated into a common society is the extent to which they intermarry."[1] Peter Blau: "High rates of intermarriage are considered to be indicative of social integration, because they reveal that intimate and profound relations between members of different groups and strata are more or less socially acceptable."[2] Leo Grebler, Joan Moore, and Ralph Guzman: "The pattern of ingroup and outgroup marriage is perhaps the most crucial indicator of the degree of social distance between an ethnic minority and the majority population."[3] Milton Gordon: "One of the most telling indexes of communal separation is the rate of intermarriage."[4] And finally, William Petersen: "The ultimate assimilation, according to many analysts, is achieved when the diverse physical types merge into a new one through successive generations of intermarriage. This was the original meaning of the melting pot. . . ."[5] These and numerous similar assertions, have the weight of common sense, formal theory, and some evidence behind them.[6]

Plan of the Chapter

The main concern of this chapter is not intermarriage *per se*, but what intermarriage reveals about assimilation. For that reason, the literature on ethnic relations receives more discussion than the literature on marriage and the family. The chapter is divided into four main sections:

- literature on intermarriage and assimilation;
- descriptive data on intermarriage rates;

149

- model to explain these rates incorporating assimilation, socio-economic status, and ethnic group membership; and
- summary and conclusion.

Intermarriage and Assimilation

Interracial marriage used to be against the law, and not until 1967 did the Supreme Court strike down antimiscegenation laws nationwide. Aversion to miscegenation was an important motive behind the early campaigns to limit immigration, and one must only recall Ross's writings to appreciate the strength of this aversion and how easily it translated into what was (purportedly) social science.

American society has changed since Ross's day, but the "rank order of discrimination" postulated by Gunnar Myrdal in the classic 1944 monograph, *An American Dilemma,* still has some validity. To summarize briefly Myrdal's thesis, the institution of race relations prevented certain interracial contacts. Contacts requiring regulation are presented in order of importance:

(1) Miscegenation involving black males and white females.

(2) Intimate social contacts (for example, interracial dancing).

(3) Use of common public facilities.

(4) Political participation of blacks.

(5) Treatment of blacks as equal to whites under the law.

(6) Black competition with whites for jobs and other means of earning a livelihood.

The above was the white rank order; the black rank order was just the reverse, Myrdal claimed. Blacks were most concerned with access to earnings and least concerned with miscegenation. Myrdal further claimed that while the institution of race relations derived from myths, the consequences are real enough: whites had built a discriminatory social structure.

Today, most people endorse the principle of equal access to government, justice, education, work, housing, and public facilities. For instance, 70% of a 1984 national sample of whites disagreed with the following statement: "There should be a law against marriage between (Negroes/blacks) and whites." More socially oriented interracial contacts are also acceptable. In response to the question, "How strongly would you object if a member of your family wanted to bring a black friend home for dinner?" 80% of the same respondents said they would not object at all.[7] This question was obviously modelled after "Guess Who's Coming to Dinner?"—a film in which a white female invites a black to meet her parents as prelude to marriage. The film caused a furor when released in 1967 but now plays on television without comment. Yet despite changes in values, and consistent with Myrdal's original pronouncement, miscegenation is still opposed.

To be sure, relatively few people now advocate laws against intermarriage. Opposition takes other guises. For example, considerably less than one-half (23%) of women would accept the marriage of a daughter to a man of a different race.[8] Black-white couples often have problems in finding housing and jobs.[9] Sometimes opposition is violent: cross burnings, poison pen letters, and threatening telephone calls. Intermarriages involving Asians, Chicanos, or groups other than blacks may be less opposed, although little formal documentation exists to support this supposition.

In light of the long historical and current antipathy to interracial marriage, one would expect to find that such unions are statistically rare; and they are. Nationwide, 99.7% of white wives have white husbands.[10]

Intermarriage and Social Distance

A well-known scale uses intermarriage to anchor one end point. In a classic research piece published in 1928, Emory Bogardus proposed a social distance measure. He asked respondents to indicate the category to which they were willing to admit, say, blacks (or some other group depending on the researcher's interest). The categories for admittance were the following:[11]

(a) United States;
(b) United States as a visitor only;
(c) Amerian citizenship;
(d) one's occupation;
(e) one's neighborhood;
(f) one's circle of personal friends; and
(g) kinship by marriage.

Taking social distance to mean the degree of intimacy allowed between members of different groups, exclusion from the country represents one end point and intermarriage the other. The Asian experience provides historical examples of these distance categories:

Categories (a) and (b): Asian exclusion laws.

Category (c): Legal prohibitions from becoming naturalized citizens.

Category (d): Attempts to preserve farming and many other professions for whites through Alien land laws and laws reserving licensor for American citizens.

Category (e): *De facto* and *de jure* (through covenants on deeds) residential segregation.

Category (f): Barring of Asians from private clubs, fraternities, and associations.

Category (g): Antimiscegenation laws.

Historically, Asians were not the only ethnic group held at a great social distance. The California legislature once seriously contemplated a law forbidding blacks to immigrate from other states. Mexican immigration quotas were kept low. Both groups were forced into segregated living areas and faced restrictions in occupational choices. They could not join many white clubs and associations, nor could they marry whites, either by law or by strong social custom.

Bogardus's surveys done in California showed that blacks, Japanese, Chinese, Hindus, and Turks were held at the greatest social distance.[12] Eastern Europeans were held at an intermediate distance. And Americans, Canadians, and northern Europeans were held at the least distance. This order of preference is highly consistent with the favoritism shown towards western Europeans by immigration law.

Although intermarriage may indicate the acceptance of a minority by the majority, the converse indication—acceptance of the majority by the minority—should be stressed more. Early writers, mostly members of the white male middle and upper classes, saw assimilation from a lofty perspecive. They assumed the minority wanted to become like the majority (a process now called Anglo conformity). Sometimes this assumption was incorrect. Before World War II, Japanese Americans who outmarried faced disapproval from family and peer group alike. Some of that disapproval may remain, not only among Japanese, but among many ethnic groups. During the 1960s, the denigrating symbolism of the banana (yellow on the outside, white on the inside) took hold. Among many Chicanos, the disparaging term *agringado* ("gringoized") was heard. And currently, an Asian minister of a large Protestant church in Los Angeles with a virtually all Asian congregation, reported that parents and youths repeatedly raise questions about intermarriage.[13] The evidence just cited is admittedly anecdotal, but one should not too lightly dismiss the possibility that the minority might reject intermarriage.

Another aspect of miscegenation is also often overlooked. Among Asians, a marriage between, for example, a Vietnamese woman and a Chinese man is considered an interracial marriage. While non-Asians might view Asians as homogenous, Asians see themselves as highly differentiated with inter-Asian hostility not at all rare. The antipathies that Koreans, Chinese, and Filipinos harbor towards the Japanese is well known. Resentment against ethnic Chinese (Chinese immigrants in Asian countries) is widespread and severe and is usually blamed on envy of Chinese economic success.[14] No one knows how strong these feelings are among American Asians, but some lingering hostilities might exist.

When contemplating the rarity of intermarriage, explanations couched in terms of racial antipathies, values, and norms come most readily to mind. Although these explanations are important, other approaches are more consistent with the emphasis of this monograph, as are discussed next.

Other Approaches to Explaining Intermarriage

Intermarriage is among the least-understood social phenomena. There is simply no good explanation for it. This state of affairs was noted almost one-half a century ago, and has not appreciably changed since then.[15] Those explanations which have been offered emphasize two broad areas: (1) a combination of homogamy-assimilation-socioeconomic status, and (2) opportunity.

Homogamy-Assimilation-Socioeconomic Status. Persons who are similar are more likely to marry than persons who are dissimilar. Homogamy, or similarity between spouses, has been documented so often that it is accepted virtually without dispute.[16]

Homogamy is related to assimilation, but not in a clear-cut fashion. As used here, assimilation refers to intergroup (not individual) similarities along specific variables. Suppose the following: (1) the majority group is highly stratified socioeconomically; (2) the minority group is homogeneously poor; (3) Anglo conformity prevails, so as the minority assimilates, it becomes like the majority; (4) then, ultimately, the minority will also become highly stratified socioeconomically. It will have moved from homogeneous poverty to heterogeneous wealth. In other words, the minority *group* becomes more like the majority group while minority *individuals* became less like each other. Thus, even if two groups are completely assimilated, that does not mean individuals are socially identical. For intermarriage, the import of this point is that assimilation does not necessarily result in homogamous marriages. Even if a group is completely assimilated, a lower-status person of the one group is not likely to marry a higher-status person of the other group.

A study of Chicano intermarriages in Los Angeles County presented data relevant to this point. The higher the occupational status of grooms, the more likely they were to outmarry: 40% of those in high-status occupations outmarried versus 21% of those in low-status occupations.[17] Another study reports similar data: of Chicano males with high occupational status, 40% were exogamous whereas of those with middle and lower status, 22% were exogamous.[18] The study con-cluded, "In other words, as Chicanos attain middle-class status, dis-tinctions based on ethnicity between them and the Anglo majority diminish and social class more accurately describes their cultural and social life than does ethnicity."[19]

Conversely, factors which reinforce ethnicity retard intermar-riage. In the case of Chicanos, these factors might be distinctive phys-ical appearance, the closeness of Mexico, continued immigration, and a large Mexican American population.

Based on data such as these, one might suspect that ethnicity is strongest among the lower classes and grows progressively weaker as one moves up the class ladder, or, in other words, an inverse relation is found between class and ethnicity. This suspicion can be given a theoretical base. One can argue as follows: lower-class status and the deprivation that goes with it prevent people from acquiring an education, thus blocking their channels to upward mobility. In addition, the poor congregate in ghettos with limited job opportunities and few contacts with the majority. Living and working among per-sons like themselves, they tend to maintain their ethnic culture, which inhibits majority contacts even more. Middle- and upper-class minor-ities encounter a much different situation. Being better educated and having higher level jobs, they interact with the majority on a collegial rather than subservient basis, live in middle-class neighborhoods, and engage in frequent and close social contacts with the majority. For them, the impact of ethnicity is consequently diminished.

This argument is reasonable, so reasonable that sometimes we forget about the lower class. Quite possibly, they have a greater poten-tial for assimilation than the middle and upper classes. Consider this possibility: for a minority to maintain its ethnic identity and structure requires counter balancing forces. Without them, the majority would absorb the minority, which is what apparently happened to some white ethnic groups.[20] That it does not happen to other groups, espe-cially nonwhites, suggests the strength of the counterbalancing forces. The most obvious counter balance is majority prejudice. Minority prejudice against the majority is another, and segregation of all kinds is still another. Forces such as these were discussed in other chapters, and so the discussion will not be repeated here.[21]

Ethnic Assimilation and Intermarriage. Some evidence on ethnic assimilation (as contrasted to socioeconomic standing) and intermar-riage is available for Mexican Americans. Grebler and associates report the following marriage certificate data for Los Angeles County.

Table 6.1
Mexican American Intermarriage

	Percent Ingroup Marriages	
Assimilation:	Grooms	Brides
Least	87	80
Intermediate	77	74
Most	70	68

From Grebler, Moore, and Guzman, p. 409, for Los Angeles County, 1963.

Least: Persons born in Mexico.
Intermediate: Persons native born of Mexican or mixed parentage.
Most: Persons native born of native parents.

Grebler assumed that the further removed persons are from the generation of immigration, the more assimilated they are. As can be seen, inmarriage rates decrease as generation increases, a finding consistent with the assumption. It is also possible that the native born have high socioeconomic status, and the combination of status and assimilation determines intermarriage. That seems to be the case. Grebler's other data shows that the third generation outmarries at the highest rate regardless of occupation.[22]

In broad outline, the thesis that assimilation leads to intermarriage applies to the groups under study. They are physically distinctive and have unique cultural backgrounds. Their histories suggest that they are not especially in favor of assimilation along all cultural and structural fronts. These factors work against intermarriage, and generally apply to all the groups. Concerning specific groups, large proportions of Filipinos and Japanese are fluent in English, a factor favoring intermarriage.[23] Japanese and Chinese Americans are close to or have attained education and income parity with whites. If the assimilation hypothesis is correct, socioeconomic parity should increase their intermarriage rates. For the three groups here under study, the Census Bureau published a special report which showed the number of persons in California with spouses of a different race.[24] Although these data are only indirect, they are instructive.

Table 6.2 shows that outmarriage rates for Chinese males and females are almost the same as the rate for Japanese males. While one might interpret these facts from any number of perspectives, an interpretation based on assimilation is difficult to maintain. That Filipinos lag behind Chinese and Japanese in income and that the Japanese rank high socioeconomically is already known. These facts do

Table 6.2
Percent of Persons With Spouse of a Different Race
(California, 1970)*

Chinese		Filipino		Japanese	
Male	Female	Male	Female	Male	Female
9	9	32	24	10	26

*From U. S. Census Bureau.

not correspond to variations in the outmarriage rates shown on the table. Findings further imply that Chinese males and females are approximately as assimilated as Japanese males, although because the rates are somewhat low (10% or lower), one might consider them nonassimilated. Why that should be the case is unknown. The same logic further leads to the conclusion that Filipino males are the most assimilated because they have the highest outmarriage rate, followed by Japanese females and Filipino females. An explanation for this ranking derived from *a priori* theory is not available.

The data illustrate still another difficulty in explaining intermarriage: inconsistent sex differences within and between groups. Japanese females outmarry at a higher rate than Japanese males (a fact well known), but Filipino males outmarry at a higher rate than both Japanese and Filipino females, while Chinese males and females outmarry at the same rate. To account for these differences and similarities, it has been suggested that Asian females are more acceptable to the dominant group than Asian males, in large part due to stereotype which depicts Asian females as highly sexual, attentive, loyal, and devoted to their families. This stereotype supposedly makes them desirable as spouses.[25] The Chinese data complicate this argument, though. Their female outmarriage rate is identical to the male rate.

Complicating matters more, it is known that about three-quarters of black-white marriages consist of a black male and white female. This is different from the pattern among other groups. Approximately one-half the marriages between whites and Chinese and whites and Japanese consists of a white male and an Asian female. If assimilation leads to intermarriage, these facts imply that black males are more assimilated than black females, and that Japanese and Chinese females are more assimilated than Japanese and Chinese males. These implications make little sense.

For blacks, alternative hypotheses are sometimes offered, as follows: A black male of high socioeconomic position, the argument runs, will marry a white female of lower position, thereby engaging in an exchange. The husband receives the caste position of the white female, and the wife receives the socioeconomic status of the black male.[26] This argument seems plausible, but an alternative is equally plausible, to wit, that the white wife receives the caste position of her black husband. If that is the case, what does the black husband receive? What is the exchange?[27] Perhaps Ira Reis came to the most accurate conclusion: "The reasons for these differences are not at all understood."[28]

Opportunity

When one shifts from the individual level of explanation to the group level, demographic characteristics bear on the topic. The sex ratio comes immediately to mind.[29] If an ethnic group has a disproportionate number of males, then every male cannot possibly be married to a female of the same group (at least not at the same time). Hence, alternatives are sought, such as picture brides (Japanese in particular) and illegal female immigration (Chinese stereotypically). When either or both of these avenues are shut, then pressures for miscegenation presumably increase. If this reasoning is correct, then early immigrants, most of whom were male and young, should have intermarried at high rates. They did not. Apparently, a skewed sex ratio alone will not produce miscegenation in the face of an antimiscegenation social structure.

Another group level consideration is size. That smaller groups outmarry more than larger groups is a well-established fact. Sociologist Peter Blau concluded the following: "The inverse relationship between group size and outmarriage has been repeatedly observed in family research, often while testing a different hypothesis."[30] In the course of developing and testing a broader theory, Blau and his associates have conducted several studies confirming this point.[31]

The core of Blau's theory is *generic heterogeneity*: the distribution of social positions along nominal positions such as race, ethnic group, sex, religion. Heterogeneity leads to intergroup contacts which lead to intermarriage. Blau and associates wrote the following:

> . . . heterogeneity promotes intergroup relations, for it means that the greater the heterogeneity the greater are the chances that any fortuitous encounter involves persons of different groups. To be sure, most casual encounters do not lead to marriage. Yet such

superficial contacts are a necessary, though not a sufficient, condition for more intimate relations to develop.[32]

In their studies of 1970 intermarriage rates in 124 of the largest metropolitan areas of the United States, Blau and associates found statistically significant relations between intermarriage and heterogeneity in national origin, language spoken in the home, region of birth, industry, and occupation. Where heterogeneity was high, intermarriage was high, with one exception. The association between black-white heterogeneity and racial intermarriage did not appear until income differences were taken into account. "The reason," they write, "is that the great economic differences between groups consolidates group boundaries and discourages intermarriage."[33] This is another way of saying that socioeconomic status is inversely correlated with ethnicity, an assumption just critiqued.

One might be tempted to say that Blau's concept of generic heterogeneity is tautologial. In a completely homogeneous society there would be no miscegenation because everyone would be the same, a point hardly disputable. Yet this tautology alone does not obviate Blau's hypothesis, because the converse does not follow. The presence of heterogeneity cannot guarantee intermarriage. As the historical review showed, California has been heterogeneous for a long while and still intermarriage has been rare. Prejudice, antimiscegenation values, laws, and other structures coupled with minority prejudice, subculture, and infrastructure formed a barrier that has, among other consequences, effectively reduced the probability of miscegenation.

Rates of Intermarriage

Interpretation of intermarriage rates can be confusing. Do figures reflect current marriages, total marriages, total persons, or married persons? Are figures based on censuses or marriage certificates? Depending on the answer, different rates result. This study uses an operational definition base on married couples and censuses. In the 1980 survey, the Census Bureau used the following definitions.

A *householder* is the person reported in column one of the Census Bureau's questionnaire, the person in whose name the housing unit was rented or purchased. If no such person existed, any adult household member older than 15 years could be the householder. Despite the similarity in terms, householder is not the same as "head of household" used in earlier censuses.

Spouse is the husband or wife of the householder, living within the household, including common law partners but not roommates of the opposite sex.

Operationally, I define *intermarriage* as any couple in which the householder's ethnicity is different from the spouse's ethnicity. This procedure overlooks married children living with their parents, but that was unavoidable. The intermarriage *rate* is the number of inter-married couples in an ethnic group as a proportion of all couples in that group. Only householders with a spouse of the opposite sex are included.

Sometimes, the residual ethnic category "others" is reported. It is a statistical aggregate consisting of persons not classified into an ethnic group. The category has little substantive meaning and will not be discussed except to note that it has a statistical consequence. Persons in the "other" category can have spouses and can be spouses, thus affecting intermarriage rates. Total sample size was 241,102 couples. Figure 6.1 displays the rates.

The graph shows two intermarriage rates: expected and observed. The observed (actual) rates indicate that Mexicans and Filipinos out-marry the most and Vietnamese the least. Recent history helps explain the Vietnamese. They have not had much time to gain a foothold in America, and have had few opportunities to intermarry. In addition, the majority came as family groups, and most family heads were already married upon arrival.[34] Although this explanation may account for the Vietnamese, it does not account for the other rates. Whites have only a slightly higher intermarriage rate than Vietnamese, yet recency of immigration cannot explain the white rate because they

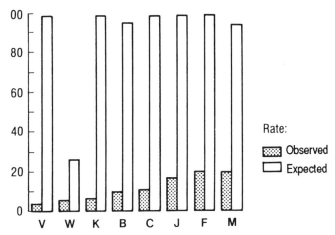

Figure 6.1 Observed and Expected Intermarriage Rates

are overwhelmingly indigenous. What could explain their rate is not apparent.

Interpreting intermarriage rates much beyond the foregoing requires extreme caution. To illustrate why, consider whites, for example, 6% of whom are intermarried and 94% of whom are not. Ethnic-racial homogamy is the overwhelming rule, but it could hardly be otherwise. The minority groups are not large enough for every white to have a nonwhite spouse. Imagine a society of 98 whites and two nonwhites. Both nonwhites marry a white. The nonwhite intermarriage rate is 100% (2/2 × 100) while the white rate is only 2.04% (2/98 × 100). Because the white rate is so low, a casual observer might conclude that whites strongly oppose intermarriage when in fact, they are intermarrying at the highest possible rate. The low rate is really due to the way numbers work. Blau makes much of the result, calling it a paradox. However, I prefer to think of it as a statistical-mathematical consequence and nothing more.[35] Even so, it must be taken into account.

The following statistical logic may be applied. If ethnic category made no difference, then the number of blacks with black spouses, for example, would be proportional to the relative size of the black group in the population. This proportionality, when converted to a percentage, becomes the "expected rate," and was calculated for each group.[36] It is shown as the clear column on the graph.[37]

With one exception, the expected rates are very high; some are 100% after rounding. They are such a tiny proportion of the total that if size were the only factor at work, virtually all group members would outmarry. In contrast, because whites are the largest group, they should outmarry at a comparatively low rate. An appreciation of the disparity between the observed and expected rates can be gained by considering the ratio of the two Table 6.3.

As the display shows, the expected white race is four-times higher than the observed rate, and that is the lowest ratio found. Close to that and forming a cluster along with whites are Filipinos, Mexicans, and Japanese. At the other end of the distribution are the Vietnamese.

Table 6.3
Ratio of Observed to Expected Intermarriage Rates

W	F	M	J	C	B	K	V
4	5	5	6	9	10	14	25

B-Black; C-Chinese; F-Filipino; J-Japanese; K-Korean;
M-Mexican; V-Vietnamese; W-White

Based on size alone, they should be outmarrying at a rate 25-times higher than their current rate. Even setting aside the Vietnamese ratio, no group approaches rate parity.

Intermarriage also varies widely by sex, as we have seen before. The figures on Table 6.4 indicate the magnitude of these variations. (For some groups, small frequencies cannot be avoided.)

This table indicates that among males, Filipinos have outmarried the most, a finding which fits the implications of Filipino American history. The little evidence available indicates that Filipino males were more aggressive than other Asians in initiating contacts with white females. The Mexican and Japanese rates are next, while the Vietnamese rate is the lowest. Interestingly, the black and Chinese rates are virtually the same. The data further indicate that the male pattern differs from the female pattern. Approximately one-third of Japanese females have spouses of a different ethnic group, the highest outmarriage rate on the table, while the lowest rates are for whites and blacks. Also displayed are the female-male ratios. Among Filipinos, Mexicans, and Chinese, females and males outmarry at approximately equal rates (ratios are near one), but among Japanese, Koreans and Vietnamese, females outmarry at two- to five-times the male rate. Among blacks and whites, though, the situation is reversed: female rates are lower than male rates. While it is difficult to discover a theoretical rationale for these differences, they are consistent with other findings.

The last descriptive point before modelling the rates concerns the ethnicity of spouses, shown on the accompanying table. (One should note that the small frequencies make judging the stability of any given figure difficult.)

Table 6.4
Observed Intermarriage Rates
Percentage*

	J	K	F	M	V	C	B	W
Males	17	6	20	18	4	11	10	6
Females	36	27	27	22	19	14	3	2
Ratio of Female to Male Rates								
	2.1	4.5	1.4	1.2	4.8	1.3	.3	.3

*Percent with a spouse of a different ethnic group.

B-Black; C-Chinese; F-Filipino; J-Japanese; K-Korean;
M-Mexican; V-Vietnamese; W-White

Table 6.5
Ethnicity of Spouses
Percentage*

Panel A: Females

Spouse	B	C	F	J	K	M	V	W	O
B	97	1	2	2	0*	0	1*	0	1
C	0*	86	1	2	1*	0*	1*	0	0*
F	0*	1*	73	1	1*	0*	1*	0	1
J	0*	1	0*	63	2*	0*	0*	0	0*
K	0*	0*	0*	1	75	0*	0*	0*	0*
M	0*	0*	1	0	0*	78	0*	2	3
V	0*	0*	0*	0*	0*	0*	81	0*	0*
W	2	10	19	28	17	17	14	95	21
O	1	1	4	2	2*	5	1*	3	74

Panel B: Males

	B	C	F	J	K	M	V	W	O
B	89	1*	0*	0*	0*	0*	0*	0	0
C	0*	89	0*	2	0*	0*	1*	0	0
F	1	1*	81	0*	0*	0*	0*	0	1
J	1	2	1*	83	3*	0*	0*	1	0
K	0*	1*	0*	1	95	0*	0*	0	0
M	1	0*	2	0*	0*	80	0*	1	3
V	0*	0*	0*	0*	0*	0*	95	0	0*
W	6	5	10	10	1*	15	2*	95	20
O	2	1*	6	3	0*	5	0*	3	76

N.B. Column percentages do not always total to 100% due to rounding. For the same reason, the outmarriage rates do not always equal the outmarriage rates that could be calculated from the data on Table 6.4

*Based on fewer than 20 cases.

B-Black; C-Chinese; F-Filipino; J-Japanese; K-Korean;
M-Mexican; V-Vietnamese; W-White

On the grounds that minority groups have more in common with each other than with the majority, one would expect intermarried minorities to have minority spouses. But on the basis of sheer numbers, one would expect the spouse to be white. As can be seen Table 6.5, the data confirm the latter expectation. Persons who do not have a spouse from the same ethnic group are most likely to have white spouses.

Modelling Intermarriage Rates

The present research is not about intermarriage *per se,* but assimilation, a concern which returns one to the opening statement of the chapter: intermarriage is the litmus test of assimilation. To study intermarriage therefore, is to study assimilation in its most extreme form. Furthermore, if assimilation is multidimensional, then intermarriage should be associated with other dimensions of assimilation. Stated that way, the relation between dimensions is nonrecursive. Assimilation along one dimension leads to intermarriage, or vice versa. This explicit concern for causal ordering predates many of the authors previously discussed, but they must have assumed that cultural and structural assimilation causally preceded intermarriage. Many of their discussions imply as much, and Bogardus's social distance scale uses the sequence explicitly. In other cases, if the ordering were not assumed, it would be difficult to see how intermarriage occurs. For these reasons, in the model to be developed, intermarriage is treated as the result rather than cause of assimilation.

Model

The dependent variable being studied, intermarriage, does not occur very often, is dichotomous (one is intermarried or not), and has limited dispersion. It is therefore difficult to statistically analyze. Data tables will be sparse, and at the extreme of sparseness, one may be trying to explain something that occurs to so few people that one has, essentially, case histories.[38] One must consequently limit the number of independent variables in the analysis, and whenever possible, use composite measures that incorporate information from several separate variables into a single number. Moreover, table sparseness, limited dispersion, and a dichotomous dependent variable limit the choice of the techniques which may be applied, and call for extra care when interpreting results. Bearing these caveats in mind, the variables incorporated into the explanation, and their operational definitions, are given below.

(1) *Assimilation.* The central variable being studied in this book is assimilation, and the basic hypothesis, therefore, is that as groups assimilate, they outmarry. If one considers intermarriage as a type of assimilation, then the hypothesis asserts one of the most fundamental assumption in ethnic studies: assimilation along one dimension leads to assimilation along other dimensions.

Assimilation was measured with the three items discussed in previous chapters: immigration, citizenship, and the ability to speak English.[39] The measures are based on the following assumptions: native born are more assimilated than those not native born; recent immigrants have not had as much time to assimilate as early immigrants (the 1970 cut-off was chosen because the 1965 Immigration Act became fully operational one year previously); naturalization signifies an emotional and political commitment to the United States; and finally, language is a key to cultural assimilation.

Based on these three measures, individuals were placed into the assimilation categories given below.

(a) Native: persons who are native born, and also thereby citizens by birth, and native English speakers.

(b) Least assimilated: persons who immigrated between 1970 and 1980, who were not citizens, and who spoke English "not well" or "not at all."

(c) Moderately assimiliated: persons who did not fall into either of the two preceding categories. These were persons who had immigrated before 1970, who were naturalized citizens, and who spoke English "well" or "very well." It might be noted that the intermediate category actually collapsed 12 subcategories into one.[40]

The above procedure reduced the number of assimilation measures from three to one, thereby reducing table sparseness. The categorization also produced the added benefit of creating a more stable measure. When multiple indicators of a concept form a composite, the amount of error in the composite should be less than if the same indicators were used separately.

(2) *Ethnicity.* We know from previous chapters that ethnic groups differ in their levels of assimilation. We also know from the data presented in this chapter that groups differ in intermarriage rates, even groups that could otherwise be equally assimilated. These bits of information suggest that group membership should be added to the explanation. Operationally, this meant including each of the groups in the analysis as a separate category.

(3) *Socioeconomic Status.* Another major structural variable important for intermarriage is socioeconomic status. Past research, however, often failed to distinguish socioeconomic mobility from assimilation. As discussed previously, the two variables—socioeconomic status and assimilation—are separate and for that reason, a separate measure of socioeconomic status is included in the model.

Researchers often use years of schooling completed to measure socioeconomic status, and it was so used here. Schooling—because it is measured in years completed—is more comparable across ethnic groups than occupation, the other commonly used status measure.[41] Just as important, education taps aspects of socioeconomic status which are particularly germane to intermarriage. Research shows that highly educated persons outmarry more than less educated persons, presumably because education decreases prejudice and because the campus provides an opportunity to meet persons of different ethnic backgrounds.

People were placed in the following educational categories: (1) high school or less (12 or fewer years of schooling completed); and (2) some college (one or more years of college completed). This cutting point was selected for statistical and theoretical reasons. Past research emphasizes the importance of higher education for intermarriage, and the cutting point between college and high school reflects that emphasis. In addition, the dividing line between high school and college is socially important. The disparaging label, "high school dropout," implies that anything less is unacceptable and, accordingly, whether a person has completed junior high or grammar school does not change that. The cutting point was statistically appropriate also, because a dichotomy was necessary to ensure that a sufficiently large number of people were in the two categories.

(4) *Interactions and Hypotheses.* Although the model may seem fairly simple, it is amply complex, especially after considering the interactions between the independent variables. When that is done, the model contains hypotheses regarding "direct effects" and "interaction effects," as follows:

(a) *Direct Effects.* Intermarriage rates result, in part, from these relationships:

- Increased assimilation leads to increased intermarriage, net of the effects of other variables in the model.
- Different groups have different intermarriage rates, net of the effects of other variables in the model.
- Increased socioeconomic status produces an increase in intermarriage rates, net of the effects of other variables in the model.

(b) *Interaction Effects.* Intermarriage rates result, in part, from the effect of these combinations of variables:

- Assimilation and ethnic group, net of the effects of other variables in the model.
- Assimilation and socioeconomic status, net of the effects of other variables in the model.
- Ethnic group and socioeconomic status, net of the effects of other variables in the model.

• Assimilation, ethnic group, and socioeconomic status, net of the effects of other variables in the model.

Research addressed to all of the above interactions has not been done, but because they are theoretical possibilities, they should be tested. Indeed, providing data on these interactions is an important contribution of this analysis.

(5) *Sex.* The final variable to be considered is sex. It is already known that within the same ethnic group, males and females outmarry at different rates, and to examine this variation, the analysis will be repeated separately for males and females. Separate analyses greatly simplify statistical procedures, as will be seen, and have no effect on the substantive interpretation of findings.

Evaluation of the Model

The logic implied by the foregoing model may be operationally summarized with a design matrix. Using the measures just discussed, an abbreviated example applicable to either males or females is shown on Table 6.6.

The design matrix both illustrates the logic of the model and shows that for each ethnic group, six combinations of variables (categories or cells) exist. Data can be fitted to this model and the goodness of fit can be evaluated with a log linear procedure using the method of maximum likelihood. (Optionally, one could reconceptualize the preceding explanation as a linear equation, and that equation could be solved using the same log linear procedures. The approach may be

Table 6.6
Example of the Design Matrix

| Ethnic Group | Assimilation | Education | Intermarried | |
			Yes	No
White	Least	High school	f*	f
White	Least	College	f	f
White	Intermediate	High school	f	f
White	Intermediate	College	f	f
White	Native	High school	f	f
White	Native	College	f	f

. . . . .
. . . . .
Repeat for each ethnic group

*Cell frequencies

especially appealing to people already familiar with regression analysis, and it parallels the regression models used in other chapters. For those reasons, the alternative is shown in the chapter appendix.)

As it turned out, unique estimates for all the parameters of the model could not be obtained because some combinations of ethnicity and assimilation produced empty cells (recall the discussion of table sparseness). Those combinations were removed to produce a *modified* model which included, as before, the direct effects of assimilation, ethnicity, and education, but only the interactive effects of assimilation and education, and ethnicity and education. Reducing a model in this way is a standard procedure with log linear analysis, and is touted as a major advantage of the technique. The modified model is the one shown on the tables.

Up to this point, the explanation has proceeded as if total prescience guided the construction of the model, but of course, it did not. Several computer passes were required to construct measures, to determine cutting points, and to ascertain table sparseness. In the process, some findings became known before predictions were firmly made, a situation which was unfortunate but unavoidable. It was unfortunate because knowing the results beforehand meant that postdiction rather than prediction was being performed, which runs contrary to the canons of science. To ameliorate the problem, data splitting was used. The data were randomly divided into two subsamples, one called an estimation sample and the other a prediction sample. Each subsample contained 120,551 couples. The exploratory computer passes were done on the estimation sample while the test of the model was performed on the prediction example.

In addition to guarding against knowing answers before making hypotheses, data splitting provides replication. Especially with sparse tables, replication adds a measure of confidence to one's conclusions. One might even argue that if a model fits a sparse table, and if the fit can be replicated, the total evidence is more compelling than if the model had been fitted to only one denser table. In the present case, the prediction data did replicate the estimation data, and so only the findings for the prediction sample are shown.

When the modified model was fitted to the prediction sample separately for males and females, the statistics on Tables 6.7 and 6.8 were obtained.

Examining these tables reveals the advantage of the log linear approach over a conventional cross-tabulation or comparison of means. Each variable or term in the explanation can be evaluated with the chi-square statistic. This statistic directly takes the relative sizes of the groups into account (and was the basis for finding the expected

Table 6.7
Statistics Associated With The Modified Model—MALES

Parameter	Degrees of Freedom	Chi-Square	Probability
Intercept	1	1,397	.00001
Ethnic group	8	7,196	.00001
Assimilation level	2	994	.00001
Education	1	12	.00004
Interactions:			
Ethnic group and education	8	239	.00001
Assimilation and education	2	133	.00001
Residual	28	2,257	.00001

rates shown previously). The intercept term represents the total number of cases divided by the total number of cells in the design matrix. For both males and females, the intercepts have large chi-squares associated with them, implying their importance. Although in most applications the intercept will be important statistically, interpreting them substantively is difficult.

Among both males and females, the variable with the largest chi-square, and by a substantial margin, is ethnicity (ethnic group). Furthermore, ethnicity combines with education to significantly effect intermarriage, although the chi-squares associated with those interaction terms are relatively small.

Interestingly, the impact of education by itself is not strong. For males, the associated chi-square is small compared to the other values on the table, while for females, the chi-square is not even statistically

Table 6.8
Statistics Associated With The Modified Model—FEMALES

Parameter	Degrees of Freedom	Chi-Square	Probability
Intercept	1	1,768	.00001
Ethnic group	8	8,397	.00001
Assimilation level	2	1,012	.00001
Education	1	5	.34500
Interactions:			
Ethnic group and education	8	539	.00001
Assimilation and education	2	33	.00001
Residual	28	1,309	.00001

significant. The interaction terms between education and assimilation have a small impact relative to other variables, but they are statistically significant. The last terms on both tables, the residuals, have large chi-squares. Even though individual terms are important, the overall fit between the models and data is not particularly good. Other variables are required, but what they might be and how they could be introduced into the already sparse data tables is not evident.

The log linear statistics provide valuable criteria for evaluating models as a whole, but no information about specific categories of people. To examine these specifics, therefore, we turn to the design matrix. The intermarriage rate, or probability, is the ratio of intermarried couples in a category to the total number of couples in that category. Because the data are so detailed, they are presented both tabularly and graphically. Table 6.9 provides information on specifics while the graphs are better for revealing overall trends. Four graphs are presented: one for each category of education and sex (Figures 6.2–6.5).

The probabilities on the table vary considerably at the extremes. At the high end, only a few of the values shown are above 50, while at the low end, almost one-half are below 10 (decimal points are omitted on the table). The log linear analysis has already shown which effects were statistically important, while this table shows that the probabilities of intermarriage are generally low on an absolute basis. There is no contradiction between these conclusions because low probabilities can be just as important, substantively, as high probabilities.

Considering overall trends, Figure 6.2 shows the data for males with a high school education or less by assimilation level. One can see that whites and blacks in the intermediate category of assimilation are more likely to intermarry than those in the other categories.[42] Essentially, the same pattern describes black and white males with some college education (Figure 6.3), and females regardless of education (Figures 6.4 and 6.5). One can further see that Japanese females with a high school education follow the same pattern as whites; that is, persons in the intermediate assimilation category are most likely to outmarry.

However, with the exception of these cases, the relation between assimilation and intermarriage is clear. All graphs show that persons in the least assimilated category have the lowest probability of intermarriage, those in the intermediate category have an intermediate probability, and those in the most assimilated category (native born) have the highest probability. Moreover, assimilation often makes a large difference. The probability of intermarriage in the native born

Table 6.9
Probability of Intermarriage

Group and Assimilation	High School Males	Females	College Male	Females
White				
Least	02	03	05	06
Intermediate	07	06	09	07
Native	06	05	05	04
Black				
Least	00*	00*	00*	00*
Intermediate	25	06	24	06
Native	08	03	13	04
Japanese				
Least	05*	28	02	05
Intermediate	06	43	13	39
Native	23	30	30	35
Chinese				
Least	01	01	07	01
Intermediate	06	10	11	15
Native	43	48	45	48
Korean				
Least	01	06	00	07
Intermediate	07	55	04	12
Native	55*	59*	65*	96*
Mexican				
Least	05	04	12	05
Intermediate	12	16	27	37
Native	48	50	70	71
Vietnamese				
Least	02	04	08	12*
Intermediate	06	43	06	19
Native	00*	00	00*	00*
Filipino				
Least	11*	10	08	06*
Intermediate	22	36	10	16
Native	65	66	80	84

Education: High school or less; some college or more.
* Fewer than 20 persons in this category.
N.B. Decimal points not shown.

category is often several times higher than the probability in the intermediate and least assimilated categories.

Even though all the graphs depict a strong relation between assimilation and intermarriage, that does not mean all probabilities are identical. Regardless of assimilation, college educated persons outmarry more than persons with a high school education, and, in general, females outmarry more than males. And even though the comparisons are being made while holding constant the effects of

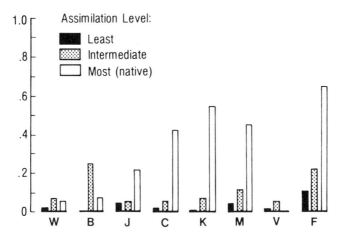

Note: Missing categories for blacks and Vietnamese

Figure 6.2: Probability of Intermarriage MALES with HIGH SCHOOL or Less

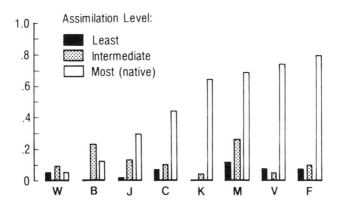

Note: Missing category for blacks

Figure 6.3: Probability of Intermarriage MALES with SOME COLLEGE or More

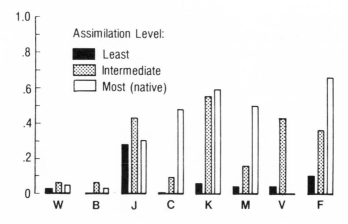

Note: Missing categories for blacks and Vietnamese

Figure 6.4: Probability of Intermarriage FEMALES with HIGH SCHOOL or Less

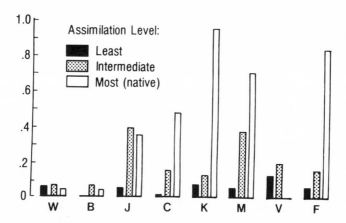

Note: Missing categories for blacks and Vietnamese

Figure 6.5: Probability of Intermarriage FEMALES with SOME COLLEGE or More

education, assimilation, and sex, the graphs clearly illustrate the strong impact of ethnicity. Different groups consistently have different probabilities of intermarriage. In a sense, none of this information is new as the log linear analysis just demonstrated that the net effects of education and sex, while important, were weaker than the net effect of assimilation, and that the net effect of ethnicity was strongest of all.

Summary and Conclusions

Findings can be summarized as follows:

- Females outmarry at a higher rate than males, except for blacks.
- No group outmarries at a rate commensurate with its size.
- Ethnicity is the most powerful predictor of intermarriage for both males and females, even after taking into account education and assimilation.

Because intermarriage indexes assimilation, studying it helps one to better understand ethnic relations, even though it is, and must be for logical reasons, rare.

When the rate of intermarriage reaches a high (but unspecified) value, the distinction between marriage and intermarriage vanishes, and so does the distinction between minority and majority.[43] Some American ethnic groups have undoubtedly reached this point, but not the groups under discussion. Their intermarriage rates are far below what would be expected on the basis of group size, while on an absolute basis, few observed rates approach even 50%.

Some exceptions should be noted, though. As previously shown on Table 6.9, the following subgroups have an intermarriage probability of .50 or higher based on 20 or more cases:

—all native born Filipinos;
—all native born Mexicans except males with a high school education; and
—Korean females with a high school education, intermediate assimilation.

While the overall outmarriage rate for some groups is relatively low, rates for these subcategories are much higher—for instance, among American born Filipinos, the outmarriage probabilities all exceed 60%. The obvious difference between Filipinos and other Asians is a Spanish heritage upon which an American influence was super-imposed. Because of this background, Filipinos are more American-ized than Japanese, Chinese, and Vietnamese despite the location of the Philippines in Asia. And because they are more Americanized, Filipinos may assimilate more easily, especially the native born and college educated who have a greater opportunity to meet non-Filipinos.[44]

Another factor is the ambiguous racial-ethnic status of Filipinos. That one scholarly treatise includes Filipino Americans with Spanish Americans while another treatise includes Filipinos with Asian Amer-icans, illustrates this ambiguity.[45] If race relations scholars disagree as to how Filipinos should be classified, it should come as no surprise to find the average person confused about the matter. One possible consequence of this ambiguity is decreased racial prejudice. Filipinos avoid the prejudice that falls upon Asians, and that may interact with ethnicity, assimilation, and socioeconomic status to further promote intermarriage.

Ambiguity also characterizes the perception of Chicanos. Like Filipinos, their racial category is not obvious, not even to the Census Bureau whose job it is to classify people. When the Bureau first pro-posed making Chicanos a separate race, the resulting protest forced the Bureau to place Chicanos among whites, a policy still followed. This ambiguity may account for the comparatively high outmarriage rate among them.

Education and Ethnicity. By itself, education had a significant but small effect in the model. This suggests that education, and by impli-cation socioeconomic status in general, might be better thought of as a facilitating variable, or one which increases the likelihood of mis-cegenation, but by itself, it is not the prime cause.

The single most influential variable was ethnic group member-ship. People's ethnicity determines the ethnicity of their spouses bet-ter than education, sex, or assimilation level. Methodological considerations help explain this result. Ethnic group membership is an unusually global measure. In part, this may be due to the global nature of the concept. Correlated with it are several ethnic factors: subcultural values, prejudices, social background, family structures, ethnic infrastructure, and more. Because ethnicity summarizes the effects of several variables, it necessarily will have a larger impact than a less global measure.

This poses less of a methodological than a conceptual problem. Methodologically, there are several techniques for controlling the cor-relates, if one so desires. However, if all possible correlates of ethnicity were included in a model along with ethnicity, then ethnicity will not have an effect. Operationally, the concept has been rendered null. But that may not be what one wants. By its very nature, ethnicity-race is a global category. All of its many correlates "come with the territory" and combined, they define ethnicity. Remove them, or control them in an equation, and there is no ethnicity left, by definition. Or to phrase it another way, if one controls enough, all things are equal. Unfortunately, it is not easy to strike the proper balance between the variables that should be introduced into a model as separate terms and those variables which should be included as part of the ethnic effect.

Assimilation. Consider, for example, a hypothetical society about which the following are true. (1) The majority does not totally suppress the possibility of intermarriage. (2) The minority does not absolutely prohibit intermarriage. (3) Any prejudices emanating from either or both the minority and majority diminish with interethnic contact. In reference to the groups under study, these assumptions may hold. History suggests that although California may not be the most open society imaginable, neither is it totally repressive. History and polling data suggest that attitudinal opposition to intermarriage has declined, while social research supports the proposition that interaction between persons of different ethnic backgrounds leads to a decline in prejudice, provided certain conditions are met, such as socioeconomic equality and common goals.[46]

Given these three assumptions, one can expect assimilation in some realms of life to result in intermarriage. The process would proceed thus: the minority must first become familiar with the customs, dress, language, values, norms, behaviors, and lifestyle of the majority group. Although cultural assimilation does not guarantee interactions with the majority (segregation could still be the rule), without cultural assimilation further interethnic relationships could very well develop.

With increased interaction, the probability of meeting persons of a different ethnic background increases, and that increases the possibility of subsequent intermarriage. Note that because intermarriage occurs at the end of the process, intermarriage is the slowest responding indicator of assimilation. One should not, therefore, expect to see rapid and dramatic changes in the rate even if assimilation proceeds apace along other dimensions.

The foregoing represents an idealized process, a scenario of what could happen given certain conditions. Over the years, those conditions have only approximately prevailed. And although caveats and incompleteness must necessarily be part of the argument, it does seem plausible.

APPENDIX

A Linear Model of Intermarriage

The explanation of intermarriage consisted of socioeconomic status, ethnicity, assimilation, sex, and some of the interactions between these variables. This explanation can be conceptualized as either a design matrix, which was done, or as a linear model bearing a resemblance to a regression equation. To begin, one can establish the following equation:

$$\text{Model I: } Y = X1$$

where Y is the intermarriage rate of the group and $X1$ is level of assimilation. Model I is basic; it contains only one independent variable. While parsimonious, it may be too simple because other variables are known to influence intermarriage. Therefore, add ethnicity, as indicated by group membership. The model becomes more complex:

$$\text{Model II: } Y = X1 + X2 + (X1 * X2)$$

where Y and $X1$ are as before, $X2$ is ethnic group, and $(X1 * X2)$ is the interaction between group and assimilation. Should ethnic group prove important, then one can conclude that regardless what effect assimilation has, other factors related to ethnic group membership still affect intermarriage. A similar statement could be made about assimilation. The interaction term allows for the possibility that neither group membership nor assimilation by themselves effect intermarriage, but only in combination with each other.

Research further suggests that socioeconomic status should be taken into account. Therefore, add it to the model:

$$\text{Model III: } Y = X1 + X2 + X3 + (X1 * X2)$$
$$+ (X1 * X3) + (X2 * X3) + (X1 * X2 * X3)$$

where terms remain as defined before and $X3$ is socioeconomic status. With $X3$ included, the model becomes far more complicated. It predicts that increased assimilation leads to increased intermarriage; that increased socioeconomic status leads to increased intermarriage; that different groups have different intermarriage rates; and that the rates differ for different combinations of assimilation and ethnic group $(X1 * X2)$, assimilation and socioeconomic status $(X1 * X3)$, ethnic group and socioeconomic status $(X2 * X3)$, and assimilation, ethnic group, and socioeconomic status $(X1 * X2 * X3)$.

Sex could be added to the linear model as another term, but at this point, introducing it would make the equation very lengthy and difficult to deal with. A mathematically equivalent alternative, and one more easily handled, is to repeat Model III for males and females separately.

The log linear procedure described earlier would produce the same statistical results if applied to the above linear model. In other words, the two approaches—as the equation shown above or as the design matrix shown previously—are mathematically equivalent and the choice between them is mostly a matter of personal aesthetics.

7

Earnings and Ethnicity

O f all the effects that discrimination and prejudice have, the effects on earnings are the most far-reaching. In American society, money places people and their families, and often their heirs, into a specific societal niche. Money measures success, denotes socioeconomic status, and determines physical comfort. Money gives one a sense of worth and is intimately linked to one's sense of self. And despite the adage that "money can't buy happiness," richer people report being happier than poorer people.[1] While money may not be the measure of all things, it is the measure of many things.

Money is so important that economists assume it measures *welfare:* a sense of well-being, happiness, and satisfaction with life.[2] "The objection to great inequality of incomes is the resulting loss of potential economic welfare," stated Dalton, a pioneering economist, more than 60 years ago.[3]

Economists have articulated several assumptions about earnings, as follows:

- Increasing earnings increases welfare.
- The relation between earnings and welfare is the same for everyone.
- Increasing earnings affects welfare independent of any other resources people may have.
- The welfare of one person (or group) is independent of any other person's (or group's) welfare.

These assumptions are especially important for ethnic relations because they bear on intergroup comparisons. If the same earnings produced more welfare for whites than for blacks, that should be taken into account; or if increased earnings actually decreased welfare, then the entire approach to ethnic equality requires restructuring. In addition, research shows that when judging their own welfare, people consider both what they already have and what others have. Judgements are not necessarily independent, a fact which has lead to the development of a large area of social psychological research.[4]

179

However, in most studies undertaken from a structural perspective, as this research is, these assumptions are commonly and noncontroversially made, often without explicit mention.

The study of money and earnings, perhaps because they are so highly quantifiable, calls attention to an issue which has gone unmentioned up to this point in the book: equality. Virtually everyone favors equality, but at the same time, virtually everyone feels comfortable in the face of great inequality. Evidently, it is not unequal wealth that people object to, but unequal opportunity. As long as people can believe that everyone has a fair chance, then success or failure can produce morally acceptable inequality. Of course, what constitutes a "fair opportunity" may not be widely agreed upon. Most people also have no objection to the inequality resulting from the unequal distribution of talent, training, and motivation. Arguing that such inequality reflects the "merit system," "standards," or "selectivity," greatly reduces the onus attached to unequally distributing rewards.[5]

While the notion of equality may be abstract, it can be nevertheless operationalized with certain statistical techniques, provided consensus on a model can be obtained. The strategy is to simultaneously equalize groups along several measures, such as education and work experience, and then to see whether the groups differ in earnings. This strategy is frequently followed, but it entails several technical steps to produce an interpretable result.

Plan of the Chapter

The chapter consists of the following sections:

- accounting for earnings inequality:
  perfect market,
  human capital,
  dual labor market, and
  split labor market;
- research task and research results; and
- summary and conclusions.

Accounting for Earnings Inequality

Several theories for unequal earnings are available, and because the current analysis draws variables from them, they will be briefly adumbrated. Probably the oldest explanations are economic.[6]

Perfect Market

According to the theory of the perfect market, only marginal productivity determines wage level (marginal productivity is the contribution to output made by a new worker). A rational profit maximizing employer will not pay a wage higher than the return (marginal product) of a worker. To do otherwise would eventually lead to financial ruin. Clearly, wage discrimination based on race, religion, creed, or any other factor not related to marginal productivity, will not exist in a perfect market. Although this argument may strike noneconomists as very optimistic, within the field of economics there is nothing controversial about it, *granted* the theoretical assumptions of a perfect market, a grant some analysts will not make.[7]

Theoretical assumptions aside, marginal productivity cannot explain the fact of unequal earnings. On average, blacks earn less than whites, women earn less than men. For this to be so, perfect market theory requires that the lesser paid groups contribute less to marginal productivity, which in turns leads to an examination of factors which might cause low marginal productivity. The most obvious factor is human capital.

Human Capital

Workers have differing amounts of experience, training, education, and ability. These characteristics are called human capital.[8] According to this theory, workers earn in accordance with their marginal prodictivity, but some contribute more, and hence earn more, because they have more human capital than others.

Sociologists have studied human capital for a long time but not under that term nor from the economists' angle. Sociologists discuss education, training, and experience as qualifications, precursors, and preparation rather than as rational investments one makes to increase one's future marginal productivity. Curiously, despite differences in theoretical orientation, economists and sociologists use much the same measures and statistical techniques.

Even including human capital (I will use the economists' term), the theory of the free market cannot very well account for the obvious discrimination that takes place. This fact has led economist Gary Becker to posit that discrimination is a matter of *taste,* or noneconomically rational behavior. He wrote the following:

> If an individual has a "taste for discrimination," he must act *as if he* were willing to pay something either directly or in the form of a

reduced income, to be associated with some persons instead of others. When actual discrimination occurs, he must, in fact, either pay or forfeit income for this privilege. . . . The magnitude of a taste for discrimination differs from person to person. . . ."[9]

Although a taste for discrimination may clarify economic theory, it adds little to sociological explanations. The concept simply reiterates that noneconomic factors influence earnings, a statement with which few noneconomists would disagree. Becker recognized this when he wrote, "the discrimination by an individual against a particular group . . . depends on the social and physical distance between them and on their relative socioeconomic status."[10] He is here discussing individuals. A little later he discusses discrimination in the market place, as follows:

> Unfortunately, it is often implicitly assumed that it [discrimination] depends *only* [on individuals who discriminate]; the arguments proceed as if a knowledge of the determinants of tastes was sufficient for a complete understanding of market discrimination. This procedure is erroneous; many variables in addition to tastes take prominent roles in determining market discrimination, and, indeed, tastes sometimes play a minor part. The abundant light thrown on these other variables by the tools of economic analysis has probably been the major insight gained from using them.[11]

Some economists disagree with Becker. In particular, Lester Thurow argues that rather than having to forfeit earnings in order not to associate with certain ethnic groups, discriminators benefit.[12] "The discriminator may prefer to hire Negro maids, Negro garbage collectors, or to work with Negroes if he can be in a position of authority. He may also prefer to hire Negro labor if it can be *exploited to increase his own profits.*"[13]

Such exploitation is easily possible because the American economy is far from perfect in the economic sense. Thurow estimated that measured in 1960 dollars (he published in 1969), whites gained (and blacks lost) between $10.5 and $20.5 billion annually from discrimination. While an imprecise estimate, even the low amount is staggering. If true, it means that whites have a huge vested interest in maintaining an unequal economic system, an interest that encourages their resistance to change. The amount also means that discrimination has a rational basis in the economic infrastructure and will be therefore extremely difficult, if not impossible, to root out of American life.

Recently, sociologists have been devoting considerable energy to analyzing human capital, economic sectors, and labor markets. Ethnic factors fit within the broader framework of production and labor, and because economists have traditionally studied these areas, sociologists have naturally drawn on their basic ideas.

Dual Economy

Many analysts divide the American economy into two basic sectors: core and periphery.[14] The *core* consists of industries which are oligopolistic, capital intensive, profitable, and have internal labor markets (long-term job tenure and mobility within a given firm or industry). The automobile industry illustrates the core. Even including imports from abroad, the number of manufacturers competing for the United States market is relatively small. Domestic manufacturers can be counted, literally, on the fingers of one hand. The industry requires huge amounts of capital to finance manufacturing plants, production, and distribution. The lead time required for design, production, and marketing new products is lengthy, forcing the industry to take a long-term perspective. Although several large car manufacturers have failed over the years, the industry has generally been profitable. The automobile industry has extensive internal labor markets: that is, employees can expect to work their entire lifetimes and rise within a single company or within the industry as a whole.

In contrast to the core, the *periphery* consists of small firms requiring relatively little capital, a short-term perspective, and few internal labor markets. The garment industry and some segments of the restaurant industry (large chains excluded) exemplify this sector. Such businesses are numerous, mostly small-scale operations, and highly competitive. Entrepreneurs can easily enter the periphery, but they often fail, and workers find few internal labor markets to protect their jobs.

The dichotomy between core and periphery does not cover all economic activities. In particular, the government does not neatly fit into either sector. By definition, government is a political entity, not a profit-maximizing one, nor must government abide by the same laws that regulate commerce. In the United States, one assumes that the government will last forever. In these respects, government is unique, fitting neither economic sector, but in other respects, government closely resembles the core. Government requires huge amounts of capital and is the single largest internal labor market in American society (the civil service and the military are full-time, life-time career routes). Another area that does not neatly fit into the dual economy scheme is agriculture, which is unfortunate because for many of the groups being studied, agriculture played a prominent role in their histories. As will be seen later, I placed agriculture in the periphery and government in the core.

Government and agriculture are not the only ambiguous cases. What is a nationwide fast food chain? By many criteria, it would be classified as part of the core sector (it requires a large capital investment, long-range planning, and is profitable). On the other hand, a fast food operation has many peripheral characteristics (episodic employment, nonunionized labor force, easily entered). Because of these and other ambiguities, some researchers maintain that the theory of the dual economy best applies to blue-collar work in heavy industries.[15]

While critics advance these points on theoretical grounds, in practice the distinction between sectors has been highly useful, and should prove useful later in this chapter.

Dual-Labor Market

Researchers often speak of two labor markets called primary and secondary. The *primary* labor market is mainly characterized by skilled or professional jobs. These jobs are stable, provide steady long-term employment, and high earnings. At the blue-collar level, unions control a major portion of the labor force, and consequently unions control entry into this market. At the white-collar level, internal labor markets provide job security as well as mobility ladders. Workers are predominantly male and white.

The *secondary* labor market is characterized by relatively unskilled and unprofessional jobs. Self-employment is more common than in the primary market. Few internal labor markets exist and unionization is not extensive. While workers may easily enter secondary occupations, employment is short term and low paying. Disproportionate numbers of females, nonwhites, and other minorities work in this labor market.

The distinction between primary and secondary labor market does not always hold. According to some, the distinction should not be between skilled and unskilled labor, but between good jobs and bad jobs, the former being largely defined by security and stability.[16] However, in most empirical research, including this piece, some control must be exerted over labor market structure in order to produce sound estimates of earnings. Past research has found the distinction between primary and secondary useful, and it be should be useful again.

Sector Market and Ethnicity

The concepts of labor market and economic sector are not mutually exclusive. The former refers to the structure of occupations, the latter to the structure of industries. Both primary and secondary labor markets exist within both core and periphery sectors. An automobile manufacturer employs lawyers and janitors. An ethnic restaurant employs bus boys and accountants. Nevertheless, different sectors should have different proportions of primary and secondary workers. In the periphery, the proportion of unskilled labor workers should be high while the opposite should be true in the core.

The most desirable economic areas are the core sector and primary market, but unfortunately for those seeking upward mobility, movement into those areas is difficult. Several barriers exist. To obtain a job in the core, one has to enter the industry, but without the requisite education, socioeconomic background, and tradition, entry is difficult. These "requirements," even if they are unofficial and do little to qualify one for a given job, act as informal filters. Unions also shelter the core labor market, and getting into a union requires, in its own way, the proper background. Furthermore, information about job opportunities in the core may not be widely available and transportation to core jobs may be expensive and tedious for people living in segregated areas. As consequences of these factors, minority representation in the core would be small without conscious discrimination by individual employers. With discrimination, it will be considerably smaller.

Conversely, minority representation in the periphery will be relatively large. The periphery is the easiest sector for a minority group to enter, but once there, any group (racial, ethnic, religious, or sexual) would not do well. Work is unpredictable; pay is low; security is rare; and advancement is limited. While a few individuals might bootstrap themselves up, only rarely can an entire group do so. When the features making the periphery difficult to leave are combined with the features making the core difficult to enter, it is no wonder that mobility between sectors is difficult.

Split-Labor Market

Sociologist Edna Bonacich coined the phrase "split-labor market" some fifteen years ago. Although the phrase is similar to "dual-labor market," the concepts are much different. A split-labor market is one in which the minority earns less than the majority even though both perform the same work.[17] Like conventional economic theory, the theory of the split-labor market assumes that employers strive to maximize profits and so pay their workers as little as possible. Striving towards that goal, employers are indifferent to ethnicity, or in Becker's terms, they have no taste for discrimination.

Even without that taste, however, discrimination occurs because a split-labor market has its own dynamics. These derive from the interplay among three major groupings: (1) employers, who desire cheap and pliant labor to maximize profits; (2) highly paid labor, consisting of current employees and small entrepreneurs; and (3) cheap labor, consisting of groups with little political or economic power. Triadic situations typically produce endemic strife, and the split-labor market is no exception.[18] Employers, being indifferent to ethnicity, will try to substitute one labor group for another on the basis of wage rates, and are perfectly willing to use cheap labor to undercut highly paid labor. As a result, whether cheap labor wants to or not, it threatens highly paid labor. To reduce the threat, highly paid labor will either (a) attempt to exclude cheap labor by, for instance, gaining legislation limiting immigration and migration, or (b) impose a caste system whereby the minority can never, under any circumstances, earn as much as highly paid labor. Paradoxically, the minority is a threat because it is powerless. If the minority becomes powerful, its economic interests coincide with that of highly paid labor, a development that works against employers who would then be deprived of cheap labor. Employers therefore favor open immigration and high mobility. The net result of this interplay is that the minority is, or remains, subordinate to highly paid labor and employers.

The theory of the split-labor market formally describes what transpired in the past, and evidence for the theory comes mostly from historical examples. Whether current labor markets in California are split, however, is another question altogether. Hopefully, the data at hand will provide some clues.

Insofar as earnings inequality divides along ethnic lines, the various theories emphasize different reasons. According to the theories of the dual economy and dual-labor market, unequal earnings result mainly from the minority being in the wrong sector or market. Switching, however, is difficult because of infrastructural barriers. Free-market theory emphasizes the employees' contribution to marginal productivity, this contribution being affected by human capital. Any inequalities then remaining are attributed to taste. Alternatively, some economists argue that employers exploit ethnic minorities and thus inequality contributes to profit. The resemblance between this point and the dynamics of the split-labor market might be noted. Both theories agree that employers gain from cheap labor and imply that inequality results less from taste than from infrastructure.

The Research Task and Research Results

Ethnicity and Economic Structures

Clear predictions follow from the concepts of the dual-labor market and dual economy: (1) workers in primary labor markets will have higher earnings than those in secondary markets; and (2) workers in core industries will have higher earnings than those in peripheral industries. These hypotheses hold true regardless of ethnicity.

As mentioned, however, sector and market are not mutually exclusive. Primary and secondary jobs exist within core and peripheral industries. This is clearly seen on the following diagram:

Economic Sector:	Core	Core	Periphery	Periphery
Labor Market:	Primary	Secondary	Primary	Secondary
Segment:	a	b	c	d
	highest earnings	?	?	lowest earnings

For lack of an agreed-upon term, let us call the combinations of sector and market an "economic segment." The highest earnings should be associated with primary occupations in the core (segment *a*) and the lowest earning associated with secondary occupations in the periphery (segment *d*). Less clear are hypotheses about primary occupations in the periphery and secondary occupations in the core (the question marks under segments *b* and *c* represent this ambiguity). One cannot hypothesize which of these segments, *b* or *c*, will have the higher earnings, so the answer must be left to the data.

Economically based theories are vague about ethnicity, often aggregating ethnic minorities with low wage earners. This is unfortunate because one cannot always assume that the causes are the same for all low-waged groups, or if the same, that they affect all groups equally. Economic structure might impact whites in one way, blacks in another, and Chicanos or Asians in still another. Human capital might produce great gains for one group but small gains for another. Some variables could even cause gains for one group and losses for another. These possible interactions call into question the appropriateness of treating all low wage earners as one homogenous group. As a consequence of these considerations, the forthcoming statistical analysis is applied to each group separately.

Operational Definitions

Before delving into analysis, a few words about operational definitions are in order. The Census Bureau reports current occupation and industry for each person aged 16 years or older with earnings. These items commonly serve to operationalize the concepts of economic sector and labor market. The gist is as follows:

Core economic sector: mining, durable manufacturing, transportation, communications and utilities, finance, insurance, and real estate. Public administration (government) was also included. While some analysts include government as a separate category, I included it in the core because the minority group sizes were so small that a more detailed classification was not feasible.

Peripheral economic sector: nondurable manufacturing, wholesale trade, retail trade, business and repair services, personal services, entertainment and recreation, professional and related services. Agriculture was included in the periphery sector, again because the sizes of the minority groups did not permit a detailed classification.

Primary labor market: managerial and professional, technical and administrative, precision production, craft and repair, printing machine operators, material moving equipment operators.

Secondary labor market: sales, clerks, service, farming and forestry, operators, fabricators and laborers.

Preliminary Findings on Economic Structure

As a first step toward ascertaining the ethnic structure of labor markets and economic sectors, consider Table 7.1. (The table shows the category "other" only to make the percentages total to 100%. The category is not discussed).

If only random influences were at work, then each group should be present in each segment in proportion to its size. The probability of that being the case is less than one in 10,000, as computed from the chi-square statistic.[19] Therefore, one can conclude that the groups

Table 7.1
Ethnic Composition of Economic Segments
(California, 1980)

Economic Sector	Core	Core	Periphery	Periphery
Labor Market	Primary %	Secondary %	Primary %	Secondary %
White	77.1	64.5	76.6	68.5
Mexican	8.1	15.2	8.4	14.1
Black	5.6	9.6	5.0	6.7
Chinese	1.5	1.1	1.8	1.7
Filipino	1.3	1.9	1.4	1.4
Japanese	1.3	1.1	1.5	1.2
Korean	.3	.4	.6	.5
Vietnamese	.3	.4	.2	.2
Other	4.5	5.8	4.5	5.7
Totals	100.0%	100.0%	100.0%	100.0%

are not randomly distributed, which is hardly surprising, and confirms a prediction that can easily be deduced from other studies.

While not randomly distributed, whites are the overwhelming majority of workers in every segment and are followed, at a considerable distance, by the next two largest groups in California: Mexicans and blacks. Within the core sector whites constitute 77% of the primary labor market but only 64% of the secondary market. A similar pattern holds for the periphery sector. In contrast, a disproportionate number of workers in secondary occupations are black and Chicano. In core secondary occupations, 15% are Chicano and 10% are black, but in core primary occupations, only 8% are Chicano and only 6% are black. The same disparity between primary and secondary markets exists in the peripheral economic sector. With regard to Asians, one can see that they are rather evenly distributed across the table, but one should bear in mind the rather small sample size.

In addition to examining ethnic composition *within* each segment, one can examine the distribution of ethnic groups *across* segments. That is, the same frequencies can be percentaged in a different direction.

Let us assume that (1) working in a secondary occupation in a peripheral industry is the least desirable segment, and that (2) whites have more power and opportunity than most minorities. From these assumptions, which seem reasonable, it follows that whites will be underrepresented and minorities overrepresented in the periphery-secondary segment. Despite the strength of the assumptions, though, the data (Table 7.2) show that the preponderance of every group,

Table 7.2
Ethnic Segments by Ethnic Group
(California, 1980)

Economic Sector Labor Market	Core Primary %	Core Secondary %	Periphery Primary %	Periphery Secondary %	Totals
White	25.0	21.1	18.4	35.5	100.0%
Mexican	14.1	26.7	11.2	48.0	100.0%
Black	19.1	32.7	12.4	35.8	100.0%
Chinese	22.3	16.8	19.7	41.1	100.0%
Filipino	19.4	28.5	16.1	36.0	100.0%
Japanese	22.5	19.7	18.8	39.0	100.0%
Korean	15.2	18.4	21.2	45.2	100.0%
Vietnamese	28.4	30.6	12.3	28.7	100.0%
Other	19.6	25.3	14.4	40.7	100.0%

including whites, is in the periphery-secondary segment. In addition, the white percentage approximates the black and Filipino percentages, and is only slightly lower than the Japanese percentage. For whatever reasons, whites have been no more successful than these minorities groups in staying out of this, the least desirable economic segment. Contrary to expectation, the Vietnamese seem to be the most successful. An explanation for this finding is not readily forthcoming.[20] At the other extreme, the most desirable segment is the core-primary, and again contrary to expectation, the white percentage is not especially large while the Vietnamese percentage is the largest of the groups. This, too, is difficult to explain.

In sum, while the groups are not randomly distributed in the economy, whites still numerically dominated every segment. Percentaging the frequencies in the other direction reveals that a disproportionate number of each group is in the periphery-secondary segment. This was not anticipated theoretically. Also not anticipated was the disproportionate number of Vietnamese in the core-primary segment. In hindsight, the Vietnamese representation may reflect the composition of Vietnamese immigration stream. Unlike previous Asian groups, many Vietnamese immigrants were middle- and upper-class people who may now be gravitating towards primary labor markets in an attempt to capitalize on their socioeconomic standing.

Earnings

The operational definition of earnings is as follows: the total annual money from wages, salaries, self-employment, and farm self-employment. The self-employed sometimes report negative earnings or losses.

When that occurred, the negative numbers were coded as .5, an arbitrarily low nonzero figure. This was done because earnings were sometimes transformed into logarithms and a negative or zero log is undefined.[21] As a preliminary step towards ordering the data, Table 7.3 compares earnings first by economic segment, and then by both economic segment and ethnicity.

The table shows the two statistics most commonly interpreted as the "average." The first, the means, are descriptively interesting and mathematically necessary for the regression techniques to be used later in this chapter. The second, the medians, are primarily of descriptive interest and show the level of earnings above or below which 50% of the group falls. One can see that ranking the economic segments by either median or mean produces the same result. The rank order, from highest to lowest earnings, follows:

Table 7.3
Annual Earnings for Economic Segments By Ethnic Group
(California, 1980)

Labor Market Economic Sector	Primary Core $	Primary Periphery $	Secondary Core $	Secondary Periphery $
Mean Earnings	17,000	14,800	10,000	7,400
White	17,900	15,500	10,700	7,900
Japanese	17,600	17,600	10,400	8,100
Chinese	16,300	15,400	9,100	6,600
Korean	14,700	14,500	7,800	7,000
Black	14,000	11,600	9,100	6,000
Filipino	13,600	14,400	9,200	6,500
Mexican	12,500	11,000	8,400	5,800
Vietnamese	9,400	8,100	6,500	4,100
Mean of means*	14,500	13,500	8,900	6,500
SD of means**	2,800	3,100	1,400	1,300
Median Earnings	16,000	11,500	8,100	4,700
White	17,000	12,000	8,900	4,700
Japanese	17,900	15,000	9,600	5,700
Chinese	16,000	12,000	8,500	4,200
Korean	13,800	11,200	7,000	4,500
Black	14,000	10,400	8,000	4,000
Filipino	13,200	14,000	9,000	5,700
Mexican	12,000	10,000	7,000	4,700
Vietnamese	9,000	3,100	6,000	2,100

*This the mean of the group means, not the mean of the economic segment.
**Standard deviation of the group means.

- core-primary
- periphery-primary
- core-secondary
- periphery-secondary

These rankings indicate that regardless of sector, earnings are highest in the primary-labor market, and further, that regardless of market, earnings are highest in the core sector. The difference between extreme mean earnings (core-primary versus periphery-secondary) is large, almost $10,000 per year. Apparently, being in the right segment has a large economic benefit, a fact already implied by several authors.

For present purposes, the breakdown by ethnicity is more pertinent. One can see that within the primary-core segment, whites have the highest earnings followed by Japanese and Chinese. There is a large difference between highest and lowest (whites compared to Vietnamese), amounting to $8,500 per year in earnings. One can also see that whites, Japanese, Chinese, and Koreans are above the mean of group means.[22] In the primary-periphery segment, the Japanese have highest mean earnings, higher than whites by $2,100 per year. Chinese rank third and again, Vietnamese rank last. The difference between the extremes is again large: $9,500 per year. In the secondary-core segment, whites rank highest and Japanese second highest. Chinese, blacks, and Filipinos have identical or near identical earnings and are slightly above the mean of all groups. Vietnamese are the lowest earning group. To find that Japanese have the highest mean earnings by a slight amount comes as a mild surprise. In the secondary-periphery segment, mean earnings are lower than in any other economic segment for every group and by a large amount, but even so, Japanese have the highest mean earnings followed by whites, while Vietnamese have the lowest mean.

The dispersion about the mean of group means is instructive (dispersion here refers to the difference between each group mean and the mean of the means). It is comparatively low in the secondary-core and secondary-periphery segments (both standard deviations are approximately $1,400). Dispersion is higher in the primary-core segment and increases higher yet in the primary-periphery segment.[23] Ethnic groups, it appears, are more equal in poverty and less equal in wealth.

The table also shows medians. They are lower than the means because extremely high values do not affect them. In general, the medians substantiate the impressions gained from studying the means, but note the position of the Vietnamese: more than one-half of all Vietnamese in the primary-periphery segment are earning less than $3,100 per year, and in the secondary-periphery segment, the value is even lower: $2,100 per year. These median values are extremely low compared to the means, which suggests that many Vietnamese are earning very little while a few Vietnamese are earning a great deal. Overall, although many groups are not well off, the Vietnamese are the least well off of any group in every segment of the economy.

These data, while simple, make a fundamental point: economic segment unquestionably affects ethnic group earnings, and the effect is fairly constant. Japanese rank either first or second in all segments, alternating in earning with whites, Chinese are either third or fourth, and Vietnamese are always last. Before seeing these findings, one might have argued that economic structure was the only important variable determining earnings, or conversely, that only ethnicity was important, but now, with data in view, one knows that *both* segment and ethnicity have important effects. On that point the data are clear.

Economic segment and ethnicity are important determinants of earnings, but several addition factors must be considered when developing a model. I have therefore divided the variables into three broad classes: control, economic structure, and human capital. They are described below.

Control variables. Variables are classified as controls when they influence earnings but are not, at the moment, of primary theoretical interest. The reason for incorporating them into the analysis is to obtain a more accurate estimate of earnings. The control variables are as follows:

(1) *Weeks worked.* The Census Bureau tabulates the number of weeks a person worked in the year previous to the census. For many persons, the opportunity to work determines their earnings (for instance, day laborers). For other persons, opportunity may be so available that they work more or fewer weeks as a matter of choice (for instance, many physicians). And for others, custom or contract determines the number of weeks worked (for instance, civil servants). Because different ethnic groups may not have the same opportunity to work, the variable was included in the analysis.

(2) *Metropolitan.* This is defined as residence in a county which the Census Bureau designates as metropolitan. Most such counties are part of an SMSA.[24] Since an SMSA is a social and economic area, one would expect jobs to be more available there than in rural areas and wages to be higher. Metropolitan residence is a binary (dummy) variable. Persons residing in a metropolitan county received a score of one; otherwise they received a score of zero.

(3) *Married.* The effect of marital status is difficult to predict. Married persons may be more highly motivated to earn but, on the other hand, marriage may hinder the acquisition of human capital

and subsequent career development. An opposite argument might be that marriage facilitates the acquisition of human capital but decreases motivation to work. Whichever argument one prefers though, that these arguments can be made means that marital status should be controlled. Currently married persons received a score of one; otherwise they received a score of zero.

(4) *Gender.* Women earn less than men, for many reasons including discrimination, and therefore, a group with proportionately more women in the labor force will have lower mean earnings. While that hypothesis has a certain reasonableness to it, note that it can be reversed. Females might be participating because males will not, or cannot, and if that is true, a high female rate should be correlated with low group earnings. To control these possible effects, gender was included in the analysis, with men receiving a score of zero and women receiving a score of one.

(5) *Native born.* This variable represents assimilation. The native born are citizens by birth, overwhelmingly native speakers of English, and socialized into American culture. They are surely more assimilated than the foreign born (the work experience-age measure, given below, also taps assimilation, but indirectly).[25] Insofar as socialization and language fluency increase one's earning potential and citizenship qualifies one for jobs closed to noncitizens, the native born should have higher earnings. Nonnative born received a score of zero and native born received a score of one.

Economic structure. As can be gathered from the lengthy discussion devoted to it earlier, economic structure has a prominent place in the explanation of earnings. The economic variables are as follows:

(1) *Economic sector.* The data have just shown that earnings vary by sector, a finding suggesting the potential importance of this variable. Persons working in peripheral industries were scored zero and those in core industries were scored one.

(2) *Labor market.* The data also showed that earnings vary by labor market, and so persons working in secondary occupations were scored zero and those in primary occupations were scored one.

Human capital. Of all the explanations for minority advancement, human capital has probably received the most attention from sociologists. Here, three critically important human capital variables are analyzed.

(1) *Work experience/age.* Work experience should be associated with higher earnings. People who have been on the job longer earn

more because they have greater seniority, job knowledge, skills, and are more firmly integrated into work-related social networks.

If work experience is measured in years, then experience must be correlated with age to some extent. For every year of experience acquired, the worker must grow at least one year older. If an alternative measure of work experience had been available, age and work experience might have been separated. But because the alternatives were not available, one can only assume that work experience was equivalent to age, minus years of education (a person accrues little or no experience while attending school) minus six years (most people enter school at approximately that age). For the foreign born, this measure is correlated with time of immigration. The longer ago a immigrant arrived, the older the immigrant must be, and so the work experience-age measure indirectly taps assimilation.

(2) *Work experience, curvilinear.* Up to some point, earnings should directly increase as experience increases (the linear effect), but at some point earnings should decrease because older workers lose wages relative to young workers (the curvilinear effect). To capture the inverted U-shaped relation between work experience and earnings, an additional work experience measure was constructed: the square of work experience.

(3) *Education.* Social scientists have studied education more than any other kind of human capital. In the present instance, education was measured with number of school years completed, beginning with zero years and ending with twenty-two years. These limits correspond to "no years" completed through "eight or more" years of college completed.

All of the preceding variables will be incorporated into a regression model, but before doing that, the descriptive statistics may prove interesting, as shown on Table 7.4.

Discussion of these findings will be brief because several were reviewed earlier in this chapter or in other chapters. Those will not be reviewed again (native born, economic sector, labor market, and education).

Weeks worked varies from group to group with Japanese working the most weeks per year (41) and Vietnamese the fewest (32). Whites, Chinese, and Filipinos work approximately 38 weeks per year while Koreans, blacks, and Mexicans work about 36 weeks per year. The plain fact that the number of weeks worked varies by ethnic group helps explain group variations in earnings.

Because the means of binary coded variables are proportions, we can also see on the table that more than 99% of several groups reside in metropolitan areas, including the Japanese who historically filled

Table 7.4
Means and Standard Deviations of Model Variables by Ethnic Group

	W	J	C	F	K	V	B	M
				Panel A: Means				
Weeks worked	38.01	40.99	38.02	38.14	35.91	31.52	35.70	35.82
Metropolitan	.95	.99	.99	.98	.99	.99	.99	.97
Married	.58	.58	.61	.67	.72	.57	.44	.59
Gender	.45	.49	.46	.53	.51	.42	.50	.42
Native born	.94	.73	.31	.18	.08	.01	.97	.55
Economic sector	.46	.42	.39	.48	.34	.59	.52	.41
Labor market	.44	.41	.42	.35	.36	.41	.32	.25
Sector-market interaction	.25	.22	.22	.19	.15	.28	.19	.14
Government worker	.16	.18	.17	.18	.08	.14	.29	.12
Self-employed	08	.10	.08	.03	.15	.04	.03	.03
Work experience	15.75	16.70	15.22	14.51	13.18	10.60	14.35	14.01
Work experience squared	48.2*	51.9*	48.9*	43.1*	31.1*	24.9*	41.8*	39.1*
Education	16.21	16.60	15.87	16.36	16.28	15.12	15.40	12.47
				Panel B: Standard Deviations				
Weeks worked	18.82	17.11	18.73	18.38	19.00	21.38	20.03	19.08
Metropolitan	.22	.11	.08	.12	.05	.09	.10	.17
Married	.49	.49	.49	.47	.45	.50	.50	.49
Gender	.50	.50	.50	.50	.50	.49	.50	.49
Native born	.24	.44	.46	.38	.26	.10	.17	.50
Economic sector	.50	.49	.49	.50	.47	.49	.50	.49
Labor market	.50	.49	.49	.48	.48	.49	.46	.44
Sector-market interaction	.43	.42	.42	.40	.36	45	.39	.35
Government worker	.36	.38	.37	.39	.27	.34	.45	.33
Self employed	.27	.30	.28	.16	.35	.19	.18	.17
Work experience	15.30	15.51	16.04	14.86	11.72	11.71	14.55	13.97
Work experience squared	68.8*	67.9*	76.5*	73.5*	46.3*	44.0*	65.1*	62.0*
Education	2.73	2.82	4.96	3.64	3.68	3.65	2.78	4.32

*Actual value divided by ten.

Metropolitan	0-reside in non-metropolitan county, 1-reside in metropolitan county.
Married	0-not currently married, 1-currently married.
Sex	0-male, 1-female.
Native born	0-no, 1-yes.
Economic sector	0-periphery, 1-core.
Labor market	0-secondary, 1-primary.
Government worker	0-non-government worker, 1-government worker.
Self-employed	0-not self employed, 1-self employed, unincorporated.
Work experience	Age minus school years completed minus six.
Education	0-never attended . . . 22 (eight or more years of college).

B-Black; C-Chinese; F-Filipino; J-Japanese; K-Korean;
M-Mexican; V-Vietnamese; W-White

an agricultural niche. In part, these high percentages may reflect the urbanization of the state as a whole. With growth, more and more counties become defined as metropolitan, and thereby encompass an increasing proportion of the population.

The data also indicate that more than two-thirds of Filipinos and Koreans were married at the time of the census while fewer than one-half of blacks were. The black rate, lowest of the groups, is consistent with other data.[26] The gender measure shows the proportion of females participating in the labor force. The Filipino and Korean proportions are the highest and the Mexican and Vietnamese proportions are the lowest. Although not theoretically anticipated, it could have been argued that the strong, traditional family orientation supposedly associated with Catholicism would lead to lower female participation rates for Chicanos and Filipinos (both groups are mostly Catholic). Contradicting the argument, however, the one group ranks high and other ranks low on this measure. Japanese have the most work experience, whites the second most, and Vietnamese the least. Because the work experience measure also taps age and assimilation, the low Vietnamese level might be a reflection of the group's low mean age and recent immigration while the opposite would be true of the Japanese.[27]

Multiple Regression Equation

Money is an interval level measure and so several multivariate techniques may be used. I opted for a regression approach because it is widely known, flexible, and extremely powerful. Just as important, regression equations may be used to compare groups while simultaneously considering both mean levels and the impact of means on earnings. The basic form of the regression equation follows:

$$Y_i = a + b_{i1}X_{i1} \ldots + b_{ik}X_{ik} \tag{1}$$

where Y is earnings, i is the respondent, k is the number of independent variables, a is a constant, and b is a regression coefficient indicating how much earnings change for each unit of change in X. Each change is a net change, taking into account the impact of other independent variables in the equation. Verbally, the bs may be described in several ways: as the amount each independent variable is "worth" in annual earnings net of the worth of other independent variables, or as the net rate at which each independent variable is translated into earnings, or as the net rate of return on the independent variable.

In each interpretation, "net" means after taking into account the other independent variables.

Many researchers transform earnings into logarithms in order to better link changes in independent variables to a proportional change in earnings.[28] This transformation usually results in a stronger outcome as measured by the explained variance (R^2). However, I did not do that. The major advantages to retaining the dependent variable in dollars rather than logarithms of dollars, are twofold. First, the coefficients (bs) are descriptively meaningful, being measured in dollars, not logarithms; and second, when not transformed, several outcomes made more sense. The signs and significance levels were more often in accord with the hypotheses (for those who wish to consider a logarithmic model, the appendix contains the appropriate table).

The analysis necessarily involves many technical details, but one should not lose sight of the basic objective, which is to analyze ethnicity. In relation to that objective, three basic outcomes are possible.

(1) Ethnicity (group membership) is the only important variable in the analysis. This suggests that ethnic related factors such as prejudice, subcultural values, and ethnic infrastructure are the predominant forces in determining earnings.

(2) Some or all of the variables in the analysis are important but ethnicity is not, thereby suggesting that ethnic-related variables have nothing to do with earnings.

(3) Ethnicity is important and so are some or all of the other variables, which suggests that both ethnic and nonethnic factors determine earnings. Past research indicates that this outcome is the most likely (and is also the most complicated to interpret).

The following table shows the results of regressing annual earnings against the independent variables just discussed.

The first point of inquiry concerns the adequacy of the equations: How well do they fit the data? The squared multiple correlation coefficients (R^2s help answer that question. As the table displays, R^2s extend from .40 to .56, values often described as low to moderate but within the size range usually found in this type of research. However, if weeks worked were removed from the equations, the R^2s) would fall to approximately .10, which is small but still significant in the statistical sense. While these equations do not fit the data as closely as one might like, they are nonetheless useful for present purposes.

The net effect of each independent variable in a regression equation may be tested against the null hypothesis that the net effect is zero, which is the same as testing the bs for statistical significance. In this test, sample size affects the number of degrees of freedom, and that number affects significance. There is no way to circumvent this problem; one must, however, be aware of it.

Table 7.5
Regression Equations for Annual Earnings
by Ethnic Group

	W	J#	C	F	K	V	B	M
R²	.45	.44	.42	.46	.40	.56	.49	.48
	Unstandardized Regression Coefficients [$1,000 units]							
Weeks worked	.27	.25	.24	.22	.24	.21	.22	.19
Metropolitan	1.26	2.17	-1.82*	1.58	2.36*	.30*	1.09	-.07*
Married	1.79	1.88	1.46	1.11	.61*	.54	.87	1.30
Gender	-6.27	-6.00	-3.26	-2.68	-3.54	-1.59	-2.55	-2.86
Native born	-1.40	.36*	1.24	.63	1.28	-2.38	.82	1.15
Economic sector	1.10	.84	1.28	.81	.79*	1.18	1.12	.99
Labor market	1.39	3.84	4.26	4.48	3.22	2.14	1.66	1.79
Sector-market interaction	.25	-.68*	.63*	-2.12	-.48*	-1.04	.82	.10*
Government worker	-2.00	-.98	.51	.41	-.32*	-.82	-.32	-.59
Self employed	.80	.48*	2.11	2.66	5.24	-.04*	.50	.76
Work experience	.44	.38	.25	.17	.30	.10	.22	.23
Work experience squared	-.08[a]	-.07[a]	-.03[a]	-.03[a]	-.06[a]	-.03[a]	-.03[a]	-.03[a]
Education	.97	.76	.48	.28	.40	.19	.59	.35
Intercept	-15.56	-15.15	-8.18	-7.08	-10.70	-4.34	-11.67	-6.22

\# The Japanese equation is the only equation not significantly different (.05 level of probability) from the white equation.
* This coefficient is not significantly different (.05 level of probability) from zero.
[a] Coefficient multiplied by ten.

B-Black; C-Chinese; F-Filipino; J-Japanese; K-Korean;
M-Mexican; V-Vietnamese; W-White

Examining the results on Table 7.5 reveals that the Japanese equation does not significantly differ from the white equation, a finding which suggests that the Japanese have assimilated in terms of earnings.[29] This possibility will be discussed later, but now and for purposes of continuity, the Japanese data will still be reported. With this one exception, all the equations statistically differed from the white equation, implying that these groups have not assimilated with regard to earnings.

The bs indicate the dollar value of the variable, and from studying them one can learn the effect of each measure on each group. To take a particular instance, one might note that for whites, each week worked is worth $270 (.27 * 1000), net of the worth of all the other variables in the equation. This figure tells us the "average net value" of weeks worked. The value for the entire year depends on the average number of weeks that were worked that year. For whites, this was 38.01 weeks (shown Table 7.4), so in total, weeks worked resulted in earnings of $10,263 ($270 * 38.01). A similar calculation was made for each variable in the white equation, and the entire process was repeated for each ethnic group. For example, weeks worked is worth $240 among Koreans, who worked an average of 35.91 weeks during the year, and therefore weeks worked resulted in $8,618 in annual earnings.

At this point, one can compare Koreans and whites as to the effect of weeks worked. Whites obviously are gaining more from the weeks they work: $10,263 versus $8,618. From subtracting the two values, the net advantage to whites is estimated at $1,645 per year. Whites accrue this advantage because they work more weeks than Koreans, and because for each week whites work, they earn more.

As the minority equation is subtracted from the white equation, a positive difference denotes a white advantage and negative difference denotes an ethnic group advantage—advantage here being used in the sense of "the dollar value is in favor of that group." Differences between intercepts (as) are difficult to interpret substantively and will be presented but not discussed. All of these calculations, while tedious, are straightforward (the appendix contains a somewhat more formal description and several references).

Approaching the problem in this way enables one to trace the etiology of an effect because one can determine whether the advantage is due to a higher mean, a higher rate of return, or some combination thereof. Quite possibly, a group can earn a greater total amount by working more weeks than another group even though the other group translates weeks worked into earnings at a higher rate. In a moment, examples of this outcome and other possibilities will be seen.

It should be explicitly mentioned that when comparing regression equations in the foregoing manner, the unit of analysis shifts from the individual to the group. The interpretation then centers on the "average" group member, average being operationalized by the mean.[30]

Table 7.6 shows the results of these calculations. The numbers in boldfaced type indicate a positive sum, or advantage for whites; those in normal type indicate an advantage for the ethnic groups. In keeping with the convention of showing the white advantage in boldfaced numbers, the differences between the white and minority intercept (as) is shown as a positive difference, although they are actually negative numbers.

Calculating the differences is a mechanical task; determining the minimum size that constitutes an advantage is far more subjective. How large a difference must exist to be called an advantage? Here, the criterion of probability is not useful because the white equation is based upon such a large sample that very small differences are statistically significant. One must therefore turn to more subjective criteria, and somewhat arbitrarily, I suggest that differences of $500 per year or less are not very meaningful in absolute terms. To indicate this, those amounts are printed in italics. While I do not wish to minimize the importance of $500 (especially in a lump sum), it seems to me that if the amount were spread over a year, it would not substantially change one group's lifestyle relative to another group's. Finally, one might recall that the Japanese equation was not significantly different from the white equation, and because of that, the Japanese are not be included in the discussion (the table nonetheless reports their data).

A pattern is evident on the table. Three variables consistently confer a relative advantage on whites. These variables are weeks worked,

Table 7.6
Earnings Advantage: Regression Estimates

Bold = white advantage, plain = ethnic group advantage
Italics = a difference of $500 or less

Whites Compared to:

	J	C	F	K	V	B	M
Intercept*	**400**	**7400**	**8500**	**4900**	**11200**	**3900**	**9300**
Weeks worked	300	**1200**	**2100**	**1700**	**3700**	**2600**	**3500**
Metropolitan	900	**3000**	*400*	1200	**900**	**100**	**1300**
Married	100	*100*	*300*	**600**	**700**	**700**	*300*
Gender	100	1300	1400	1000	2200	1600	1600
Native born	1600	1700	1400	1400	1300	2100	1900
Economic sector	200	0	*100*	*200*	*200*	*100*	*100*
Labor market	1000	1200	1000	600	*300*	*100*	*200*
Sector market interaction	200	*200*	*500*	*100*	*400*	*100*	0
Government worker	100	*200*	*400*	*300*	*200*	*200*	*200*
Self employed	0	*100*	0	700	*100*	0	0
Work experience	500	**3000**	**4400**	**2900**	**5800**	**3700**	**3600**
Work experience squared	300	2200	2600	2200	3200	2700	2600
Education	3000	**8100**	**11000**	**9200**	**12700**	**6500**	**11300**

*I do not interpret the intercept, but some readers may wish to do so. Signs are omitted, but except for the difference between intercepts, a negative difference would indicate an advantage for the ethnic group and a positive difference an advantage for whites. Recall that the Japanese equation is not statistically different from the white equation, and therefore is not marked in bold or italics.

B-Black; C-Chinese; F-Filipino; J-Japanese; K-Korean;
M-Mexican; V-Vietnamese; W-White

work experience, and education. Weeks worked will be discussed in some detail to illustrate the analysis. Note on Table 7.4 that whites, Chinese, and Filipinos all work approximately 38 weeks per year while the remaining groups work 35 or fewer weeks per year. All other things being equal, the greater the number of weeks worked, the greater the earnings. This confers an advantage on these groups relative to other groups.

However, all else is not equal, which is the reason for performing the regression analysis. The second factor is the net rate at which weeks worked is translated into earnings, or the net value of a week of work. The regression coefficient (Table 7.5) is an estimate of that value, and one can see that the white coefficient is .27, or expressed in dollars, $270 per year after allowing for the effects of the other variables in the equation. This is the highest rate of any group. Thus, the white advantage derives from the combination of a relatively high mean level weighted by a very high coefficient.

Whites also gain relative to the other groups from work experience. The etiology of this effect is similar to that of weeks worked. The white mean is slightly higher than the mean of all other groups and at the same time, whites have a higher rate of return than any other group. To illustrate: the white regression coefficient is almost four-times larger than the Vietnamese coefficient, and almost two-times larger than the coefficients for Filipinos, blacks, and Mexicans. Primarily as a result of this high return, whites accrue a substantial advantage from their work experience.

Of all the variables in regression equations, education consistently confers the largest advantage on whites, the dollar values varying from $6,500 (whites with blacks) to $12,700 (whites with Vietnamese). Because all groups, except Chicanos, have approximately the same average amount of education, the only way whites could gain an advantage from education is to have a higher rate of return. And, in fact, the white regression coefficient is three- to four-times higher than the ethnic group coefficients. It is not the amount of education that produces the white advantage, but the value.

Not all variables favor whites. Three variables consistently favor the ethnic groups: gender, native born, and the curvilinear component of work experience. Consider gender. All the gender coefficients are negative, meaning that women earn less than men. However, the white coefficient is large, being from two- to four-times larger than any ethnic coefficient, while at the same time, the proportion of white women in the labor force is not exceptional. This combination results in the ethnic groups losing less than whites, thereby gaining the net advantage of gender.

Due to a similar etiology, the impact of being native born also confers a relative advantage on the ethnic groups. The original hypothesis was that being native born would increase earnings. That is the case for all groups except whites and Vietnamese. The Vietnamese situation is unique and the number of native born Vietnamese is so small (1%) that comparisons might be statistically suspect. That possibility does not apply to the white population though. Native born whites earn less than their foreign born counterparts (the white regression coefficient is negative while the coefficients for the other groups are positive). As a result, this negative coefficient produces an earnings advantage for the ethnic groups. The third variable consistently favoring the ethnic groups is the curvilinear component of work experience. As anticipated, the coefficients are negative, indicating that curvilinear work experience decreases mean earnings. While the white coefficient is not particularly large, whites have more work experience than most other groups, and when that amount is weighted by the negative coefficient, whites generally lose more, thus producing a relative gain for the ethnic groups.

Married persons earn more than the unmarried, a finding which is true for every group under study, except among Koreans (the coefficient is not statistically significant). Although the impact of marriage is high for whites, the proportion of married whites in the work force is relatively low. This low proportion offsets the impact of the white coefficient. A different outcome describes other groups. It makes no difference—that is, the dollar value of the advantage is less than $500—when whites are compared to Chinese, Filipinos, and Mexicans, and only a modest difference exists when compared to Koreans, Vietnamese, and blacks.

The labor market also has a mixed effect. It confers an advantage on Chinese and Filipinos, and to a lesser degree, on Koreans. While their proportions in the primary labor market are smaller than the white proportion, these ethnic groups translate their market positions into earnings at a higher rate than whites, resulting in an advantage for them. The same effects, however, are not large enough to produce a net advantage for Vietnamese, blacks, and Mexicans.

One of the more interesting negative findings concerns the self-employed. For the Vietnamese, being self-employed has no effect on annual earnings (the regression coefficient is small and insignificant), but among all other groups, the self-employed earn more than those who are not self-employed, and furthermore, among Asians, the self-employed earn considerably more than among whites (Table 7.5). These findings are in accord with what one would expect. Interestingly, however, when these effects are combined with the proportion of each group that is self-employed, no major advantage is conferred on either the ethnic groups or on whites. The one exception is Koreans. They gain a modest amount relative to whites.

Several variables consistently produce no advantage at all. These variables are economic sector, the interaction between sector and market, and being a government worker. This should not be interpreted to mean that these variables are not important determinants of earnings. For example, except for Koreans, core workers earn more than periphery workers, and among most groups, government workers earn less than nongovernment workers. Such findings were originally anticipated on theoretical grounds. Unanticipated was the general lack of impact of the sector-market interaction. As often as not, the coefficients are not significantly different from zero. From a statistical perspective, this may be the result of "multicollinearity": the presence of the one interaction term and the two separate terms that comprise it means all three terms are correlated, and hence the impact of any given term is diluted.

In addition to providing data on earnings, these negative findings emphasize the importance of examining not only the impact of variables on earnings, but also the impact of the variables on earnings *across* groups. Sometimes a variable that is critically important within a group produces no comparative advantage.

Summary and Conclusions

The data were presented as a net dollar advantage going to either whites or to an ethnic group. While this was not the only way the data might have been presented, it was consistent with the focus on assimilation. The major empirical findings may be summarized as follows:

* Earnings are higher in the core sector of the economy than in the periphery and higher in the primary labor market than in the secondary market.
* However, the highest earnings are in the core-primary segment of the economy; second highest in the periphery-primary segment; third highest in the core-secondary segment; and lowest in the peripheral-secondary segment. These rankings hold true when earnings are broken down by ethnic group.
* Japanese have the highest earnings, by a small amount, of any group. Vietnamese have the lowest earnings.

- The Japanese regression equation was the only one not significantly different from the white equation. This suggests that the Japanese are now assimilated, but because assimilation is multidimensional, the suggestion applies only to earnings.
- Whites consistently gain relative to the ethnic groups from weeks worked, work experience, and education.
- The ethnic groups consistently gain relative to whites from gender, being native born, and the curvilinear component of work experience.
- The other variables had either mixed or null effects. Sometimes they conferred an advantage on whites, sometimes on the ethnic groups, and sometimes they had almost no impact one way or another.

The fact that the equations for the ethnic groups differed significantly from the white equation (except for the Japanese) means there is an interaction between ethnicity and variables in the equations; to wit, ethnicity affects earnings.

Conclusions about the split-labor market are more difficult to draw. To determine whether a market is split requires data showing that ethnic groups are paid less than the majority for performing identical work. Data of that precision were not available. If, however, one is willing to loosen that strict criterion to situations of unequal earnings between majority and ethnic group even after taking into account similarity of occupation, human capital, economic segment, and other relevant control variables, then the present data suggest something akin to a split-labor market exists. There is a decidedly strong ethnic effect on earnings.

A reduction in the earnings gap between majority and ethnic group results from a combination of effects, as follows:

(1) *Positive Rate Gain:* both majority and ethnic group are at the same level on a variable that produces a gain in earnings, and the ethnic group converts that variable at a higher rate than the majority.

(2) *Negative Rate Gain:* both majority and ethnic group are at the same level on a variable that produces a loss in earnings, and the ethnic group converts that variable at a lower rate than the majority.

These possibilities sensitize one to the etiology of an effect, and further suggest that the past emphasis on the sheer quantity of human capital is no longer appropriate. An ethnic group must not only have as much human capital as the majority, but must translate it into earnings at a higher rate than the majority, otherwise equality of earnings will not result.

The implications of this point might be disquieting, especially regarding education. Conventional sociological wisdom holds that education is the key to upward mobility. The present findings do not negate the conventional wisdom, but they do modify it. Persons with more education have better life chances than persons with less education, but one might now question whether education will inevitably lessen the gap between majority and minority. If majority and minority acquire equal amounts of education, and if the benefits of education accrue in roughly the same linear fashion to both groups, then education will have little direct effect on achieving equality of earnings. This is another version of the "Alice in Wonderland" phenomenon, but now translated from regression equations. The minority must run faster (the coefficient) just to maintain the current gap in earnings.[31]

If, as many economists assume, absolute earnings determine welfare (life satisfaction), then the minority will be in a better position than before—"Alice in Wonderland" not withstanding. But if the assumption is incorrect, then a whole new realm of speculation opens up. According to several social psychological theories, welfare results from relative comparisons. The minority judges its welfare by the welfare of the majority. Hence, as long as the gap remains, minority welfare remains unchanged regardless of absolute levels of earnings.[32] Because the present data are not related to this argument, it must be left in the realm of speculation.

The final comment concerns the numerous differences that were found. Native-born blacks earned more than foreign-born blacks, but native-born whites earned less than foreign-born whites. Filipinos in metropolitan counties earned more than Filipinos in rural counties, but living in a metropolitan area made no difference for Chinese, Koreans, Vietnamese, and Mexicans. These examples, and others, emphasize the myriad and complex differences within and between ethnic groups, and therefore, the broadest implication of this analysis may be the simplest and most obvious: generalizing from any given group to all groups is an extremely dangerous undertaking.

APPENDIX

Between-Group Comparisons

Most often, regression analysis is used to estimate the net effect of an independent variable, as measured by the partial regression slope, or regression coefficient (b). The coefficient is represented in the unit of the dependent variable. If the dependent variable is measured in pounds, then the *b* is in pounds; if the dependent variable is in dollars, then the *b* is in dollars. This interpretation of regression is fundamental, and based on it, regression equations can be used to compare groups. Consider this approach with simplified notation. So one will have a concrete case to deal with, suppose earnings are regressed against the independent variables in the model for whites and Chicanos, to obtain:

$$Y_i = a + b_{i1}X_{i1} \ldots + b_{ik}X_{ik} \quad \text{(1) white}$$

$$Y_i = a + b_{i1}X_{i1} \ldots + b_{ik}X_{ik} \quad \text{(2) Chicano}$$

These are conventional regression equations. If means are substituted for the *X*s, the following holds:

$$Y_w = a + b_1X_{wl} \ldots + b_kX_{wk} \quad \text{(2) white}$$

$$Y_c = a + b_1X_{cl} \ldots + b_kX_{ck} \quad \text{(3) Chicano}$$

where Y_w and Y_c are the mean of earnings of whites and Chicanos, *b* is from equations (1) or (2) respectively, and X_m and X_c are the white and Chicano means of the *X*s, and *k* is the number of independent variables. In this form, the equation relates mean earnings to mean levels of the independent variables, and the net contribution of an independent variable is given by the combined weight of the regression coefficient (*b*) and variable mean. This calculation can be carried out for each group separately, the results subtracted term by term, and summed:

$$\text{sum } (Y_w - Y_c) = \text{sum } (a_w + a_c) + (b_1X_{w1} - b_1X_{c1})$$
$$+ \ldots (b_kX_{wk} - b_kX_{ck})$$

The difference between white and Chicano mean earnings will equal the sum of the differences between the product of the means and coefficients. Or, the differences indicate how much of an advantage one group has over another.[33]

These procedures are the equivalent of generating a regression equation that contains all the aforementioned independent variables, a dummy variable representing each ethnic group, and all the interaction terms between the independent variables and the ethnic group dummy variables, as follows:

$$Y = a + b_1X_1 \ldots + b_2X_2 + b_3D_3 + b_kD_k$$
$$+ b_4(D_1 * X_1) + \ldots b_k(D_3 * X_k)$$

where the terms are defined as before, D is a dummy variable representing an ethnic group, scored one or zero, and the terms in parenthesis are the interactions between the dummy variable and the other independent variables. Each minority can be so scored, and the appropriate interaction terms generated. While mathematically non-controversial, if all the independent variables, dummy variables, and interaction terms were placed in a single equation, the equation becomes unwieldly because it is so long. Also, such an equation introduces interpretative difficulties about the R^2s and about multicollinearity.

If one wants to measure the effect of a particular ethnic group, that information is already contained in the regression equations presented on Table 7.5. One simply subtracts the intercepts of the white and minority equation. The resulting value will equal the value of D_k if the above equation were solved.[34]

Logarithmic Transformation

The following table contains the results of the regression analysis of the logarithmic transformed measure of earnings.

Table 7.7
Regression Equations for Log of Annual Earnings

	W	J#	C	F	K	V	B	M
R^2	.65	.62	.62	.63	.59	.67	.68	.63

Unstandardized Regression Coefficients [log units]								
Weeks worked	.13	.13	.13	.12	.14	.14	.14	.13
Metropolitan	.24	-.14*	-.54	-.14*	1.61*	-.25*	-.19	-.25
Married	-.12	-.08*	-.02*	.04*	-.08*	-.22*	.06	.12
Gender	-.45	-.42	-.19	-.32	-.48	-.32	-.25	-.30
Native born	-.37	.31	.14	.04*	.15*	-.32*	.18	.13
Economic sector	.09	.18	.13	.07*	.38	.56	.20	-.03*
Labor market	-.01	.15	.19	.32	.21*	-.49	.19	-.01*
Sector-market interaction	.19	.13*	.14*	-.35	-.32*	.08*	-.07*	.15
Government worker	-.03	.05*	-.09*	-.07*	-.07*	.39	-.03*	.07

Table 7.7 (cont.)

Self employed	-.25	.07*	-.30	-.61	.08*	-1.26	-.31	-.19
Work experience	.04ᵃ	-.01ᵃ	.05ᵃ *	.04ᵃ *	.06ᵃ *	-.05	-.01	-.01ᵃ *
Work experience squared	-.05ᵇ	-.03ᵇ	-.04ᵇ	-.03ᵇ	-.04ᵇ *	.08ᵇ	.01ᵇ	.01ᵇ
Education	.06	.03	.02	.01*	.02ᵃ *	.03*	.04	.01
Intercept	2.41	2.79	3.26	3.46	1.08	2.66	2.04	3.04

\# The Japanese equation is the only equation not significantly different (.05 level of probability) from the white equation.
* This coefficient is not significantly different (.05 level of probability) from zero.
ᵃ Raw coefficient times ten.
ᵇ Raw coefficient times one-hundred.

B-Black; C-Chinese; F-Filipino; J-Japanese; K-Korean;
M-Mexican; V-Vietnamese; W-White

8

Ethnic Group Success

T his chapter discusses the broader conceptual issues surrounding assimilation, paying extra attention to Japanese Americans as an example of ethnic exceptionalism. A revised explanation for their upward mobility is offered, which is then used to shed light on the situation of the other groups under study.

Plan of the Chapter

The chapter has the following sections:

- summary of findings;
- definition of *ethnic group success*;
- explanations of ethnic group success;
- an alternative explanation;
- ethnic economic arena and Japanese American success; and
- the future.

Summary of Findings

To this point in the study, the census data have been presented by topic, such as by residential segregation or demographic potential. An alternative arrangement is to organize the material by ethnic group, an arrangement which facilitates making comparisons between ethnic groups. Because the present chapter will be addressing such comparisons, that is now the more useful arrangement. The major findings, as reorganized, are summarized below.

211

Vietnamese

With one major exception, the Vietnamese occupy the lowest rung of the stratification ladder and give little indication of rapid assimilation; they have the lowest earnings and the lowest occupational rankings; they have the lowest naturalization rate; they are poorest in English. They have low demographic potential: they are young and have a high dependency ratio, high fertility, and are an expansive population.

However, contrary to what the preceding list implies, Vietnamese are relatively well educated.

The obvious explanation for the Vietnamese is their traumatic history. As refugees fleeing their homeland, they do not resemble the typical immigrants of the past.

Mexican Americans

Mexican Americans have demographic and socioeconomic profiles similar to the Vietnamese, except for education. Chicanos rank low on that measure, and their prospect for upward mobility is poor.

Blacks, Chinese, Filipinos, and Koreans

Blacks, Chinese, Filipinos, and Koreans hold an intermediate position. The position of blacks is particularly interesting in light of their historical background. No group played a more dramatic role in the civil rights movement, and no other group was the focus of as much national attention. Whether the current position of blacks can be causally attributed to the civil rights movement is not known, but regardless of cause, the fact remains that blacks are no longer the deprived population they once were. To be sure, they have not achieved parity with whites—a point worth emphasizing—but that does not alter their ranking.

Japanese

Japanese rank highest of all the ethnic groups. They outmarry at the highest rate; they are very near or exceed whites on socioeconomic measures; almost three-fourths are native born. They have high demographic potential: a high mean age, a constrictive population pyramid, low job-squeeze ratio, and low fertility rate.

The success of Japanese is truly extraordinary, for they were subjected to some of the most vicious, systematic, and long-term discrimination ever heaped upon any American minority. Hostility

went beyond interpersonal slights, it involved the entire legal appa-
ratus of the government. Yet somehow, Japanese Americans over-
came those barriers to become an ethnic exception, the only nonwhite
group to have ever made it in America.

How did they do it?

This straightforward question requires a complex answer. It is
also a fundamental question, so fundamental that one wonders why
it was overlooked for so long. Before that question can be addressed,
however, one must examine what is meant by *success*.

Definition of Ethnic Group Success

The concept of *upward mobility* requires some clarification because
making intergroup comparisons is easily misinterpreted as prejudice.
A first step towards defining what *success* means in this context is to
recall Milton Gordon's analysis. He said that the majority imposes its
socioeconomic structure on the minority, and that the imposition
occurs even if the minority is isolated structurally but assimilated
culturally.[1] Based on this point, one can think of assimilation as occurring along the following three basic dimensions:

(1) *Subcultural,* referring to practices, norms, values, and customs.

(2) *Structural,* referring to the interactions governed and rendered
routine, such as marriage and friendship.

(3) *Socioeconomic,* referring to standings on education, occupation, and income.

Consider each of these dimensions in relation to success. If a
minority group assimilates into the majority and thereby loses its
subculture, one probably would not regard that as success. To do so
would imply that the culture lost was inferior to the culture gained.
Similarly, to regard structural assimilation as success implies that the
ethnic group is somehow inferior to the majority. For example, a
group may outmarry in perfect proportion to its size, but that does
not mean that majority group spouses are better than those of the
ethnic group.

Socioeconomic assimilation, however, has a much different con-
notation. To say that a group has achieved levels of education, income,
and occupation commensurate with the majority is not pejorative. In
the case of the groups studied here, all were originally below the
majority, so socioeconomic assimilation meant an increase in the
group's standard of living and was in keeping with the American value
system.

Based on the foregoing distinctions, I use *assimilation* with reference to cultural and structural matters, and *success* (or its opposite, *failure*) with reference to socioeconomic matters.

Explanations of Ethnic Group Success

Several perspectives for viewing ethnic group success exist, but even after more than a century of debate, the broadest and most enduring perspective is assimilation. At its base, the issue still is this: can *they* be like *us*? From Israel Zangwill's idealistic vision of America as the melting pot to the current debate over the new immigration policy, *they* and *us* remain the central issue. Thus, the broader meaning of this study can be revealed by comparing what the data show and imply to widely held ideas about assimilation and success. In carrying out this task, having directly comparable data on different groups is very valuable, indeed.

Discrimination-Prejudice

The most common explanation for ethnic failure is prejudice-discrimination. The ethnic group fails because the majority discriminates. As one writer neatly stated:

> One of the most fascinating aspects of our species is the extraordinary physical and cultural diversity of its members. Yet this diversity is often a source of conflicts and inequality, because human relations are all too often conducted on the basis of the differences rather than the similarities between groups.[2]

If relations are based on differences, then the more different a group is, the more it will be discriminated against. From this it follows that nonwhite groups, being both subculturally and physiologically different, will be more discriminated against than white ethnic groups, who are only subculturally different. This argument has a certain appeal, but, for all its appeal, the argument has a serious empirical flaw: highly visible groups who have succeeded. As has been amply documented throughout this study, Japanese Americans are virtually indistinguishable from the majority along socioeconomic measures, but they are highly distinguishable physiologically. While not as successful as the Japanese, Chinese Americans also contradict the discrimination argument. Explaining these exceptions is difficult. Stanley Lieberson writes the following:

Although handicapped by very deep forms of discrimination, the descendants of both Japanese and Chinese immigrants occupy much more favorable positions presently than do blacks. This is a puzzle . . . but it does not necessarily mean one has to go as far as Banfield[3] . . . who argues the importance of race is exaggerated, that most white-black differences are due to background and that, indeed, such gaps can be explained by nonracial factors. He goes on to argue that what is taken to be race prejudice is often really class prejudice.[4]

Even if Banfield is correct, that does not help us very much, for one then must explain class prejudice. The basis for the prejudice simply is pushed one step further back, and possibly out of sight, but that does not constitute an explanation.

Methodologically, a strict test of the discrimination argument requires that groups be matched on all possible causal variables except visibility, a requirement impossible to satisfy in the case of nonwhites.[5] But even setting aside the methodological problem, why should distinctiveness make a group an object of discrimination? Why not argue the opposite? Why should not a group be favored because of its distinctiveness?

Lieberson answers these questions by arguing that competition between majority and minority for resources, jobs, and power forms the impetus for intergroup hostility. In the course of the competition, group differences become the visible focus of the contention, something to hang the hostility on. Outsiders (including social scientists) can easily but mistakenly conclude that the differences are the cause of the hostility, when, in fact, the reverse is true: the competition caused the differences to become salient.[6]

The present data, both historical and statistical, are consistent with Lieberson's argument, although they cannot definitively prove it. The Japanese and Chinese were initially welcomed as valuable additions to the labor pool, and not until they started competing with white labor did anti-Asianism emerge as a powerful political force. Although one will never know what would have happened without the competition, one can surmise that the Chinese and Japanese would have succeeded more quickly and to a greater degree than they did.

Exogenous Factors

Another group of explanations coalesce around what I call *exogenous factors*: historical forces over which the affected groups had little or no control. Perhaps, if one prefers, one might call these factors *luck*.

Early Japanese were emigrating from an industrializing nation on the verge of becoming a major military power, and the Japanese government took a keen interest in emigration. Dispatches sent by Japanese diplomats in the United States often complained of the poor image that lower class immigrants presented to the American public, and proposals to limit immigration to a better "quality" of person were sometimes made.[7] In contrast to the Japanese, Chinese and Mexicans were emigrating from countries that had little power and that were not in a position to protect their emigrants. For blacks, the country in question was the United States, but until fairly recently, the federal government did little to protect their rights. They were, in a sense, "abandoned." Filipinos were not as much abandoned as rejected. The federal government limited immigration and encouraged Filipinos already in the United States to leave the country. The Vietnamese are a curious case. The United States government was responsible for their immigration, and it is reasonable to suppose that the Vietnamese have benefitted from the government's concern. So, in an odd way and despite the passage of decades, the Vietnamese resemble the Japanese in that both groups have had at least some government support.

In attempting to protect its emigrants, the Japanese government was only partially successful. The Japanese government could not prevent the Gentlemen's Agreement, the 1924 Immigration Act, the Alien Land Law, and discrimination in housing, employment, and everyday life. Unless one posits a snowballing process whereby small acts by the Japanese government near the turn of the century eventually worked their way through history to become major influences much later, government interventions cannot account for the current success of Japanese Americans.

Cultural Factors

Culture is a common explanation for ethnic success. Indisputably, cultural differences exist, and these differences may facilitate or retard upward mobility. In the case of Japanese Americans, a widely echoed assertion is that their subculture stresses education, a stress buttressed by the Japanese family. In his analysis of Japanese American subculture, Harry Kitano writes as follows:

> A major decision might include the parent sacrificing his own pleasures in order to send his son to college, so that the story of an aging parent living practically on bread and water in order that his children

could gain a college education is not an unusual one in the Issei culture.[8]

Another example is the pooling of family resources. Older brothers and sisters and their families would collectively finance the education of a younger (usually male) sibling.

Also frequently mentioned is the Japanese penchant for hard work. This trait is much admired and is part of the broader value system of the Confucian ethic. According to the ethic, success results from work, perseverance, and study. One research piece even suggests that Japanese Americans have so strongly internalized the ethic that is has become a personality trait.[9] Although less frequently mentioned, the Confucian emphasis on stoicism and pragmatism is surely important too. If sacrifice and suffering are necessary for success, then one sacrifices and suffers without complaint. This stoicism, the willingness to quietly "bear the unbearable," is important enough to have a separate Japanese name: *gaman*.

Japanese Americans are also noted for valuing entrepreneurship. Because many Japanese did establish privately owned businesses (including farms), the value must be true by definition. The implication, though, is that less successful groups do not have a similar subcultural value. Blacks and Chicanos, especially, are not noted for entrepreneurship and have not been as successful as the Japanese.

Self-help is another cultural value. Very rarely did even indigent Japanese Americans seek aid from the government. They turned to their kin and community, and suffered through the hardship (*gaman*). Supporting this value in a material way were ethnic organizations, most notably the *fujinkai*, a club composed of persons who immigrated from the same area of Japan. In addition to providing conviviality and friendship, the *fujinkai* was a welfare organization. For example, it took up collections for families hard hit by personal disasters. *Fujinkai* members visited the sick and lent personal help in times of distress. The *fujinkai* often sponsored another self-help device: the *tanamoshi*. Members would contribute a monthly amount of money to a pool, and periodically, different members could "borrow" (the specific details varied) the pool for their own use. In effect, the *tanamoshi* was an ethnically organized, informal credit union. (Similar devices are called the *hui* among the Chinese and the *gyeh* among Koreans).[10] The Japanese also followed the custom of the *koden*: giving monetary gifts at important events, such as weddings or funerals. The sum of the *koden* might be considerable, and it was intended, in the case of weddings, to provide the couple with a start in life, and in the case of death, to help allay the expenses of the funeral.

All of these subcultural values and customs must have had some impact on assimilation and success, but unfortunately, one does not know precisely to what extent, nor does one know if the impact was greater for some groups than others. Japanese subculture stressed education, for example, but no one knows the extent to which the groups differed on this value. And even if the differences were known, they might not account for the differences in success. That is an empirical question yet to be answered.

A broader conceptual issue still remains: the breadth of the argument. Subculture includes so many behaviors, values, and institutions—virtually everything—that almost anything can be read into it. If a group succeeds, then observers cull the subculture for traits that engender success. If a group fails, then observers cull the subculture for traits that engender failure. In either case, because subculture is so inclusive, observers can almost always find some traits that support the subcultural argument. Lieberson writes as follows:

> Why are two or more groups different with respect to some characteristic or dependent variable? Presumably, they differ in their values or in some norm. How do we know that they differ in their values or norms? The argument then frequently involves using the behavioral attribute one is trying to explain as the indicator of the normative or value difference one is trying to use as the explanation. A pure case of circular reasoning!"

There is, in addition, a political aspect to this circular reasoning. Early anti-Asianists offered subculture as the reason Asians would never succeed, while modern observers offer the same subculture as the reason Asians have succeeded. Although one might acknowledge the role of subculture as a contributing factor and perhaps even as a causal factor, scientifically documenting those roles has not been possible.

Demographic-Ecological Factors

The data showed that Asians are consistently less segregated than blacks at every level of education. Because the data were limited, residential segregation, socioeconomic status, and detailed ethnicity could not be measured at the same time, an unfortunate fact which precluded making all the comparisons one would have liked.

Residential segregation indisputably exists, but its effect on success is quite disputable. One might argue that the integration of housing leads to integration along other fronts, such as clubs, schools, and work.[12] This is reasonable, yet the argument can be reversed and still be reasonable: before a group can residentially integrate, it must have the resources to do so, and to attain those resources, the group must first achieve socioeconomic parity with the majority.

Contrary to either hypothesis, however, residential segregation seems not to have much impact at all. The most successful groups, the Japanese and Chinese, were highly segregated in the past, perhaps even more than blacks, Chicanos, and Vietnamese are now. For all its evils—which I will not minimize—residential segregation does not distinguish between ethnic group success and failure. This conclusion is further bolstered by the data showing that Asians, the most successful group, are residentially segregated even after allowing for the effects of education and income.

Another demographic-ecological factor is group size. One might hypothesize that smaller groups assimilate faster than larger groups because smaller groups pose less of a threat to the majority; or alternatively, one might hypothesize that smaller groups assimilate more slowly because they command fewer resources and power. These hypotheses were directly assessed by the data on residential segregation, and indirectly, by the entire analysis of this study. The weight of evidence favored the former hypothesis.[13]

Economic Factors

Human Capital. One of the most popular explanations for the success of certain groups is human capital. Asians, the argument goes, have succeeded because they have a great deal of human capital, mostly in the form of education. The present data showed that Filipino and Korean Americans have the most formal eduation, but they are not the most successful groups. Apparently, the effect of human capital is more complex than realized.[14] The analysis showed that whites convert their education into earnings at a higher rate than the other groups. Human capital, though valuable to the minority, is more valuable to the majority.

This is sobering. It means that education is necessary for success but will not solve the problem of inequality. To achieve the same *total* return on their education, the minority must acquire more education than the majority—which is another way of saying that the minority must be overqualified to compete for the same salaries, which is a form of discrimination.

Time is another important factor related to success. The processes of achieving socioeconomic parity require time. A new group faces the inevitable necessity of adapting to a new culture while the host group must adapt to a new group. The resulting problems, whether minor or major, cannot be resolved instantaneously. For example, Vietnamese fishermen who settled on the Gulf Coast encountered severe discrimination, much of it originating from conflicts with whites over norms of "fair" competition. Nowadays, however, these problems have greatly abated as both groups have learned to accommodate the other.[15] Working out the accommodation took time.

Time is important for another reason. The groups studied here were welcomed as long as they filled lower echelon jobs and the economy was prosperous, but when the economy changed, the welcome changed. Thus, groups that arrived during prosperity had a good opportunity to gain a foothold in the economy, and the long-term impact might have been substantial. The Chinese arrived during the Gold Rush and during the railroad construction. Jobs were plentiful, and the Chinese were welcomed. Some of the money acquired during those periods may have been used to finance the small Chinese businesses that rapidly emerged when the welcome changed to hostility. Although this hypothesis cannot be empirically verified for a lack of records, it seems plausible and it helps explain how the Chinese managed to establish their economic foothold. The quick movement of Japanese into independent farming may have been similarly financed by the earnings accumulated during the period of welcome.[16]

Even though discrimination, subculture, and exogenous factors are frequently offered as explanations for ethnic group success, the explanations are not completely satisfactory. Attempts to apply them to different groups in a comparative fashion revealed their lack of generality, a lack that is a serious flaw in scientific explanation. Rather than attempting to "patch" the explanations to fit each group, I suggest that a better approach is to ground an explanation in the material, pragmatic, and economic necessities of social survival.

Assumptions of an Alternative Explanation

According to anthropologist Marvin Harris, explanations for human behavior should begin with the ". . . simple premise that human social life is a response to the practical problems of human existence."[17]

Cultural materialism, the formal name of Harris's theory, relies heavily on the intellectual tradition of Karl Marx, who wrote in a brief but key passage, "The mode of production in material life determines the general character of the social, political and spiritual processes of life."[18] Stated so succinctly, the power of this statement is easily overlooked, but it reverses the commonplace notion that ideas, or superstructure, are the driving force behind society.

This notion has been the center of much, and often bellicose, debate. For current purposes, one does not have to agree that cultural materialism turns on its head the notion that "ideas change the world" in order to accept that much ethnic group behavior is due to material concerns, the exact amount remaining an empirical question and varying according to circumstances.

Consistent with the emphasis on the material basis of behavior, goes the emphasis on infrastructure. This concept is used in several ways by different authors, and moreover, in the parlance of politics it seems to have a different meaning altogether. Here, I think of infrastructure as follows:

(1) Divisions, proc₋ sses, and relationships that occur at the infrastructural level constitute the core of ethnic relationships. Historically, economic concerns have been dominant. From them, political and legal concerns have flowed. Two notions underlie the emphasis on economic concerns.

(2) Economic relations are the driving force, the engine, of American society. As the historical review has emphasized, whenever ethnic groups clashed with white economic interests, a barrage of antiminority responses occurred, both infrastructural (for example, exclusion laws), and superstructural (for example, stereotypes).

(3) Economic concerns would not be so important for ethnic relations were it not for the obvious fact that the economic pie is too small; there is not enough wealth to satisfy everyone. And further, if one assumes that human desires feed on themselves, that the more people get, the more they want, then the pie will never be large enough. The very act of satisfying one level of wants opens the way to another level. While the possibility of never ending wants poses an interesting philosophical issue, it suffices for present concerns that in the past, pr⁻ᶜ⁻nt, and the near future, groups must compete with each other fᴏᵣ a share of the "good life" that is not abundant enough for all to have as much as they want.

Here the concern is with groups defined according to ethnic criteria such as race, language, religion, and custom. These are highly visible, distinctive, and easily maintained groupings. Other groups also compete for a share of the pie: management versus workers, women versus men, the elderly versus the young. Thus, when viewed broadly, ethnic group competition is a variation on an ongoing, omnipresent competition for scarce economic resources.

The above sketch, although unquestionably preliminary, still promises to be highly useful. It forms the base of the specific explanation to be presented next. Constructed upon this base will be a theory specifying the way ethnic group success comes about. The theory will first be presented in generic terms, and then applied to

Japanese Americans. They were selected because, of the groups studied, they are the most successful; consequently, they most require explanation. The implications of the theory for the other groups will be drawn out after that.

A Theory of Ethnic Group Success and Exceptionalism

The theory proposed here introduces the idea of an ethnic hegemonization and an ethnic economic arena, and in so doing, adapts and builds upon the concepts of an internal labor market, sheltered labor market, middleman minority, vertical economic integration, and ethnicity. These concepts were introduced before, but one must know how they are modified for present purposes.

Internal Labor Market. Persons trapped in secondary labor markets may assimilate culturally, but their chances for socioeconomic success are dim. Despite the evidence, however, the assertion fails to explain all ethnic group success and failure. Japanese were small entrepreneurs, truck farmers, and laborers. In a few cases, these entrepreneurs became extremely wealthy, but they were exceptions and individual attributes such as motivation, intelligence, and luck can explain their success. The same attributes, however, cannot explain the course of an entire ethnic group, and so one must explore other concepts. The notion of an internal labor market provides a useful starting point.

An internal labor market has several features, but the following are of particular relevance for understanding ethnic relations:

(1) The internal labor market exists within a broader infrastructure, such as government, large firm, union, or industry.

(2) The broader infrastructure shelters the market and its workers from the vagaries of economic change and political attack. The sheltering, while not total, is substantial.

(3) The market provides at least some upward mobility for some workers.

(4) Workers spend most or all of their careers within this labor market.

The most important feature of an internal labor market is "sheltering." Marcia Freedman, for instance, has described sheltering mechanisms which ". . . protect jobs from competition, and mitigate the effects of both intermittent work schedules and cyclical layoffs."[19] Because of the sheltering, an internal labor market is a desirable economic niche and one over which much ethnic hostility can develop, as exemplified by the attempts of blacks to enter construction trades.

Middleman Minority. A middleman minority can be thought of as an ethnic group which has the position of mediating economic endeavors, usually as wholesalers.[20] The minority thus acts as a buffer between consumers and producers, and often takes on the characteristics of a petite bourgeoisie. The theory of the middleman minority advances the understanding of ethnic success, but it nevertheless has a weakness: why should the majority cede a middleman position to the minority in the first place? Throughout history, the majority has managed to keep minorities out of these positions, and one expects a ceding only under exceptional circumstances, as when the ethnic group can perform a task forbidden to the majority (such as money lending), or if the ethnic group has a monopoly on specific skills and knowledge, or if the position is not very lucrative. Other than these circumstances, one expects the minority to take the middleman position only if the minority can muster enough power to counter majority resistance. How a minority gets the power is, in large part, the explanation for minority success.

Ethnic Saturation. A situation wherein disproportionate (often extremely disproportionate) numbers of a given minority work in a given occupation, I call ethnic saturation. Common observation will reveal examples of occupations mostly filled by a single minority group. Perhaps less common than before, one cannot but notice the disproportionately large number of blacks working as airport porters, or the various minorities driving taxies, or the preponderance of Mexicans in field work. While being a member of the ethnic group is not a legal requirement to enter the occupation (indeed, such a requirement might be illegal), membership seems to be a *de facto* advantage.

Ethnic saturation may increase employment opportunities for the group, but it does not necessarily lead to socioeconomic advancement. The Chicano saturation of stoop labor is an illustration. The only resource Chicanos command is their own labor, and that resource gives them little power because it is in such long supply. Consequently, Chicanos suffer all the consequences of being in a secondary labor market: low pay, little advancement, negligible job security, episodic employment, and an absence of internal labor markets.

Ethnic Hegemonization. By this term I mean a situation wherein a given group saturates an economic arena and obtains some control (power) over the arena. Both saturation and power are necessary. A group might become powerful by controlling the key positions of an economic arena, and at the same time, not saturate the industry or occupation, such as the growers who control agriculture or the whites who control the South African gold mines. This pattern is typical of the majority and relatively rare for a minority. To be successful, minorities have had to follow another path. They have had to hegemonize an entire economic arena, *both* horizontally and vertically *and* forge an economic interface with the majority.

Even if an ethnic group can hegemonize only a narrow band of an industry, hegemonization provides several benefits, among them the following:

(1) The minority finds protection from discrimination. Outside the arena, group members may be penalized by persons who refuse to hire them, promote them, or otherwise do business with them. Within the arena, because nearly everyone belongs to the same ethnic group, discrimination is not a factor (the problem may be the reverse: ethnic group members discriminating against nonmembers).

(2) An ethnic economic arena provides power. Once an arena is hegemonized, the majority must either deal with the ethnic group or suffer some losses (this assumes, of course, that the majority wants what the minority has).

(3) The ethnic economic arena provides organizational sheltering. Unions, to illustrate, have historically been hostile towards minorities, but within an ethnic economic arena, a union must accept the minority if it wishes to build membership. Additional sheltering comes from firms. They may have internal labor markets and the strength to withstand political and economic upheavals.

(4) Just as an organization provides stronger shelter than an individual, an economic arena as a whole provides stronger shelter than a single organization. While one part of the arena might be experiencing hard times, the effects on another part of the arena might be less. A decline in production will hurt producers, but retailers may benefit from the resulting price increases. An arena gains strength in another way. On the whole, an entire economic arena is more important to the broader economy than any single firm and so, if a minority hegemonizes an entire arena, the minority's power will almost certainly increase.

(5) An ethnic economic arena provides an extended ladder of upward mobility. Minorities can advance to higher level positions within the arena without being hindered by prejudice and discrimination.

(6) Compaction within the economic arena reinforces ethnicity. By saturating the arena, group members are thrown into daily and

routine contact with each other. The necessity to disperse into a broader culture is reduced, thereby the necessity to assimilate is reduced.

Although the benefits of hegemonization have just been discussed for ethnic minorities, those benefits are not minority group specific. They would accrue to any group that has hegemonized the arena, including the majority. This raises the same issue that was raised about the middleman minority: why would the majority cede an economic arena to the ethnic group? And the response is the same: if the minority has but little political, social, or economic power, the majority will not cede it. Tọ hegemonize the arena, the minority must have some kind of leverage, either an independent power base, special knowledge and skills, or a willingness to engage in businesses that the majority will not, or cannot, engage in.

Applying the underlying ideas of materialism and infrastructure in the above manner results in an explanation that might be called "emergent": actions by individuals result in structural cohesiveness. This point might be better understood through illustration. In the classic theory of free enterprise, each individual, by maximizing his or her own gain, contributes to the maximum benefit of all and does so without being aware of it or, in Adam Smith's classic statement, "Every individual . . . intends only his own security, only his own gain. And he is in this led by an *invisible hand* to promote an end which was not part of his intention." In an analogous way, minority and majority individuals, by promoting their own economic ends, unknowingly spin off beneficial consequences for the groups as a whole.

The concepts of hegemonization and economic arenas are powerful tools. The following application to the case of Japanese Americans is intended more to illustrate this power rather than to formally prove the theory (proof would require an entirely different data set and so go far beyond the confines of this study). In addition to illustrating the concepts, the application illustrates how ethnicity combines with infrastructure and materialism to promote group success.

Ethnic Hegemonization and Japanese American Success

The importance of agriculture in Japanese American history is difficult to overstress, and the application of the concept builds on that fact.[21] The argument is basically simple: (1) Japanese American success resulted from their hegemonization of an arena of the produce industry; (2) hegemonization was possible cause of certain material and economic characteristics of the produce business; and (3) ethnicity was transformed into an economic asset.]

[Japanese American agriculture rested on a narrow base, and the very narrowness gave the Japanese a competitive advantage. For example, Japanese farmers planted specialized crops that were labor intensive; they mustered family help to reduce labor costs; they applied scientific farming techniques; they rented or sometimes purchased marginal lands that would respond to their farming methods; they carefully brought their crops to the market at propitious times. They were willing to move when it was economically advantageous to do so, and the Japanese population quickly shifted, one may recall, from northern California to southern California. Somewhat paradoxically, the mobility of Japanese farmers was stimulated by laws intended to reduce their competitive advantage, the Alien Land Laws. Those Japanese farmers who could not acquire direct or indirect title to their lands were not economically rooted to any one agricultural area.]

[Some scholars maintain the land laws effectively stunted the growth of Japanese agriculture while others maintain that the impact was relatively minor.[22] In either case, however, the laws did not drive the Japanese out of agriculture as the anti-Japanists hoped they would. A major reason was economic. White farmers found they could earn more by leasing lands to the Japanese than by working the land themselves. Ironically, while the majority of Californians favored the land laws, many white farmers, who were supposedly being protected by the land laws, opposed them.] Says Yamato Ichihashi, whose early study of the Japanese in California provides much benchmark data, ". . . landlords sold their lands because they received good prices for them. The expansion in leasing was effected for similar reasons."[23] [Local authorities were responsible for enforcing the land laws, but because a minority of whites opposed them, they were not always rigorously enforced in some areas.] Writes Elliot Mears in his 1928 study, "It cannot be denied that over the state there is a general lack of enforcement of the combined acts of 1913, 1920, and 1923 [various alien land laws]."[24]

Japanese could make a profit on marginal lands because of their approach to farming and so they hegemonized a narrow but important arena of agriculture production. They came to account for 10% of the state's production while constituting less than 2% of the state's population.

Any group that depends on another group to buy its output is at a disadvantage, for if the buying group can afford not to buy, then the selling group must either accept low offers or go out of business. This applies ethnically. A minority that must sell to, or work for, the majority is in a weak position. If, for reasons of prejudice, politics, or economic rationality, the majority refuses to deal with the minority, the minority is rendered helpless. So, while the Japanese could farm efficiently, they still needed a dependable outlet for their crops—they needed the services of a trustworthy middleman.

As it turned out, the overwhelming bulk of produce grown in California was distributed (jobbed) through the two wholesale markets in Los Angeles. Collectively, this wholesale outlet was called *the market*, but it was not a single entity; rather, it was a collection of individual companies located next door to each other, sharing a common street and common services, such as lighting, plumbing, and security. Japanese companies dominated the "San Pedro" market, and penetrated the "Central Avenue" wholesale market to a lesser extent (that market remained largely dominated by non-Japanese wholesalers). Japanese wholesale brokerage companies (called "houses") varied in size from a single "stall" (area with a roof) run by one or two persons with one delivery truck, to multistall companies with dozens of employees, trucks and drivers.

Japanese hegemonization of a portion of the market was possible because the produce business had several unique economic characteristics. Produce wholesaling was, first of all, a relatively easy business to enter. Middleman wholesalers required comparatively small (as businesses go) amounts of capital. The business involved transferring goods, so large investments in production facilities were not required. Produce was sold on consignment. Farmers were payed a percentage of the sale only if the broker could sell their crops. This substantially reduced the capital tied up in inventory and also reduced the amount required to start a wholesale brokerage house. Entry into the business, while certainly not easy, was not out of the question.

The characteristics of produce itself facilitated Japanese hegemonization. Factors outside anyone's direct control, notably the weather, affect supply and hence price. Produce is perishable and requires fast transportation, which was especially critical before the development of modern, large-scale refrigeration. These characteristics meant that supply and prices were uncertain and always quickly changing, and speed was at a premium. A crop might be moved from farm to wholesale market to retail market long before all the formal paperwork—receipts, invoices, bills of lading, contracts—caught up. A formal, legalistic, bureaucratic system could not keep up with the movement of the merchandise itself. For such a system to function smoothly, word-of-mouth, telephone conversations, and "understandings"—trust—had to be the basis for business transactions.

Trust was also required because the farmer might be hundreds of miles from the point of sale, with no way to directly monitor the wholesaler. If the trust requirement was only one-sided, then the relationship between farmer and wholesaler might have been unstable, but offsetting that was the necessity for the wholesaler to trust the farmer. The wholesaler did not know to which house the farmer was sending his crop, and without an assured supply, a wholesaler might have little to sell and consequently little income. Because the San Pedro market was small, wholesalers would eventually find out which houses were being supplied by which farmers, but there was little they could do about it in the short run. The market moved too quickly. Whether the wholesale produce business was unique in its requirements for informal trust is difficult to know. The point here, though, is that trust was required and that ethnicity reinforced it.

The Japanese community, it must be emphasized, was small. Friendship networks overlapped with kinship networks to reinforce each other. Even if people did not know each other personally, they became known by reputation, and indirectly, through common friends, relatives, participation in ethnic clubs, and through other ethnic organizations. Face was quickly gained and lost, and with its loss, a person's family lost face as well. In this way, the ethnic community monitored and sanctioned behavior, forcing members to behave in certain ways. Sometimes, social networks extended over long distances, from one part of California to another.[25]

In the produce business, this was no accident. It was consciously reinforced. The reinforcements might be monetary, as when wholesalers made loans to farmers, a practice that lessened the farmer's dependence on outside financial institutions, but tightened the bond to wholesalers. Occasionally, kinship reinforced the linkages. Farmer and wholesaler might be related. Farmers also visited the market and were given the "royal" treatment: taken to dinner and on deep sea fishing trips, of which they were especially fond. Each house had its "field man," a person (often an owner) who periodically visited various farms, arranging business details and cementing informal relations. The field man traditionally brought gifts with him, and was eagerly awaited by the farmer's children.

Ethnicity reinforced trust in another way. Speaking of the *Issei*, Ivan Light writes, "In the Japanese economy, work was largely available only through the mediation of kin and *kenjin*. To receive a job in the Japanese-American economy was to become the recipient of a benevolence bestowed upon one by virtue of social connections."[26] This meant that the recipient incurred an obligation to the person who bestowed the favor, binding both to each other, and within the confines of the ethnic community, the bond was difficult to set aside.

Although outsiders might have viewed this process as nepotism or clannishness, insiders viewed it as the fulfillment of moral obligations.

Just because trust was necessary in the produce business does not mean all Japanese Americans were virtuous. Surely, many individuals were not virtuous but even so, the larger community forced people to outwardly conform regardless of their inner preferences. In this way, the trustworthiness of the group as a whole exceeded that of any individual.

Ethnically enforced trust, while necessary, was not sufficient to guarantee success. The Japanese community could hardly consume all the produce that Japanese farmers were growing and jobbing through the San Pedro market. Japanese houses had to have other customers; they had to economically interface with white retail consumers. Before World War II, Japanese produce retailers—fruit stands and vegetable stands—were common, and were supplied by Japanese. Moreover the Japanese were dealing in a commodity, not a brand item. Lettuce is lettuce; cucumbers are cucumbers. Even if customers preferred not to buy Japanese grown produce, they had no convenient way of knowing if they were.[27] The unpredictability of farming also contributed to the willingness of white retail merchants to do business with Japanese wholesalers. During times of short supply, there was not enough produce to satisfy all demands, and buyers for retail outlets were forced to deal with Japanese houses or do without. Unpredictability necessitated give and take: buying more than required when the market was long in order to obligate the wholesaler when the market was short. Because produce moved quickly, these relationships were cemented by informal personal contacts developed over many years of business dealings. And as a last resort, Japanese wholesalers had an ethnic outlet, Japanese fruit and vegetable stands, when the quality of produce was bad or in oversupply. Although they could not absorb a large oversupply, they could help.

In short, the unpredictability of supply, the necessity for quick movement of the crop, the necessity to rely on trust, the commodity nature of produce, and the presence of small Japanese retail outlets all combined to increase the economic power of Japanese wholesalers vis-à-vis white buyers. Regardless of prejudices, both parties were linked to each other through economic necessity.

Hegemonization opened an avenue of upward mobility. Within the economic arena of produce, Japanese could rise to higher positions. A common career path was to start as a swamper (the person who moved produce crates and loaded trucks) to a helper (the person who aided a salesman), to salesman (the person who, as the title implies, was responsible for selling to retailers). Only a few achieved the higher positions, and even fewer became owners, but no matter how little room there was at the top, anti-Japanese discrimination was not a factor.

A few farmers also became wealthy when the lands they owned turned out to be highly sought by real estate developers. This may have disproportionately happened to Japanese because their farms were often located near major metropolitan areas, and as the metropolis expanded, it overflowed into Japanese lands. For instance, before World War II, many Japanese farmed the open expanses near Gardena, California, an area which is now an older suburb of Los Angeles.

Hegemonization also modulated the vagaries of the produce business. By its very nature, farming is unpredictable. Weather may play havoc with one farm area while favoring another area. Decisions made a year or more previously about which crops to plant may lead to overproduction or underproduction in the current year. Produce wholesalers may have financed losing crops or built intricate sales relationships with supermarket chains that went out of business. All of these, and other, economic risks are partially offset by ethnic hegemonization. While the Japanese farmers who invested in a bad crop might have suffered losses in a given year, the wholesale jobbers were not so dependent on just one crop, and could compensate by emphasizing other products. In this way, the ethnic economy, and by extension, the entire ethnic group, was better able to withstand economic reversals.

As long as ethnic businesses deal with other ethnic businesses, the group as a whole will gain even if an individual business loses. What counts as expenses to one ethnic business counts as revenues to another ethnic business. One ethnic business loses customers but another ethnic business gains those same customers. In this way, money remains within the ethnic community, a situation that differs from that found among blacks and Chicanos. They have long complained that white businesses drain money from their communities. Of course, at some point the minority must interface with the majority or the minority will be living entirely on its own wash, which is hardly a favorable economic prospect.

⌈Ironically, Japanese discrimination against other ethnic groups was prevalent. A scattering of Mexican and blacks were employed by Japanese houses, but always in lower echelon jobs as swampers, and occasionally, as truck drivers. They were considered "casual" workers. When business slowed, as it did during the winter, they were the first to be laid off and the last to be rehired.⌉

⌊At the time when Japanese Americans were being subjected to intense discrimination, they were finding some organizational shelter within their arena of the produce business.⌋After controversy and struggle, Local 630 of the Teamsters Union accepted Japanese American workers. During World War II, they were permitted to "withdraw" from the union for the duration of the internment, a device which enabled them to reenter Local 630 without penalty after the war. The internment also suggests some limits. Hegemonizing an important economic arena should protect the group from attack, and it did—but only to a point. Some people argued that the Japanese contribution to farm production was too valuable to lose during wartime, and therefore they should not be interned. Obviously, key decision-makers felt otherwise.

Two additional factors should be mentioned. The first is education. It goes hand-in-hand with the process of hegemonizing an economic arena. Facility with communication, mathematics, taxation, accounting, and human relations contributes to business success, and not surprisingly, ethnic groups engaged in entrepreneurial activities have valued education. The second is demographic composition. Despite the frightful predictions once made by demographers, the size of the Japanese American population has remained tiny, so tiny that they can be accommodated in a comparatively small economic arena. The Japanese, despite hegemonizing a part of the produce industry, were never remotely close to saturating it. Had the situation been otherwise, had the Japanese population been larger relative to the arena they were attempting to command, their success might not have occurred.

Japanese Americans are now in the processing of moving out of ethnic economic arenas and into the mainstream economy. They are becoming physicians, dentists, optometrists, accountants, insurance brokers. Even so, William Petersen has claimed they have typically chosen professions that permit them to enter private practice catering to the populace at large but with a fall-back possibility of catering to the ethnic community.[28] His claim was made almost 20 years ago and was based on a perusal of records at the University of California, Berkeley. Currently, the necessity for a fall-back position has declined, one would think, and will continue to decline into the future.

The Future

The concept of ethnic hegemonization and the case of Japanese Americans suggest scenarios for the other groups studied here. The Chinese restaurant business is instructive. Although it might seem natural for the Chinese to dominate the Chinese arena of the restaurant industry, one does not have to be Chinese. One need only think of all the non-Mexicans and faceless corporations in the Mexican food business, such as Taco Bell, to realize that the nature of the economic arena determines ethnic hegemonization, not ethnicity.

What makes Chinese food unique in this respect is that while being one of the most popular cuisines in the world, Westerners are not familiar enough with it to cook it.[29] The Chinese thus have an immediate basis for ethnically hegemonizing the business—they have knowledge others do not have. Managing the business aspects of a Chinese restaurant also requires knowledge of Chinese culture. Chinese restaurateurs must purchase supplies in bulk from Chinese export-import wholesalers, and knowing the language and the Chinese norms of business is helpful. Further, the very fact that a Chinese restaurant is Chinese confers an advantage. Customers expect to find Chinese waiters, cooks, and other employees, and they are channelled into the business through ethnic networks of kin and friends.

In broad stroke, the situation found in the Chinese restaurant business resembles the Japanese situation just discussed. In both cases, ethnicity is converted into an economic asset, and ethnic hegemonization is vertical. There are also broad differences. First, if learning Chinese cooking were the only prerequisite to successfully running a Chinese restaurant, other groups might eventually enter the business. Some Asian groups have already done so by a back door route, including both their specific ethnic foods and Chinese food on the same menu. They serve Chinese food in order to broaden their customer base. Second, Japanese hegemonization was particularly strong at the production and wholesale level, mostly out of the public eye, and with a staple commodity. In contrast, the Chinese restaurant must directly cater to the white public on the basis of ethnicity, and an outburst of anti-Chinese racism would hurt them severely. More benignly, the popularity of ethnic foods goes in cycles, and a simple change in taste could be disastrous to the Chinese restaurant industry.

In some respects, the situation found among Korean Americans is similar, in embryonic form, to that found among the Japanese and Chinese. Anecdotal evidence coupled with the present data imply that Korean Americans have opted for small scale, entrepreneurial activity. They have moved into retailing electronics, clothing, and dry goods. Whether they can hegemonize this economic arena is not clear, but they might. With so many of these products now being imported from Korea, ethnicity will give Korean Americans an advantage over other groups in establishing supply links with distributors in Korea. Moreover, ethnicity may reinforce the trust which acts as a social collateral in many business transactions, particularly those spanning the Pacific Ocean.

Mexican Americans have saturated portions of manual labor

markets, but have not hegemonized them. Consequently, they do not have access to higher echelon positions, and they do not have much control over their economic future. Scenarios about Filipino and Vietnamese Americans are less clear, largely for lack of information. Apparently, Vietnamese have created ethnic enclaves, but they may not be able to hegemonize ethnic economic arenas which interface with the majority population. In addition to all the problems of any immigrant group, Vietnamese have the problem of being cast off by their government for political reasons. They may, therefore, find it impossible to establish commercial ties to Vietnam, ties which could become the basis for ethnically hegemonizing an economic arena. While Filipinos do not face the same political problem, they are not currently hegemonizing any particular economic arena, and what the future holds for them is difficult to foresee.

In some regards, blacks are the most puzzling group under study. They were the main focus of the civil rights movement and their success to this point might be attributed to a national concern for equality supported by government-mandated programs and laws. If that is the case, it implies that some minorities can succeed without ethnically hegemonizing an economic arena. To test that possibility, future research must apply the concept of hegemonization to blacks. Given their geographic diversity and sheer size, no single economic arena may account for their current level of socioeconomic assimilation. Rather than being a single group, blacks may be divided into a melange of ethnic-historical-geographic-socioeconomic groupings, a diversity masked by their common race.

Success does not mean that prejudice has vanished, a point repeatedly made here and further exemplified by American Jews. The "problem," according to the anti-Semite, is that Jews are *too* successful. The infamous quota systems that were, and still undoubtedly are in existence, reflect this contention. To the anti-Semite, Jewish piety is Zionism, the profit motive is greed, a strong family orientation is clannishness. Upward mobility may lead to socioeconomic attainment, but it does not necessarily lead to acceptance.

Japanese Americans may soon encounter this paradoxical consequence of success. Already one hears that the Japanese are *too* smart and work *too* hard. This is an old contention lodged against early Japanese farmers, and against any immigrant group that successfully competes with the majority. In the case of physically visible minorities, another catch-22 is at work. Unlike white ethnics, the Japanese cannot become invisible; they cannot disappear into the white mass. If Japanese fail, then their failure can serve to justify hostility and their physiology reveals their identity. But if they succeed, then their success promotes envy, and again, their physiology reveals their identity. Viewed this way, white ethnic groups have a significant advantage because once they succeed, their whiteness enables them to hide their success.

Dual Culture

Milton Gordon, whom I have much discussed, said that an ethnic group can assimilate culturally but not structurally. In view of what happened to Japanese Americans, his statement requires modification. Even by the second generation, Japanese Americans were gaining in income and education, waiting for the white doors to open, which they did, after World War II. Nowadays, Japanese Americans are beginning to assimilate structurally, at least that is a common interpretation of their intermarriage rates. This means that if Japanese Americans are to keep their cultural heritage, it will have to be on the symbolic and voluntary level. Whether that happens remains to be seen, but if it does, it will have interesting implications. It would mean a situation in which the ethnic group has assimilated structurally and socioeconomically, but has chosen to maintain a *dual culture*: one is the culture of the dominant group into which the ethnic group is socialized in the course of everyday life, and the other is the specific culture of the ethnic group, which is consciously maintained.

Somehow, the two cultures must be balanced. Undoubtedly the majority culture predominates in most situations, but in certain symbolic situations, the ethnic culture comes forth, as at ethnic festivals. If that were all, then the concept of a dual culture would not be much, if any, different from the concept of symbolic ethnicity. But dual culture runs deeper, it involves everyday life and self identity. Certain figures of speech, food preferences, household items, and other aspects of lifestyle bear the ethnic stamp, deliberately, and are maintained and consciously integrated into the group's lifestyle.

Dual cultured persons, it must be emphasized, are not marginal, trapped between two cultures and unable to make a choice. Quite the opposite, they have chosen to be dual cultured and identify with the ethnic role they have chosen.

Somewhat ironically, to be dual cultured requires socioeconomic success. A poor minority group does not have the resources necessary to resist cultural assimilation. The group has no choice but to use the public schools and other majority institutions, and to partake of the majority's popular culture. A poor immigrant group, therefore, will be culturally swallowed by the majority. On the other hand, a wealthier ethnic group has the means to resist acculturation. It can support language schools, it can import cultural artifacts (such as foods, clothing, books, art objects), it can afford periodic visits to the home country, it can travel long distances for cultural festivals and social gatherings. Thus, as the group succeeds, it can increasingly afford to maintain a dual culture. This may happen, or perhaps is already happening, to later generations of Japanese Americans who now consciously support Asian political groups, culture centers, and academic departments, and who try to learn rudiments of the language, Japanese fine arts, or judo and karate. While these activities may not require great riches—the second generation of Japanese participated in many of these activities—all require some discretionary wealth.

The thesis of the dual culture implies that the concepts of cultural pluralism and assimilation will eventually require adjustment. A group could assimilate socioeconomically and structurally while at the same time, move off at an obtuse angle by consciously maintaining a dual culture.

The analysis presented in this monograph is a beginning of explanation, not an end. Many questions remain unanswered. At minimum, one must know the following:

(1) What is the relation between ethnic group success and prejudice? Minority group success often inspires majority hostility. Japanese success in agriculture did nothing to mitigate discrimination; indeed, their success promoted the Alien Land Laws, the prohibition against Japanese becoming naturalized citizens, and the halting of immigration. This raises a rather pessimistic question: can an ethnic group succeed, be accepted, and be visible at the same time?

(2) Why did the Japanese enter agriculture while other ethnic groups did not? Several groups—Chicanos, Filipinos, Chinese—did become agriculture laborers, but they were not able to vertically hegemonize that economic arena.

(3) What was the precise quantitative importance of the various Japanese economic arenas—from production through retailing?

(4) What role did the expansion of California agriculture as a whole have in Japanese success? Japanese were fortunate in that they immigrated just when the state was becoming the largest grower of produce in the world, and the Japanese rode the boom. Of course, other ethnic groups lived in California at that time and they missed the boom—an obvious fact, but one which needs to be more fully explained.

(5) Not all Japanese Americans worked in the produce business. Many established small businesses, mostly catering to the local Japanese community. Others went into gardening, chick sexing, flower farming, and still others found employment wherever they could. A

few went into the professions, largely serving other Japanese. What was the relation between this activity, ethnic economic hegemonization, and success?

(6) What impact did the internment of World War II have? Entrenched in agriculture and small businesses, the Japanese lost everything. One might reasonably hypothesize that any group would be economically devastated, its community shattered, its resources depleted, its motivation deadened. Yet after the war, the Japanese reached higher levels of success than before. How did they do that?

When these questions are answered, an explanation for Japanese American success will be close at hand. The explanation would be a fascinating narrative account and would go beyond Japanese Americans per se, to be a general theory for ethnic group success. Few theories can be more timely, for new immigration policy is creating new Americans in wholesale number, and few issues can be more important than this, a most basic and elusive one: How can Americans get along with each other?

Notes

Prologue

1. Slaves and indentured servants, excepted.
2. Some are slightly rewritten.
3. Lindsey, Robert, "Resentment of Japanese is Growing Because of Surplus in Trade, Poll Finds," *New York Times,* April 6, 1982: Y–13.
4. Clendinen, Dudley, "Race and Blind Justice Behind Mixup in Court," *New York Times,* November 3, 1985: Y–13.
5. Lindsey, Robert, "Debate Growing On Use of English," *New York Times,* July 21, 1986: 1.
6. *New York Times,* November 26, 1986: Y–12.
7. "Dramatic Drops for Minorities," *Time,* November 11, 1985: 84.
8. "At Sanyo's Arkansas Plant the Magic Isn't Working," *Business Week,* July 14, 1986: 51.
9. Yoshihashi, Pauline, "Renaming for a Hero is Disputed," *New York Times,* August 18, 1986: Y–8.

Chapter 1

1. Myrdal, Gunnar, *An American Dilemma.* New York: Pantheon Books, 1972: 75; originally published by Harper and Row, 1944.
2. Simpson, George Eaton, and J. Milton Yinger, *Racial and Cultural Minorities: An Analysis of Prejudice and Discrimination,* Fifth Edition. New York: Plenum Press, 1985: 104–106.
3. Myrdal, pp. 75–76.
4. Myrdal, p. 76.
5. Myrdal originally called this a "vicious circle" but renamed it the "principle of cumulation" to allow for the upward spiral, Myrdal, p. 75, note b.
6. The last chapter contains a more detailed discussion of these points.
7. I emphasize that the term success is being here used in this very narrow way.

8. Thernstrom, Stephen (ed.), *Harvard Encyclopedia of American Ethnic Groups.* Cambridge, Massachusetts: The Belknap Press of Harvard University Press, 1980.

9. *Harvard Encyclopedia,* p. vi.

10. Petersen, William, *Population,* Third Edition. New York: Macmillan Publishing Co., 1975: 98.

11. Petersen, William, "Chinese Americans and Japanese Americans" in Sowell, Thomas (ed.), *Essays and Data on American Ethnic Groups.* Washington, D. C.: The Urban Institute, 1978: 65–106.

12. Ross, Edward Alsworth, *The Old World in the New: The Significance of Past and Present Immigration to the American People.* New York: The Century Co., 1914; *Harvard Encyclopedia,* p. 154.

13. Ross, p. 303.

14. Ross, Edward Alsworth, *The Changing Chinese: The Conflict of Oriental and Western Cultures in China.* New York: The Century Co., 1911: 47.

15. Steiner, Jesse Frederick, *The Japanese Invasion: A Study in the Psychology of Inter-Racial Contacts.* Chicago: A. C. McClurg & Co., 1917: vi.

16. Park, Robert E., "Our Racial Frontier on the Pacific," reprinted in *Race and Culture: Essays in the Sociology of Contemporary Man.* New York: The Free Press, 1950: 150.

17. Park, p. 151.

18. McKenzie, R. D., *Oriental Exclusion: The Effect of American Immigration Laws, Regulations, and Judicial Decisions Upon the Chinese and Japanese on the American Pacific Coast.* Chicago: University of Chicago Press, 1928.

19. McKenzie, p. 181.

20. McKenzie, p. 180.

21. Quoted in *Harvard Encyclopedia,* p. 493.

22. Kallen, Horace M., *Culture and Democracy in the United States: Studies in the Group Psychology of the American Peoples.* New York: Boni and Liveright, Publishers, 1924: 43.

23. Gordon, Milton M., *Assimilation in American Life: The Role of Race, Religion, and National Origins.* New York: Oxford University Press, 1964: 158.

24. Gordon, p. 159.

25. Lieberson, Stanley, *Ethnic Patterns in American Cities.* New York: The Free Press of Glencoe, 1963: 9 (italics added).

26. Jiobu, Robert M., and Harvey H. Marshall, Jr., "Urban Structure and the Differentiation Between Blacks and Whites," *American Sociological Review* 36 (August 1971): 638–649.

27. The answer to both questions seems to be yes. Jiobu, Robert M., and Harvey H. Marshall Jr., "Minority Status and Family Size: A Comparison of Explanations," *Population Studies* 31 (November 1977): 509–517. Marshall, Harvey H. Jr., and Robert M. Jiobu, "An Alternative Test of the Minority Status Hypothesis," *Pacific Sociological Review* 21 (April 1978): 221–237. Also see, Marshall, Harvey, H. Jr., and James Sinnot, "Urban Structure and the Black/White Fertility Differential: Examination of the 'Assimilationist' Model," *Social Science Quarterly* 52 (December 1971): 586–601.

28. Goldscheider, Calvin, *Population, Modernization, and Social Structure.* Boston: Little, Brown and Company, 1971: Part 3.

29. Alba, Richard D., *Italian Americans: Into the Twilight of Ethnicity.* Englewood Cliffs, New Jersey: Prentice-Hall, Inc, 1985: 150.

30. Gans, Herbert J., "Symbolic Ethnicity," in Gans, Herbert J., Nathan Glazer, Joseph R. Gusfield, and Christopher Jencks (eds.), *On the Making of Americans: Essays in Honor of David Riesman.* University of Pennsylvania Press, Inc., 1979: 204.

31. Dormon, James H., "Louisiana's Cajuns: A Case Study in Ethnic Group Revitalization," *Social Science Quarterly* 65 (December 1984): 1043–1057.

32. Hansen, Marcus Lee, "The Problem of the Third Generation Immigrant," *Commentary* (November 1952): 492–500.

33. Jiobu and Marshall, 1977.

34. Kelley, Jack, and Eric Brazil, "Indochinese Drift Across the U.S.," *USA Today,* December 17, 1984: 6A.

35. Clancy, Paul, "Magnet City Draws Waves of Immigrants," *USA Today,* May 13, 1985: 1.

36. "Oriental Silence Stifles Gang Probe," *Columbus Dispatch,* September 11, 1977: 5.

37. Andersen, Kurt. Reported by Benjamin W. Cate with the Los Angeles Bureau, *Time,* June 13, 1983: 21.

38. Andersen, p. 21.

39. Andersen, p. 24.

40. Givens, Ron, "Asian-Americans: The Drive to Excel," *Newsweek: On Campus,* April 1984: 8.

41. Tokaji, Ted, M. D., personal communication.

42. Tukey, John W., *Exploratory Data Analysis.* Reading, Massachusetts: Addison-Wesley Publishing Company, 1977: 51.

43. Tufte, Edward R., *The Visual Display of Quantitative Information.* Cheshire, Connecticut: Graphics Press, 1983.

Chapter 2

1. Crouchett, Lorraine Jacobs, *Filipinos in California: From the Days of the Galleons to the Present.* El Cerrito, California: Downey Place Publishing House, Inc., 1982: 9.

2. Moore, Joan and Harry Pachon, *Hispanics in the United States.* Englewood Cliffs, New Jersey: Prentice-Hall, 1985: 23.

3. Moore and Pachon, p. 23.

4. Moore and Pachon, p. 23.

5. Moore, Joan W., with Alfredo Cuellar, *Mexican Americans.* Englewood Cliffs, New Jersey: Prentice-Hall, Inc., 1970.

6. McWilliams, Carey, *North from Mexico: The Spanish-Speaking People of the United States.* Philadelphia: J. B. Lippincott Company, 1949: 167, 169.

7. McWilliams, p. 168.

8. Camarillo, Albert, *Chicanos in a Changing Society: From Mexican Pueblos to American Barrios in Santa Barbara and Southern California, 1848–1930.* Cambridge, Massachusetts: Harvard University Press, 1979: 215.

9. See Chapter 7.

10. Jones, Maldwyn Allen, *American Immigration.* Chicago: University of Chicago Press, 1960: 291.

11. Bryan, Samuel, "Mexican Immigrants in the United States," *The Survey*, September 7, 1912; reprinted in Moquin, Wayne (ed.), with Charles A. Van Doren, *A Documentary History of the Mexican Americans.* New York: Praeger Publishers, 1971: 265.

12. Personal communication.

13. Moquin, p. 294; Meier, Matt S., and Feliciano Rivera, *The Chicanos: A History of Mexican Americans.* New York: Hill and Wang, A Division of Farrar, Straus and Giroux, 1972: Chapter 9.

14. Prago, Albert, *Strangers in Their Own Land: A History of Mexican-Americans.* New York: Four Winds Press, 1973: 175.

15. McWilliams, p. 52.

16. Romo, Ricardo, *East Los Angeles: History of a Barrio.* Austin, Texas: University of Texas Press, 1983: 23.

17. Meier and Rivera, p. 79.

18. Moore, p. 19.

19. Romo, p. 27.

20. Moore and Pachon, p. 23.

21. Camarillo, p. 132.

22. Meier and Rivera, pp. 81–82.

23. Prago, pp. 111–112.

24. Moore, p. 22.

25. Mazón, Mauricio, *The Zoot-Suit Riots: The Psychology of Symbolic Annihilation.* Austin, Texas: University of Texas Press, 1984.

26. Robinson, Cecil, *With the Ears of Strangers: The Mexican in American Literature.* Tucson, Arizona: University of Arizona Press, 1963: 33.

27. Moore, p. 3.

28. Katz, William Loren, *The Black West.* Garden City, New York: Doubleday & Company, Inc., 1971: 18.

29. U. S. Bureau of the Census, *Historical Statistics of the United States, Colonial Times to 1970, Bicentennial Edition, Part 1.* Washington, D. C.: U. S. Government Printing Office, 1975: Table A 195–209.

30. Lapp, Rudolph, *Afro-Americans in California.* San Francisco: Boyd & Fraser Publishing Company, 1979: 26.

31. Beasley, Deliah L., *The Negro Trail Blazers of California.* New York: Negro Universities Press, 1969: 188; originally published in 1919.

32. Romo, p. 64.

33. Thernstrom, Stephan (ed.), *The Harvard Encyclopedia of American Ethnic Groups.* Cambridge, Massachusetts: The Belknap Press of Harvard University Press, 1980: 14.

34. Lapp, p. 27.

35. Reported in Lapp, pp. 33–34.

36. Reported in Lapp, p. 34.

37. Lapp, p. 36.

38. Goode, Kenneth G., *California's Black Pioneers: A Brief Historical Survey.* Santa Barbara, California: McNally & Loftin, Publishers, 1973: 133.

39. Jiobu, Robert M., "Earnings Differentials Between Whites and Ethnic Minorities: The Cases of Asian Americans, Blacks, and Chicanos," *Sociology and Social Research* 61 (October 1976): 24–38.

40. Goode, p. 65.

41. Goode, p. 75.

42. Lapp, p. 8.

43. Katz, p. 122.

44. Sung, Betty Lee, *Mountain of Gold: The Story of the Chinese in America.* New York: The Macmillan Company, 1967: 1.

45. Book, Susan W., *The Chinese in Butte County, California: 1860–1920.* San Francisco: R and E Associates, 1976: 9.

46. I recognize that the word *coolie* may be derogatory. I mean no offense by it, but it was the commonly used word until fairly recently. The same is true of *Chinaman.*

47. Saxton, Alexander, *The Indispensable Enemy: Labor and the Anti-Chinese Movement in California.* Berkeley, California: University of California Press, 1971: 63. Saxton is also the source for the other figures cited in this section.

48. Kingston, Maxine Hong, *China Men.* New York: Alfred A. Knopf, 1977: 131.

49. Tsai, Shih-shan Henry, *China and the Overseas Chinese in the United States, 1868–1911.* Fayetteville, Arkansas: University of Arkansas Press, 1983: 31.

50. *Ho Ah Kow vs. Matthew Nunan,* Opinion of the Circuit Court of the United States for the District of California, delivered July 7, 1879. San Francisco: J. L. Rice & Co., Law Printers and Publishers, 1879: 3–4.

51. Jones, p. 249.

52. de Bary Nee, Victor G., and Brett de Bary Nee, *Longtime Californ': A Documentary Study of an American Chinatown.* New York: Pantheon Books, 1973: 33.

53. de Bary Nee and de Bary Nee, p. 37.

54. Sandmeyer, Elmer Clarence, *The Anti-Chinese Movement in California.* Urbana, Illinois: University of Illinois Press, 1973.

55. Miller, Stuart Creighton, *The Unwelcome Immigrant: The American Image of the Chinese, 1785–1882.* Berkeley, California: University of California Press, 1969.

56. Miller, p. 147.

57. Miller, p. 147.

58. The economic accomplishments of Japanese industry are almost always attributed to imitative capacity rather than creativity.

59. Lyman, Stanford M., *The Asian in North America.* Santa Barbara, California: ABC-Clio, Inc., 1977: 121.

60. *Issei*: pronounced "E" (short *e* sound) "say." *Nisei*: pronounced "Knee-say." *Sansei*: pronounced "San" (long *a* sound) "say."

61. Petersen, William, *Japanese Americans: Oppression and Success.* New York: Random House, 1971: 15, 20.

62. Data for 1880–1940 are from Thomas, Dorothy Swaine, *The Salvage: Japanese American Evacuation and Resettlement.* Berkeley, California: University of California Press: 1952: Table 3. Thomas took her data from the U. S. Census.

63. Petersen, p. 20; Modell, John, *The Economics and Politics of Racial Accommodation: The Japanese of Los Angeles, 1900–1942.* Urbana, Illinois: University of Illinois Press, 1977: 18.

64. Ichihashi, Yamato, *Japanese in the United States.* New York: Arno Press and the New York Times, 1969: 110; originally published by the Stanford University Press, 1932.

65. Wilson, Robert A., and Bill Hosokawa, *East to America: A History of the Japanese in the United States.* New York: William Morrow, 1980: 66.

66. These figures do not "add up." The sum of 10,000 railroad workers plus 12,000 to 15,000 service workers plus 30,000 agriculture workers exceeds the reported total Japanese population of California circa 1909–1910. I do not know the source of the discrepancy.

67. Personal communication.

68. Wilson and Hosokawa, p. 118.

69. Petersen, p. 32.

70. Petersen, p. 33.

71. Bailey, Thomas A., *Theodore Roosevelt and the Japanese-American Crisis: An Account of the International Complications Arising from the Race Problem on the Pacific Coast.* Palo Alto, California: Stanford University Press, 1934.

72. Because Korea was a Japanese protectorate, the Gentlemen's Agreement applied to Koreans too.

73. Modell, Chapter 3.

74. Wilson and Hosokawa, p. 115.

75. Irwin, Wallace, *Letters of a Japanese Schoolboy ("Hashimura Togo").* New York: Doubleday, Page & Company, 1909: 48–49.

76. Irwin, Wallace, *Seed of the Sun.* New York: George H. Doran Company, 1921: 55–56.

77. Kyne, Peter B., *Pride of Palomar.* New York: Cosmopolitan Book Corporation, 1921: 38–41.

78. Burma, John H., *Spanish-Speaking Groups in the United States.* Durham, North Carolina: Duke University Press, 1954: 140.

79. Crouchett, p. 34.

80. Melendy, Brett, *Asians in America: Filipinos, Koreans and East Indians.* Boston: Twayne Press, 1977: 46–47.

81. Melendy, p. 46.

82. Melendy, p. 61.

83. Montero, Darrel, *Vietnamese Americans: Patterns of Resettlement and Socioeconomic Adaptation in the United States.* Boulder, Colorado: Westview Press, 1979.

84. Kelly, Gail Paradise, *From Vietnam to America: A Chronicle of the Vietnamese Immigration to the United States.* Boulder, Colorado: Westview Press, 1977: 44–47.

85. Kelly, p. 41.

86. Perhaps *never* is too strong a word.
87. Saxton, p. 259.
88. Miller.

Chapter 3

1. Petersen, William, *Population*, Third Edition. New York: Macmillan Publishing Co., 1975: 1.

2. Darnton, Robert, *The Great Cat Massacre and Other Episodes in French Cultural History.* New York: Basic Books, Inc., Publishers, 1984: 257. One should note that Darnton has reservations about the *Annales* approach.

3. Tien, Yuan H., "Changing Trends in the Chinese-American Population," *Human Biology* 30 (September 1958): 201–209.

4. U. S. Bureau of the Census, *Japanese, Chinese, and Filipinos in the United States, Subject Reports* PC(2)–1G. Washington, D. C.: U. S. Government Printing Office, 1973: 119.

5. Kim, Hyung-chan, "Koreans," in Thernstrom, Stephan (ed.), *Harvard Encyclopedia of American Ethnic Groups.* Cambridge, Massachusetts: The Belknap Press of Harvard University Press, 1980: 604.

6. Compare with Petersen, Chapter 3.

7. See the following article and the references therein: Day, Lincoln H., "Minority-Group Status and Fertility: A More Detailed Test of the Hypothesis," *The Sociological Quarterly* 25 (Autumn 1984): 456–472.

8. Easterlin, Richard A., *Birth and Fortune: The Impact of Numbers on Personal Welfare.* New York: Basic Books, Inc., Publishers, 1980.

9. "To America with Skills," *Time,* July 8, 1984: unpaginated.

10. Jiobu, Robert M., "Earnings Differentials Between Whites and Ethnic Minorities: The Cases of Asian Americans, Blacks, and Chicanos," *Sociology and Social Research* 61 (October 1976): 24–38.

11. U. S. Bureau of the Census, *Persons of Spanish Origin in the United States,* March 1979. Current Population Reports, Series P–20, No. 354. Washington, D. C.: U. S. Government Printing Office, 1980: 14.

12. Caplan, Nathan, "Working toward Self-sufficiency," *ISR Newsletter,* Spring/Summer 1985: 4,5,7. Ann Arbor, Michigan: University of Michigan, Institute for Social Research.

Chapter 4

1. For example, Robertson, Ian, *Sociology,* Second Edition. New York: Worth Publishers, Inc., 1981: Chapter 11.

2. See Miller, Delbert C., *Handbook of Research Design and Social Measurement,* Second Edition. New York: McKay, 1970: 170–171.

3. The index is given by:
$$ID = 1/2 \ [\text{sum} \ [abs \ (W - M)]]$$
where *ID* is the index of dissimilarity, *abs* is the absolute value, *W* is the

percent of whites in a given category of a given distribution, and M is the corresponding value for a minority group. This index is also used in Chapter 5.

4. A considerable literature exists on this index and it is discussed in greater detail in Chapter 5. When used in a purely descriptive fashion, some of the issues do not apply.

5. As far as I know, no sampling distribution exists for the index of dissimilarity. Consequently, a computer program was written to draw repeated random samples. From these samples, index values were computed and a sampling distribution could then be constructed. I thank Richard Haller for developing the program.

6. See Chapter 2.

7. See Chapter 1, especially the work of Ross.

8. It is not totally clear who is counted in this category. Presumably, persons who are employees of their own corporations are categorized as private wages and salary workers. See: U. S. Bureau of the Census, *Census of Population and Housing, 1980: Public-Use Microdata Samples, Technical Documentation.* Washington, D. C.: U. S. Government Printing Office, 1983: K–10.

9. Sue, Stanley, "Asian Americans and Educational Pursuits: Are the Doors Beginning to Close?" *P/AAMHRC Research Review* 4 (July/October 1985): 25.

10. U. S. Bureau of the Census, *America's Black Population, 1970–1982: A Statistical View,* PIO/POP–83–1. Washington, D. C.: U. S. Government Printing Office, 1983.

11. The Chinese have the lowest percentage finishing high school, yet the Chinese median exceeds the black median. This is a statistical anomaly, and it illustrates the importance of examining both the distribution and central tendency before coming to firm conclusions.

12. *Time,* October 7, 1985: 55.

13. Lindsey, Robert, "Debate Growing on Use of English," *New York Times,* July 21, 1986: 1, 8.

14. Personal observation.

15. Castro, Tony, "Something Screwy Going on Here," *Sports Illustrated,* July 8, 1985: 34.

16. Personal observation.

17. I have heard it used by professors at the university faculty club.

Chapter 5

1. Blackwell, James E., *The Black Community: Diversity and Unity,* Second Edition. New York: Harper & Row, Publishers, 1985: Chapter 6.

2. Alihan, Milla A., *Social Ecology.* New York: Columbia University Press, 1938.

3. Liebow, Elliot, *Talley's Corner: A Study of Negro Street Corner Men.* Boston: Little, Brown and Company, 1966.

4. Shevky, Eshref, and Wendell Bell, *Social Area Analysis: Theory, Illustrative Application and Computational Procedures*. Palo Alto, California: Stanford University Press, 1955; Bell, Wendell, "Economic, Family, and Ethnic Status: An Empirical Test," *American Sociological Review* 1 (February 1955): 44–52; Anderson, Theodore, and Lee L. Bean, "The Shevky-Bell Social Areas: Confirmation of Results and a Reinterpretation," *Social Forces* 40 (December 1962): 119–124.

5. Robinson, W. S., "Ecological Correlations and the Behavior of Individuals," *American Sociological Review* 15 (June 1950): 351–357; Menzel, Herbert, "Comments on Robinson," *American Sociological Review* 15 (October 1950): 674.

6. The index of dissimilarity is defined as follows:

$$ID = \frac{1}{2} \; [abs \; sum \; (W_i - Y_i)]$$

where W is the percent of whites in census tract i, Y is percent of a given ethnic group, *abs* is the absolute value, and the *sum* is across all census tracts in the SMSA.

7. Taeuber, Karl E., and Alma F. Taeuber, *Negroes in Cities: Residential Segregation and Neighborhood Change*. Chicago: Aldine Publishing Company, 1965: Appendix A.

8. For example: Winship, Christopher, "A Revaluation of Indexes of Residential Segregation," *Social Forces* 55 (June 1977): 1058–1066; Cortese, Charles F., R. Frank Falk and Jack K. Cohen, "Further Considerations on the Methodological Analysis of Segregation Indices," *American Sociological Review* 41 (August 1979): 630–637; Kestenbaum, Bert, "Notes on the Index of Dissimilarity: A Research Note," *Social Forces* 59 (September 1980): 275–280.

9. Taeuber and Taeuber, p. 196.

10. Lundgren, Terry Dennis, "Comparative Study of All Negro Ghettos in the United States." Unpublished Ph.D. Dissertation, Columbus, Ohio, Department of Sociology, The Ohio State University, 1976.

11. Jiobu, Robert M., and Harvey H. Marshall, "Urban Structure and the Differentiation Between Blacks and Whites," *American Sociological Review* 36 (August 1971): 638–649; Marshall, Harvey, and Robert Jiobu, "Residential Segregation in United States Cities: A Causal Analysis," *Social Forces* 53 (March 1975): 449–460.

12. See Hwang and Murdock for a study of Spanish, white, and black mixes in residential segregation, and for an example of an different statistical index: Hwang, Sean-Shong, and Steve H. Murdock, "Residential Segregation in Texas in 1980," *Social Science Quarterly* 63 (December 1982): 737–748.

13. Grebler, Leo, Joan W. Moore, and Ralph C. Guzman, *The Mexican-American People: The Nation's Second Largest Minority*. New York: The Free Press, A Division of the Macmillan Company, 1970: Appendix G.

14. Grebler, Moore, and Guzman, Appendix G.

15. Grebler, Moore, and Guzman, Appendix G; Taeuber and Taeuber, Appendix A.

16. For an alternative approach, see Hwang and Murdock.

17. Income was taken from the Microdata sample, 1980—the same data set used in Chapter 4 and elsewhere.

18. Frisbie, Parker W., and Lisa Neidert, "Inequality and the Relative Size of Minority Populations: A Comparative Analysis," *American Journal of Sociology* 82 (March 1977): 1007–1030.

19. Blalock, Hubert M., Jr., *Toward a Theory of Minority-Group Relations.* New York: John Wiley & Sons, Inc., 1967: 143.

20. Frisbie and Neidert.

21. See Chapter 8 regarding cultural materialism.

22. Blalock, p. 148.

23. I should point out that I do not follow Blalock's terminology. I define intent as an attitudinal or cognitive variable. It is a component of prejudice in contrast to discrimination, which is a behavioral variable.

24. Compare with Chapter 4.

25. Coleman, James S., Sara D. Kelly, and John A. Moore, *Trends in School Segregation, 1968–73.* Washington, D. C.: The Urban Institute, 1975. I refer to this as the Coleman index but the index originated some forty years ago. See Williams, Josephine J., "Another Commentary on So-Called Segregation Indices," *American Sociological Review* 13 (June 1948): 298–303.
The index is given by:

$$S_{ij} = sum_k \, (n_{ki} * P_{ki}) \, / \, sum_{ki} \, n_{ki}$$

where i is the minority, j is the majority, n is the number of minority members living in census tract k, p is the proportion of whites in tract k.

26. A standardized version of this index is formally identical to several common measures: *eta* squared, *phi* squared, the correlation ratio, and R squared in the analysis of variance. See Kestenbaum; Blalock, Hubert M., Jr., *Social Statistics*, Second Edition. New York: McGraw-Hill Book Company, 1972: Chapter 16.

27. Belsley, David A., Edwin Kuh, and Roy E. Welsch, *Regression Diagnostics: Identifying Influential Data and Sources of Collinearity.* New York: John Wiley & Sons, 1980: Chapter 2.

28. See Chapter 2 on historical background.

29. Note that the correlation between relative and absolute size ranged from a high of $-.88$ (among Chinese) to a low of $-.25$ (among Chicanos). The high value might possibly cause concern. Fortunately, though, the model is being replicated across six other ethnic groups whose data show no signs of excessive collinearity.

30. Marshall and Jiobu. A statistical tautology might be present. The Coleman index contains the white proportion (P_{ki}), but that should, if anything, increase the correlation.

31. Tukey, John W., *Exploratory Data Analysis.* Reading, Massachusetts: Addison-Wesley Publishing Company, 1977: Chapter 3.

32. Park, Robert E., "The City: Suggestions for the Investigation of Human Behavior in the Urban Environment," in Park, Robert E., and Ernest W. Burgess, *The City.* Chicago: University of Chicago Press, 1967: 10, 27, italics added and order rearranged; originally published by the University of Chicago Press, 1925.

33. Park, Robert E., "The Urban Community as a Spatial Pattern and a Moral Order," in Burgess, E. W. (ed.), *The Urban Community.* Chicago, University

of Chicago Press, 1962: 9; originally published by the University of Chicago Press, 1926.

34. Grebler, Moore, and Guzman, p. 271.

35. Massey, Douglas S., "Social Class and Ethnic Segregation: A Reconsideration of Methods and Conclusions," *American Sociological Review* 46 (October 1981): 649.

36. Gordon, Milton M., *Assimilation in American Life: The Role of Race, Religion, and National Origins.* New York: Oxford University Press, 1964: 247.

37. Wright, Gwendolyn, *Building the Dream: A Social History of Housing in America.* New York: Pantheon Books, 1981: xviii.

38. Massey points out that studies employing the method of indirect standardization have supported the ethnic status argument and studies using direct standardization have supported the socioeconomic status hypothesis. His data strongly suggest the superiority of direct standardization, a superiority long noted by demographers. However, while he cogently explains how the two methods work in the case of estimating residential integration, he fails to explain why each method supports the hypothesis it does.

39. As far as I know, there is no mathematical way to tease out of the data that which has not been reported. Moreover, even if that were possible, I am not sure it would be ethical to do so.

40. This differs from the Public-Use Microdata samples used elsewhere in the book. For some analyzes, the Hispanic counts are subtracted from the white counts, but if one wishes to employ socioeconomic measures in the same analysis, that procedure is of no help.

41. Midpoints of the Census categories were used. Income in 1979: $2,500; 6,250; 8,750; 12,500; 17,500; 22,500; 30,000; 42,500; 65,000; for all persons in the labor force. Because the last category was open-ended, the last midpoint was estimated on the basis of tables of income constructed from the Public-Use Microdata samples used previously. The estimation admittedly contained a certain amount of arbitrarines.

Education: School years completed: 4 years, 10, 12, 14, 19; for all persons aged 25 years or older. The last open-ended category was estimated in the same manner as income.

42. This procedure has been referred to as direct standardization. It (the procedure) should not be confused with the "direct standardization" techniques taught in demography textbooks. See Massey.

43. A strict interpretation of significance testing requires that the null hypothesis not be rejected for the positive significant slopes, because those slopes are opposite the *a priori* prediction.

44. See Chapter 2.

45. There are a few exceptions to this statement. The presence of one's servants close at hand might be convenient, but that implies such a subservient role for the minority that it would hardly qualify as "integration" in the sense that the term is usually used.

46. It is worth noting that in the long run, *everything might* come true.

47. National Opinion Research Center, *General Social Surveys, 1972–1984: Cumulative Codebook.* Chicago: University of Chicago, 1984.

48. For several studies, see: Deutscher, Irwin, *What We Say/What We Do: Sentiments & Acts.* Glenview, Illinois: Scott, Foresman and Company, 1973.

49. Douglas, Jack D., *Existential Sociology.* New York: Cambridge University Press, 1977.

Chapter 6

1. Bogue, Donald J., *Principles of Demography.* New York: John Wiley & Sons, Inc., 1969: 358.

2. Blau, Peter, Carolyn Beeker, and Kevin M. Fitzpatrick, "Intersecting Social Affiliations and Intermarriage," *Social Forces* 62 (March 1984): 591.

3. Grebler, Leo, Joan W. Moore, and Ralph C. Guzman, *The Mexican-American People: The Nation's Second Largest Minority.* New York: The Free Press, A Division of the Macmillan Company, 1970: 405.

4. Gordon, Milton, *Assimilation in American Life: The Role of Race, Religion, and National Origins.* New York: Oxford University Press, 1964: 165.

5. Petersen, William, *Population,* Third Edition. New York: Macmillan Publishing Company, Inc., 1975: 129.

6. Some analysts distinguish between interracial marriage and miscegenation. However, according to the *Oxford American Dictionary,* miscegenation refers either to "marriage or interbreeding of races, especially of whites with nonwhites." Here I use the words miscegenation and intermarriage synonymously to mean marriage and to include both ethnic and racial groups.

7. Percentages calculated from: National Opinion Research Center, *General Social Surveys, 1972–1984.* Chicago: University of Chicago, National Opinion Research Center, July, 1984.

8. National Opinion Research Center data, 1982; Roper poll of women, 1985. Reported in the *Columbus Dispatch,* October 26, 1985: 5A.

9. Simpson, George Eaton, and Milton J. Yinger, *Racial and Cultural Minorities: An Analysis of Prejudice and Discrimination,* Fifth Edition. New York: Plenum Press, 1985: 304.

10. Reiss, Ira L., *Family Systems in America,* Third Edition. New York: Holt, Rinehart and Winston, 1980: 332–336.

11. Bogardus, Emory S., *Immigration and Race Attitude.* Lexington, Massachusetts: D. C. Health, 1928. I have rephrased Bogardus's wording.

12. The presence of Hindus on the survey may require explanation. For a brief period, Asian Indians, or Hindus, were immigrating to California, setting off an anti-Hindu campaign.

13. Personal communication.

14. Crossette, Barbara, "Prejudice is One of Asia's More Common Afflictions," *New York Times,* December 29, 1985: 2E.

15. Merton, Robert K., "Intermarriage and Social Structure," *Psychiatry* 4 (August 1941): 361–374.

16. Blau, Peter M., Terry C. Blum, and Joseph E. Schwartz, "Heterogeneity and Intermarriage," *American Sociological Review* 47 (February 1982): 45–62.

17. Grebler, Moore, and Guzman, p. 411.

18. Murgia, Edward, *Chicano Intermarriage: A Theoretical and Empirical Study.* San Antonio, Texas: Trinity University Press, 1982: 24.

19. Murgia, p. 24.

20. Recall the discussion in Chapter 1.

21. See Chapter 5.

22. Grebler, Moore, and Guzman, p. 409, 411.

23. See Chapter 4.

24. U. S. Bureau of the Census, *Subject Reports: Japanese, Chinese, and Filipinos in the United States,* PC(2)1G. Washington, D. C.: U. S. Government Printing Office, 1973; Tables 5, 20, 35.

25. See Kitano, Harry H. L., and Wai-tsang Yeung, "Chinese Interracial Marriage," in Cretser, Gary A., and Joseph J. Leon (eds.), *Intermarriage in the United States.* New York: The Haworth Press, 1982: 35–48. A recent account is: Belkin, Lisa, "The Mail-Order Marriage Business," *New York Times Magazine,* May 11, 1986: 28.

26. Merton.

27. Porterfield, Ernest, *Black and White Mixed Marriages.* Chicago: Nelson-Hall, 1975: 85–97.

28. Reiss, p. 332.

29. Simpson and Yinger, p. 301.

30. Blau, Blum, and Schwartz, p. 47.

31. Blau, Peter M., *Inequality and Heterogeneity: A Primitive Theory of Social Structure.* New York: The Free Press, a division of Macmillan Publishing Co., Inc., 1977; Blum, Terry C., "Racial Inequality and Salience: An Examination of Blau's Theory of Social Structure," *Social Forces* 63 (March 1984): 607–617; Blau, Blum, and Schwartz.

32. Blau, Blum, and Schwartz, p. 47.

33. Blau, Blum, and Schwartz, p. 58.

34. For example, see Kelly, Gail Paradise, *From Vietnam to America: A Chronical of the Vietnamese Immigration to the United States.* Boulder, Colorado: Westview Press, 1977: 44–45.

35. This point has been recognized for a long time. For a review, see Blau, Chapter 2.

36. For another example of this procedure, see Blum.

37. This is the same computation used to determine the expected frequencies in Pearson's chi-square.

38. For example, Gordon, Albert I., *Intermarriage: Interfaith, Interracial, Interethnic.* Boston: Beacon Press, 1964.

39. See Chapter 4.

40. Each of the three measures had two intermediate categories, or $3 * 2 * 2 = 12$ subcategories.

41. For example, Grebler, Moore, and Guzman, Chapter 17.

42. No blacks were in the least assimilated category, nor were any Vietnamese in the most assimilated category.

43. Petersen.

44. Stevens, Gillian, and Gray Swicegood, "The Linguistic Context of Ethnic Endogamy," *American Sociological Review* 52 (February 1987): 73–82.

45. Burma treats Filipinos as Spanish speaking, while the Census Bureau includes them with Asians. See Burma, John H., *Spanish-Speaking Groups in the United States*. Durham, North Carolina: Duke University Press, 1954; U. S. Bureau of the Census, *Japanese, Chinese, and Filipinos in the United States*.

46. Research on the contact hypothesis is voluminous. A summary is provided in Simpson and Yinger, Chapter 17.

Chapter 7

1. Easterlin, Richard A., "Does Money Buy Happiness?" *The Public Interest* 30 (Winter 1973): 3–10.

2. Schwartz, Joseph, and Christopher Winship, "The Welfare Approach to Measuring Inequality," in Schuessler, Karl F. (ed.), *Sociological Methodology, 1980*. San Francisco: Jossey-Bass, 1979: 1–36.

3. Dalton, H., "The Measurement of the Inequality of Incomes," *Economic Journal* 30 (1920): 349–361.

4. Easterlin.

5. Heilbroner, Robert L., and Lester C. Thurow, *Economics Explained*. Engelwood Cliffs, New Jersey: Prentice-Hall, Inc., 1982: Chapter 18.

6. Jacobs, David, "Unequal Organizations or Unequal Attainments? An Empirical Comparison of Sectoral and Individualistic Explanations for Aggregate Inequality," *American Sociological Review* 50 (April 1985): 166–180; Becker, Gary S., *Human Capital*. New York: Columbia University Press, 1964.

7. See Bibb, Robert, and William H. Form, "The Effects of Industrial, Occupational, and Sex Stratification on Wages in Blue-Collar Markets," *Social Forces* 55 (June 1977): 974–996.

8. Becker, 1964.

9. Becker, Gary S., *The Economics of Discrimination*, Second Edition. Chicago: University of Chicago Press, 1971: 14, 16.

10. Becker, 1971, p. 16.

11. Becker, 1971, p. 18.

12. Thurow, Lester C., *Poverty and Discrimination*. Washington, D. C.: The Brookings Institution, 1969.

13. Thurow, p. 117; italics added.

14. Several different terms have been used: primary-secondary, split-intact, center-periphery, monopoly-competitive, concentrated-unconcentrated. For simplicity, I will use core and periphery. For a review, see Gordon, David M., *Theories of Poverty and Underemployment: Orthodox, Radical, and Dual Labor Market Perspectives*. Lexington, Massachusetts: D. C. Heath and Company, 1972.

15. Form, William, personal communication.

16. Piore, Michael J., *Birds of Passage: Migrant Labor and Industrial Societies*. Cambridge, Great Britain: Cambridge University Press, 1979: Chapter 2.

17. Bonacich, Edna, "A Theory of Ethnic Antagonism: The Split Labor

Market," *American Sociological Review* 37 (October 1972): 547–559. Also, Makabe, Tomoko, "The Theory of the Split Labor Market: A Comparison of the Japanese Experience in Brazil and Canada," *Social Forces* 59 (March 1981): 786–809.

18. Simmel provides the classic treatment of triadic relationships. See: Simmel, Georg, *Conflict and the Web of Group-Affiliations,* Bendix, Reinhard, and Kurt Wolff (trans.). Glencoe, Illinois: The Free Press, 1955.

19. Chi-square = 14,584, p = .0001 with df = 24.

20. See Chapter 4.

21. For a review of measures, see Fossett, Mark, and Scott J. South, "The Measurement of Intergroup Income Inequality: A Conceptual Review," *Social Forces* 61 (March 1983): 855–871.

22. The mean of the group means is not the same as the mean within the economic segment. The same is true regarding medians.

23. The foregoing statements could have been made in terms of homogeneity rather than dispersion as the one is the opposite of the other.

24. See Chapter 5 for a discussion of Standard Metropolitan Statistical Areas.

25. See Chapter 4.

26. For example, see: Bureau of the Census, *Statistical Abstract of the United States, 1984.* Washington, D. C.: U. S. Government Printing Office, 1983: Tables 52–55.

27. See Chapter 3.

28. Cotton, Jeremiah, "Decomposing Income, Earnings, and Wage Differentials: A Reformulation of Method," *Sociological Methods & Research* 14 (November 1985): 201–216.

29. This test and variations of it are commonly used, often under different names. For example, see Dixon, W. J. (Chief Editor), *BMDP Statistical Software,* 1985 Printing. Berkeley, California: University of California Press, 1985: Chapter 13; Jiobu, Robert M., "Earnings Differentials Between Whites and Ethnic Minorities: The Cases of Asian Americans, Blacks, and Chicanos," *Sociology and Social Research* 61 (October 1976): 24–38.

30. There is a large literature on this and the closely related topic of "decomposition." Several methods of decomposition have been proposed but as yet, no single method has been singled out as the best method. See Jiobu; Cotton; Jones, F. L. and Johnathan Kelley, "Decomposing Differences Between Groups: A Cautionary Note on Measuring Discrimination," *Sociological Methods & Research* 12 (February 1984): 323–343; Mayer, Susan E., and Kriss A. Drass, "Assessing Discrimination: A Boolean Approach," *American Sociological Review* 49 (April 1984): 221–234; Allison, Paul D., "Measures of Inequality," *American Sociological Review* 43 (December 1978): 865–880.

31. This does not mean, of course, that education is valueless. It will always be necessary for upward mobility, but it will not be sufficient.

32. Schwartz and Winship. Jiobu, Robert M., "Violence in Urban Society," in Schwirian, Kent P. (ed.), *Contemporary Topics in Urban Sociology.* Morristown, New Jersey: General Learning Press, 1977: 402–459.

33. See Cotton.

34. Kmenta, Jan, *Elements of Econometrics*. New York: The Macmillan Company, 1971: Chapter 11.

Chapter 8

1. Chapter 1.
2. Robertson, Ian, *Sociology*, Second Edition. New York: Worth Publishers, Inc., 1981: 279.
3. Banfield, Edward C., *The Unheavenly City: The Nature and Future of Our Urban Crisis*. Boston: Little, Brown, 1968.
4. Lieberson, Stanley, *A Piece of the Pie: Blacks and White Immigrants Since 1880*. Berkeley, California: University of California Press, 1980: 6.
5. Taeuber, Karl E., and Alma F. Taeuber, "The Negro as an Immigrant Group: Recent Trends in Racial and Ethnic Segregation in Chicago," *American Journal of Sociology* 69 (January 1964): 374–382.
6. Lieberson, 1980, p. 382.
7. Wilson, Robert A., and Bill Hosokawa, *East to America: A History of the Japanese in the United States*. New York: William Morrow, 1980: 47.
8. Kitano, Harry H. L., *Japanese Americans: The Evolution of a Subculture*, Second Edition. Engelwood Cliffs, New Jersey: Prentice-Hall, Inc., 1976: 43.
9. Caudill, William, and George De Vos, "Achievement, Culture and Personality," *American Anthropologist* 58 (December 1956): 1102–1126.
10. Light, Ivan H., *Ethnic Enterprises in America: Business and Welfare Among Chinese, Japanese, and Blacks*. Berkeley, California: University of California Press, 1972: Chapter 2; "Money Pool: It's There When Koreans Need It," *New York Times*, September 29, 1986: Y–9.
11. Lieberson, p. 8.
12. Taeuber and Taeuber.
13. Lieberson, Stanley, and Mary Waters, "Ethnic Mixtures in the United States," *Social Science Research* 70 (October 1985).
14. Wilson, Kenneth L., and Alejandro Portes, "Immigrant Enclaves: An Analysis of Labor Market Experiences of Cubans in Miami," *American Journal of Sociology* 86 (September 1980): 295–319.
15. For example, "Vietnamese Find Ally in Texas: Time," *New York Times*, September 29, 1986: Y–7.
16. I am currently developing a project to explore this issue, tentatively entitled, "An Incredible Story: The Japanese of California." In this regard, Broom and Riemer provide data that might prove useful: Broom, Leonard, and Ruth Riemer, *Removal and Return: The Socio-Economic Effects of the War on Japanese Americans*. Berkeley, California: University of California Press, 1949.
17. Harris, Marvin, *Cultural Materialism: The Struggle for the Science of Culture*. New York, Random House, 1979: ix.
18. Marx, Karl, quoted in Harris, p. 55.

19. Freedman, Marcia K., *Labor Markets: Segments and Shelters*. Montclair, New Jersey: Allanheld, Osmun & Co., Publishers, Inc., 1976: 130.

20. Bonacich, Edna, and John Modell, *The Economic Basis of Ethnic Solidarity: Small Business in the Japanese-American Community*. Berkeley, California: University of California Press, 1980.

21. See Wilson and Hosokawa.

22. Petersen, William, *Japanese Americans: Oppression and Success*. New York: Random House, 1971, p. 53.

23. Ichihashi, Yamato, *Japanese in the United States*. New York: Arno Press, 1969: 195–196; originally published by the Stanford University Press, 1932.

24. Mears, Eliot Grinnel, *Resident Orientals on the American Pacific Coast: Their Legal and Economic Status*. Chicago: The University of Chicago Press, 1928: 253.

25. This point is made in reference to urban communities by Wellman, Barry, and Barry Leighton, "Networks, Neighborhoods, and Communities: Approaches to the Study of the Community Question," *Urban Affairs Quarterly* 14 (March 1979): 363–390.

26. Light, p. 78–79.

27. The commodity-like anonymity of produce has also made it difficult for agricultural unions to enforce boycotts at the retail level.

28. Petersen, 1971: 115–116.

29. Light, Ivan, and Charles Choy Wong, "Protest or Work: Dilemmas of the Tourist Industry in American Chinatowns," *American Journal of Sociology* 80 (May 1975): 1342–1368.

References

Alba, Richard D., *Italian Americans: Into the Twilight of Ethnicity.* Englewood Cliffs, New Jersey: Prentice-Hall, Inc, 1985.

Alihan, Milla A., *Social Ecology.* New York: Columbia University Press, 1938.

Allison, Paul D., "Measures of Inequality," *American Sociological Review* 43 (December 1978): 865–880.

Andersen, Kurt. Reported by Benjamin W. Cate, with the Los Angeles Bureau, *Time*, June 13, 1983: 18–25.

Anderson, Theodore, and Lee L. Bean, "The Shevky-Bell Social Areas: Confirmation of Results and a Reinterpretation," *Social Forces* 40 (December 1962): 119–124.

Bailey, Thomas A., *Theodore Roosevelt and the Japanese-American Crisis: An Account of the International Complications Arising from the Race Problem on the Pacific Coast.* Palo Alto, California: Stanford University Press, 1934.

Banfield, Edward C., *The Unheavenly City: The Nature and Future of Our Urban Crisis.* Boston: Little, Brown, 1968.

Beasley, Delilah L., *The Negro Trail Blazers of California.* New York: Negro Universities Press, 1969; originally published in 1919.

Becker, Gary S., *The Economics of Discrimination,* Second Edition. Chicago: University of Chicago Press, 1971.

———, *Human Capital.* New York: Columbia University Press, 1964.

Belkin, Lisa, "The Mail-Order Marriage Business," *New York Times Magazine,* May 11, 1986: 28–29.

Bell, Wendell, "Economic, Family and Ethnic Status: An Empirical Test," *American Sociological Review* 1 (February 1955): 44–52.

Belsley, David A., Edwin Kuh, and Roy E. Welsch, *Regression Diagnostics: Identifying Influential Data and Sources of Collinearity.* New York: John Wiley & Sons, 1980.

Bibb, Robert, and William H. Form, "The Effects of Industrial, Occupational, and Sex Stratification on Wages in Blue-Collar Markets," *Social Forces* 55 (June 1977): 974–996.

Blackwell, James E., *The Black Community: Diversity and Unity, Second Edition*. New York: Harper & Row, Publishers, 1985.

Blalock, Hubert M., Jr., *Social Statistics*, Second Edition. New York: McGraw-Hill Book Company, 1972.

———, *Toward a Theory of Minority-Group Relations*. New York: John Wiley & Sons, Inc., 1967.

Blau, Peter, Carolyn Beeker, and Kevin M. Fitzpatrick, "Intersecting Social Affiliations and Intermarriage," *Social Forces* 62 (March 1984): 585–605.

———, *Inequality and Heterogeneity: A Primitive Theory of Social Structure*. New York: The Free Press, a division of Macmillan Publishing Co., Inc., 1977.

———, Terry C. Blum, and Joseph E. Schwartz, "Heterogeneity and Intermarriage," *American Sociological Review* 47 (February 1982): 45–62.

Bloom, Leonard, and Ruth Riemer, *Removal and Return: The Socio-Economic Effects of the War on Japanese Americans*. Berkeley, California: University of California Press. 1949.

Blum, Terry C., "Racial Inequality and Salience: An Examination of Blau's Theory of Social Structure," *Social Forces* 63 (March 1984): 607–617.

Bogardus, Emory S., *Immigration and Race Attitude*. Lexington, Massachusetts: D. C. Health, 1928.

Bogue, Donald J., *Principles of Demography*. New York: John Wiley & Sons, Inc., 1969.

Bonacich, Edna, and John Modell, *The Economic Basis of Ethnic Solidarity: Small Business in the Japanese-American Community*. Berkeley, California: University of California Press, 1980.

———, "A Theory of Ethnic Antagonism: The Split Labor Market," *American Sociological Review* 37 (October 1972): 547–559.

Book, Susan W., *The Chinese in Butte County, California: 1860–1920*. San Francisco: R and E Associates, 1976.

Bryan, Samuel, "Mexican Immigrants in the United States," The Survey, September 7, 1912; reprinted in Moquin, Wayne (ed.), with Charles A. Van Doren, *A Documentary History of the Mexican Americans*. New York: Praeger Publishers, 1971.

Burma, John H., *Spanish-Speaking Groups in the United States*. Durham, North Carolina: Duke University Press, 1954.

Business Week, "At Sanyo's Arkansas Plant the Magic Isn't Working," July 14, 1986: 51–52.

Camarillo, Albert, *Chicanos in a Changing Society: From Mexican Pueblos to American Barrios in Santa Barbara and Southern California, 1848–1930.* Cambridge, Massachusetts: Harvard University Press, 1979.

Caplan, Nathan, "Working toward Self-sufficiency," *ISR Newsletter,* Spring/ Summer 1985: 4,5,7. Ann Arbor, Michigan: University of Michigan, Institute for Social Research.

Castro, Tony, "Something Screwy Going on Here," *Sports Illustrated,* July 8, 1985: 30–37.

Caudill, William, and George De Vos, "Achievement, Culture and Personality," *American Anthropologist* 58 (December 1956): 1102–1126.

Clancy, Paul, "Magnet City Draws Waves of Immigrants," *USA Today,* May 13, 1985: 1.

Clendinen, Dudley, "Race and Blind Justice Behind Mixup in Court," *New York Times,* November 3, 1985: Y–13.

Coleman, James S., Sara D. Kelly, and John A. Moore, *Trends in School Segregation, 1968–73.* Washington, D.C.: The Urban Institute, 1975.

Columbus Dispatch, "Oriental Silence Stifles Gang Probe," September 11, 1977: 5.

Cortese, Charles F., R. Frank Falk, and Jack K. Cohen, "Further Considerations on the Methodological Analysis of Segregation Indices," *American Sociological Review* 41 (August 1979): 630–637.

Cotton, Jeremiah, "Decomposing Income, Earnings, and Wage Differentials: A Reformulation of Method," *Sociological Methods & Research* 14 (November 1985): 201–216.

Crossette, Barbara, "Prejudice is One of Asia's More Common Afflictions," *New York Times,* December 29, 1985:2E.

Crouchett, Lorraine Jacobs, *Filipinos in California: From the Days of the Galleons to the Present.* El Cerrito, California: Downey Place Publishing House, Inc., 1982.

Dalton, H., "The Measurement of the Inequality of Incomes," *Economic Journal* 30 (1920): 349–361.

Darnton, Robert, *The Great Cat Massacre and Other Episodes in French Cultural History.* New York: Basic Books, Inc., Publishers, 1984.

Day, Lincoln H., "Minority-Group Status and Fertility: A More Detailed Test of the Hypothesis," *The Sociological Quarterly* 25 (Autumn 1984): 456–472.

de Bary Nee, Victor G., and Brett de Bary Nee, *Longtime Californ': A Documentary Study of an American Chinatown.* New York: Pantheon Books, 1973.

Deutscher, Irwin, *What We Say/What We Do: Sentiments & Acts.* Glenview, Illinois: Scott, Foresman and Company, 1973.

Douglas, Jack D., *Existential Sociology.* New York: Cambridge University Press, 1977.

Dormon, James H., "Louisiana's Cajuns: A Case Study in Ethnic Group Revitalization," *Social Science* Quarterly 65 (December 1984): 1043–1057.

Easterlin, Richard A., *Birth and Fortune: The Impact of Numbers on Personal Welfare.* New York: Basic Books, Inc., Publishers, 1980.

———, "Does Money Buy Happiness?" *The Public Interest* 30 (Winter, 1973): 3–10.

Fossett, Mark, and Scott J. South, "The Measurement of Intergroup Income Inequality: A Conceptual Review," *Social Forces* 61 (March 1983): 855–871.

Freedman, Marcia K., *Labor Markets: Segments and Shelters.* Montclair, New Jersey: Allanheld, Osmun & Co., Publishers, Inc., 1976.

Frisbie, Parker W., and Lisa Neidert, "Inequality and the Relative Size of Minority Populations: A Comparative Analysis," *American Journal of Sociology* 82 (March 1977): 1007–1030.

Gans, Herbert J., "Symbolic Ethnicity," in Gans, Herbert J., Nathan Glazer, Joseph R. Gusfield, and Christopher Jencks (eds.), *On the Making of Americans: Essays in Honor of David Riesman.* University of Pennsylvania Press, Inc., 1979.

Givens, Ron, "The Drive to Excel," *Newsweek: On Campus*, April 1984: 4–13.

Goldscheider, Calvin, *Population, Modernization, and Social Structure.* Boston: Little, Brown and Company, 1971.

Goode, Kenneth G., *California's Black Pioneers: A Brief Historical Survey.* Santa Barbara, California: McNally & Loftin, Publishers, 1973.

Gordon, Albert I., *Intermarriage: Interfaith, Interracial, Interethnic.* Boston: Beacon Press, 1964.

Gordon, David M., *Theories of Poverty and Underemployment: Orthodox, Radical, and Dual Labor Market Perspectives.* Lexington, Massachusetts: D. C. Heath and Company, 1972.

Gordon, Milton M., *Assimilation in American Life: The Role of Race, Religion, and National Origins.* New York: Oxford University Press, 1964.

Grebler, Leo, Joan W. Moore, and Ralph C. Guzman, *The Mexican-American People: The Nation's Second Largest Minority.* New York: The Free Press, A Division of the Macmillan Company, 1970.

Hansen, Marcus Lee, "The Problem of the Third Generation Immigrant," *Commentary* (November 1952): 492–500.

Harris, Marvin, *Cultural Materialism: The Struggle for the Science of Culture.* New York, Random House, 1979.

Heilbroner, Robert L., and Lester C. Thurow, *Economics Explained.* Engelwood Cliffs, New Jersey: Prentice-Hall, Inc., 1982.

Ho Ah Kow v. Matthew Nunan, Opinion of the Circuit Court of the United States for the District of California, delivered July 7, 1879. San Francisco: J. L. Rice & Co., Law Printers and Publishers, 1879.

Hwant, Sean-Shong, and Steve H. Murdock, "Residential Segregation in Texas in 1980," *Social Science Quarterly* 63 (December, 1982): 737–748.

Ichihashi, Yamato, *Japanese in the United States.* New York: Arno Press and the New York Times, 1969; originally published by the Stanford University Press, 1932.

Irwin, Wallace, *Letters of a Japanese Schoolboy: ("**Hashimura Togo**").* New York: Doubleday, Page & Company, 1909.

———, *Seed of the Sun.* New York: George H. Doran Company 1921.

Jacobs, David, "Unequal Organizations or Unequal Attainments? An Empirical Comparison of Sectoral and Individualistic Explanations for Aggregate Inequality," *American Sociological Review* 50 (April 1985): 166–180.

Jiobu, Robert M., "Earnings Differentials Between Whites and Ethnic Minorities: The Cases of Asian Americans, Blacks, and Chicanos," *Sociology and Social Research* 61 (October 1976): 24–38.

———, "Violence in Urban Society," in Schwirian, Kent P. (ed.), *Contemporary Topics in Urban Sociology.* Morristown, New Jersey: General Learning Press, 1977: 402–459.

———, and Harvey H. Marshall, Jr., "Minority Group and Family Size: A Comparison of Explanations," *Population Studies* 31 (November 1977): 509–517.

———, and Harvey H. Marshall, Jr., "Urban Structure and the Differentiation Between Blacks and Whites," *American Sociological Review* 36 (August 1971): 638–649.

Jones, F. L., and Johnathan Kelley, "Decomposing Differences Between Groups: A Cautionary Note on Measuring Discrimination," *Sociological Methods & Research* 12 (February 1984): 323–343.

Jones, Maldwyn Allen, *American Immigration.* Chicago: University of Chicago Press, 1960.

Kallen, Horace M., *Culture and Democracy in the United States: Studies in the Group Psychology of the American Peoples*. New York: Boni and Liveright, Publishers, 1924.

Katz, William Loren, *The Black West*. Garden City, New York: Doubleday & Company, Inc., 1971.

Kelley, Jack, and Eric Brazil, "Indochinese Drift Across the U.S.," *USA Today*, December 17, 1984: 6A.

Kelly, Gail Paradise, *From Vietnam to America: A Chronical of the Vietnamese Immigration to the United States*. Boulder, Colorado: Westview Press, 1977.

Kestenbaum, Bert, "Notes on the Index of Dissimilarity: A Research Note," *Social Forces* 59 (September 1980): 275–280.

Kim, Hyung-chan, "Koreans," In Thernstrom, Stephan (ed.), *Harvard Encyclopedia of American Ethnic Groups*. Cambridge, Massachusetts: The Belknap Press of Harvard University Press, 1980: 601–606.

Kingston, Maxine Hong, *China Men*. New York: Alfred A. Knopf, 1977.

Kitano, Harry H. L., *Japanese Americans: The Evolution of a Subculture*, Second Edition. Engelwood Cliffs, New Jersey: Prentice-Hall, Inc., 1976.

———, and Wai-tsang Yeung, "Chinese Interracial Marriage," in Cretser, Gary A., and Joseph J. Leon (eds.), *Intermarriage in the United States*. New York: The Haworth Press, 1982: 35–48.

Kmenta, Jan, *Elements of Econometrics*. New York: The Macmillan Company, 1971.

Kyne, Peter B., *Pride of Palomar*. New York: Cosmopolitan Book Corporation, 1921.

Lapp, Rudolph, *Afro-Americans in California*. San Francisco: Boyd & Fraser Publishing Company, 1979.

Lieberson, Stanley, *Ethnic Patterns in American Cities*. New York: The Free Press of Glencoe, 1963.

———, *A Piece of the Pie: Blacks and White Immigrants Since 1880*. Berkeley, California: University of California Press, 1980.

———, and Mary Waters, "Ethnic Mixtures in the United States," *Social Science Research* 70 (October 1985): 43–52.

Liebow, Elliot, *Talley's Corner: A Study of Negro Street Corner Men*. Boston: Little, Brown, and Company, 1966.

Light, Ivan H., *Ethnic Enterprises in America: Business and Welfare Among Chinese, Japanese, and Blacks*. Berkeley, California: University of California Press, 1972.

————, and Charles Choy Wong, "Protest or Work: Dilemmas of the Tourist Industry in American Chinatowns," *American Journal of Sociology* 80 (May 1975): 1342–1368.

Lindsey, Robert, "Debate Growing on Use of English," *New York Times*, July 21, 1986: 1, 8.

————, "Resentment of Japanese is Growing Because of Surplus in Trade, Poll Finds," *New York Times*, April 6, 1982: Y–13.

Lundgren, Terry Dennis, *Comparative Study of All Negro Ghettos in the United States*. Unpublished Ph.D. Dissertation, Columbus, Ohio: Department of Sociology, The Ohio State University, 1976.

Lyman, Stanford M., *The Asian in North America*. Santa Barbara, California: ABC-Clio, Inc., 1977.

Makabe, Tomoko, "The Theory of the Split Labor Market: A Comparison of the Japanese Experience in Brazil and Canada," *Social Forces* 59 (March 1981): 786–809.

Marshall, Harvey, H. Jr., and Robert M. Jiobu, "Residential Segregation in United States Cities: A Causal Analysis," *Social Forces* 53 (March 1975): 449–460.

————, and Robert M. Jiobu, "An Alternative Test of the Minority Status Hypothesis," *Pacific Sociological Review* 21 (April 1978): 221–237.

————, and James Sinnot, "Urban Structure and the Black/White Fertility Differential: Examination of the 'Assimilationist' Model," *Social Science Quarterly* 52 (December 1971): 586–601.

Massey, Douglas S., "Social Class and Ethnic Segregation: A Reconsideration of Methods and Conclusions," *American Sociological Review* 46 (October 1981): 641–650.

Mayer, Susan E., and Kriss A. Drass, "Assessing Discrimination: A Boolean Approach," *American Sociological Review* 49 (April 1984): 221–234.

Mazon, Mauricio, *The Zoot-Suit Riots: The Psychology of Symbolic Annihilation*. Austin, Texas: University of Texas Press, 1984.

McKenzie, R. D., *Oriental Exclusion: The Effect of American Immigration Laws, Regulations, and Judicial Decisions Upon the Chinese and Japanese on the American Pacific Coast*. Chicago: University of Chicago Press, 1928.

McWilliams, Carey, *North from Mexico: The Spanish-Speaking People of the United States*. Philadelphia: J. B. Lippincott Company, 1949.

Mears, Eliot Grinnell, *Resident Orientals on the American Pacific Coast: Their Legal and Economic Status*. Chicago: The University of Chicago Press, 1928.

Meier, Matt S., and Feliciano Rivera, *The Chicanos: A History of Mexican Americans.* New York: Hill and Wang, a Division of Farrar, Straus and Giroux, 1972.

Melendy Brett, *Asians in America: Filipinos, Koreans and East Indians.* Boston: Twayne Press, 1977.

Menzel, Herbert, "Comments on Robinson," *American Sociological Review* 15 (October 1950): 674.

Merton, Robert K., "Intermarriage and Social Structure," *Psychiatry* 4 (August 1941): 361–374.

Miller, Delbert C., *Handbook of Research Design and Social Measurement,* Second Edition. New York: McKay, 1970.

Miller, Stuart Creighton, *The Unwelcome Immigrant: The American Image of the Chinese, 1785–1882.* Berkeley, California: University of California Press, 1969.

Modell, John, *The Economics and Politics of Racial Accommodation: The Japanese of Los Angeles, 1900–1942.* Urbana, Illinois: University of Illinois Press, 1977.

Montero, Darrel, *Vietnamese Americans: Patterns of Resettlement and Socioeconomic Adaptation in the United States.* Boulder, Colorado: Westview Press, 1979.

Moore, Joan, with Alfredo Cuellar, *Mexican Americans.* Englewood Cliffs, New Jersey: Prentice-Hall, Inc., 1970.

————, and Harry Pachon, *Hispanics in the United States.* Englewood Cliffs, New Jersey: Prentice-Hall, 1985.

Murgia, Edward, *Chicano Intermarriage: A Theoretical and Empirical Study.* San Antonio, Texas: Trinity University Press, 1982.

Myrdal, Gunnar, *An American Dilemma.* New York: New York: Pantheon Books, 1972; originally published by Harper and Row, 1944.

National Opinion Research Center, *General Social Surveys, 1972–1984: Cumulative Codebook.* Chicago: University of Chicago, 1984.

New York Times, "Money Pool: It's There When Koreans Need It," September 29, 1986: Y–9.

————, "Vietnamese Find Ally in Texas: Time," September 29, 1986: Y–7.

Park, Robert E., "The City: Suggestions for the Investigation of Human Behavior in the Urban Environment," in Park, Robert E., and Ernest W. Burgess, *The City.* Chicago: University of Chicago Press, 1967; originally published by the University of Chicago Press, 1925.

————, "Our Racial Frontier on the Pacific," reprinted in *Race and Culture: Essays in the Sociology of Contemporary Man*. New York: The Free Press, 1950.

————, "The Urban Community as a Spatial Pattern and a Moral Order," In Burgess, E. W. (ed.), *The Urban Community*. Chicago: University of Chicago Press, 1962; originally published by the University of Chicago Press, 1926.

Petersen, William, "Chinese Americans and Japanese Americans," in Soweli, Thomas (ed.), *Essays and Data on American Ethnic Groups*. Washington, D. C.: The Urban Institute, 1978.

————, *Japanese Americans: Oppression and Success*. New York: Random House, 1971.

————, *Population*, Third Edition. New York: Macmillan Publishing Company, Inc., 1975.

Piore, Michael J., *Birds of Passage: Migrant Labor and Industrial Societies*. Cambridge, Great Britain: Cambridge University Press, 1979.

Porterfield, Ernest, *Black and White Mixed Marriages*. Chicago: Nelson-Hall, 1975.

Prago, Albert, *Strangers in Their Own Land: A History of Mexican-Americans*. New York: Four Winds Press, 1973.

Reiss, Ira L., *Family Systems in America*, Third Edition. New York: Holt, Rinehart and Winston, 1980.

Robertson, Ian, *Sociology*, Second Edition. New York: Worth Publishers, Inc., 1981.

Robinson, Cecil, *With the Ears of Strangers: The Mexican in American Literature*. Tucson, Arizona: University of Arizona Press, 1963.

Robinson, W. S., "Ecological Correlations and the Behavior of Individuals," *American Sociological Review* 15 (June 1950): 351–357.

Romo, Ricardo, *East Los Angeles: History of a Barrio*. Austin, Texas: University of Texas Press, 1983.

Ross, Edward Alsworth, *The Changing Chinese: The Conflict of Oriental and Western Cultures in China*. New York: The Century Co., 1911.

————, *The Old World in the New: The Significance of Past and Present Immigration to the American People*. New York: The Century Co., 1914.

Sandmeyer, Elmer Clarence, *The Anti-Chinese Movement in California*. Urbana, Illinois: University of Illinois Press, 1973.

Saxton, Alexander, *The Indispensable Enemy: Labor and the Anti-Chinese Movement in California*. Berkeley, California: University of California Press, 1971.

Schwartz, Joseph, and Christopher Winship, "The Welfare Approach to Measuring Inequality," in Schuessler, Karl F. (ed.), *Sociological Methodology, 1980.* San Francisco: Jossey-Bass, 1979: 1–36.

Shevky, Eshref, and Wendell Bell, *Social Area Analysis: Theory, Illustrative Application and Computational Procedures.* Palo Alto, California: Stanford University Press, 1955.

Simmel, Georg, *Conflict and the Web of Group-Affiliations,* Bendix, Reinhard, and Kurt Wolff (trans.). Glencoe, Illinois: The Free Press, 1955.

Simpson, George Eaton, and Milton J. Yinger, *Racial and Cultural Minorities: An Analysis of Prejudice and Discrimination,* Fifth Edition. New York: Plenum Press, 1985.

Steiner, Jesse Frederick, *The Japanese Invasion: A Study in the Psychology of Inter-Racial Contacts.* Chicago: A. C. McClurg & Co., 1917.

Stevens, Gillian, and Gray Swicegood, "The Linguistic Context of Ethnic Endogamy," *American Sociological Review* 52 (February, 1987): 73–82.

Sue, Stanley, "Asian Americans and Educational Pursuits: Are the Doors Beginning to Close?" *P/AAMHRC Research Review* 4 (July/October 1985): 25.

Sung, Betty Lee, *Mountain of Gold: The Story of the Chinese in America.* New York: The Macmillan Company, 1967.

Taeuber, Karl E., and Alma F. Taeuber, *Negroes in Cities: Residential Segregation and Neighborhood Change.* Chicago: Aldine Publishing Company, 1965.

———, "The Negro as an Immigrant Group: Recent Trends in Racial and Ethnic Segregation in Chicago," *American Journal of Sociology* 69 (January 1964): 374–382.

Thernstrom, Stephen (ed.), *Harvard Encyclopedia of American Ethnic Groups.* Cambridge, Massachusetts: The Belknap Press of Harvard University Press, 1980.

Thomas, Dorothy Swaine, *The Salvage: Japanese American Evacuation and Resettlement.* Berkeley, California: University of California Press, 1952.

Thurow, Lester C., *Poverty and Discrimination.* Washington, D. C.: The Brookings Institution, 1969.

Tien, Yuan H., "Changing Trends in the Chinese-American Population," *Human Biology* 30 (September 1958): 201–209.

Time, "Dramatic Drops for Minorities," November 11, 1985: 84.

———, "To America with Skills," July 8, 1984: unpaginated.

Tsai, Shih-shan Henry, *China and the Overseas Chinese in the United States, 1868–1911.* Fayetteville, Arkansas: University of Arkansas Press, 1983.

Tufte, Edward R., *The Visual Display of Quantitative Information*. Cheshire, Connecticut: Graphics Press, 1983.

Tukey, John W., *Exploratory Data Analysis*. Reading, Massachusetts: Addison-Wesley Publishing Company, 1977.

U. S. Bureau of the Census, *America's Black Population, 1970–1982: A Statistical View*, PIO/POP–83–1. Washington, D. C.: U. S. Government Printing Office, 1983.

————, *Census of Population and Housing, 1980: Public Use Microdata Samples, Technical Documentation*. Washington, D. C.: U. S. Government Printing Office, 1983.

————, *Historical Statistics of the United States, Colonial Times to 1970, Bicentennial Edition, Part 1*. Washington, D. C.: U. S. Government Printing office, 1975.

————, *Japanese, Chinese, and Filipinos in the United States, Subject Reports* PC(2)–1G. Washington, D. C.: U. S. Government Printing Office, 1973.

————, *Persons of Spanish Origin in the United States, March 1979, Current Population Reports*, Series P–20, No. 354. Washington, D. C.: U. S. Government Printing Office, 1980.

————, *Statistical Abstract of the United States, 1984*. Washington, D. C.: U. S. Government Printing Office, 1983.

Wellman, Barry, and Barry Leighton, "Networks, Neighborhoods, and Communities: Approaches to the Study of the Community Question," *Urban Affairs Quarterly* 14 (March 1979): 363–390.

Williams, Josephine J., "Another Commentary on So-Called Segregation Indices," *American Sociological Review* 13 (June 1948): 298–303.

Wilson, Kenneth L., and Alejandro Portes, "Immigrant Enclaves: An Analysis of Labor Market Experiences of Cubans in Miami," *American Journal of Sociology* 86 (September 1980): 295–319.

Wilson, Robert A., and Bill Hosokawa, *East to America: A History of the Japanese in the United States*. New York: William Morrow, 1980.

Winship, Christopher, "A Reevaluation of Indexes of Residential Segregation," *Social Forces*, 55 (June 1977): 1058–1066.

Wright, Gwendolyn, *Building the Dream: A Social History of Housing in America*. New York: Pantheon Books, 1981.

Yoshihashi, Pauline, "Renaming for a Hero is Disputed," *New York Times*, August 18, 1986: Y–8.

Index